Minneapolis

Currents of Change

Minneapolis
Currents of Change

by Mark Soderstrom · Kristina Sauerwein · Penny Suess

This book was produced in cooperation with the Minneapolis Regional Chamber of Commerce. Cherbo Publishing Group gratefully acknowledges the chamber's important contribution to *Minneapolis: Currents of Change*.

Cherbo Publishing Group would also like to thank Bonnie Carlson, president of the Bloomington Convention & Visitors Bureau, for her assistance.

CPG *cherbo* publishing group, inc.

president	JACK C. CHERBO
executive vice president	ELAINE HOFFMAN
editorial director	CHRISTINA M. BEAUSANG
managing feature editor	MARGARET L. MARTIN
feature editor	ERICA RHEINSCHILD
senior profiles editor	J. KELLEY YOUNGER
profiles editor	LIZA YETENEKIAN SMITH
associate editor	SYLVIA EMRICH-TOMA
proofreader	BENJAMIN PROST
profiles writers	LINDA CHASE
	SYLVIA EMRICH-TOMA
	KATHLEEN GILBERT
	COREY HEFFERNAN-HOUCHIN
	TERRAN LAMP
	BETH MATTSON-TEIG
	DAN REINES
	KRISTINA SAUERWEIN
	STEFANIE SPIKELL
	BARBARA STAHURA
	PENNY SUESS
	DIANE VER STEEG-ANDERSON
	LIZA YETENEKIAN SMITH
	STAN ZIEMBA
art director	PERI A. HOLGUIN
designer	THEODORE E. YEAGER
profiles designers	NELSON CAMPOS
	JOEL VENDETTE
photo editor	WALTER MLADINA
digital color specialist	ART VASQUEZ
sales administrator	JOAN K. BAKER
profile services supervisor	PATRICIA DE LEONARD
profile services coordinator	LESLIE E. SHAW
administrative assistants	KELLY PASSALAQUA
	BILL WAY
regional sales manager	RICHARD R. FRY
publisher's representatives	SUSAN C. ADAMS
	RANDY S. FRAHM

Cherbo Publishing Group, Inc.
Encino, California 91316
© 2005 by Cherbo Publishing Group, Inc.
All rights reserved. Published 2005
Printed by Friesens
Altona, Manitoba, Canada,
and Neche, North Dakota, USA

Library of Congress Cataloging-in-Publication data
Soderstrom, Mark et al.
A pictorial guide highlighting 19th-through-21st-century
Minneapolis economic and social history.
Library of Congress Control Number: 2005928843
ISBN 1-882933-64-8

Visit the CPG Web site at www.cherbopub.com.

The information in this publication is the most recent available, has been carefully researched to ensure accuracy, and has been reviewed by the sponsor. Cherbo Publishing Group, Inc. cannot and does not guarantee either the correctness of all information furnished it or the complete absence of errors, including omissions.

Downtown Minneapolis skyway

Ice-skating on a Minneapolis lake

The landmark Murray's Restaurant with the Wells Fargo tower at right

Biking at Lake Harriet

Table of Contents

Corporations and Organizations Profiled

The following organizations made a valuable commitment to the quality of this publication. The Minneapolis Regional Chamber of Commerce gratefully acknowledges their participation in *Minneapolis: Currents of Change*.

Business Visionaries

The following companies and organizations are innovators in their fields and have played a prominent role in this publication, as they have in the Minneapolis community.

U.S. Bancorp
U.S. Bancorp Center
800 Nicollet Mall, Minneapolis, MN 55402
Steve Dale, Senior Vice President of Media Relations
Phone: 612-303-0784; Fax: 612-303-0735
E-mail: steve.dale@usbank.com
Web site: www.usbank.com

LINDQUIST&VENNUM PLLP

Lindquist & Vennum PLLP
4200 IDS Center, 80 South Eighth Street, Minneapolis, MN 55402
Phone: 612-371-3211; Fax: 612-371-3207
Web site: www.lindquist.com

Minnesota Vikings
9520 Viking Drive, Eden Prairie, MN 55344
Phone: 952-828-6500; Fax: 952-828-6575
Web site: www.vikings.com

MINNESOTA VIKINGS

select ◆ comfort.
CREATOR OF THE SLEEP NUMBER® BED

Select Comfort Corporation
6105 Trenton Lane North, Minneapolis, MN 55442
Tamara K. Nystuen, Senior Director of Corporate
Communications and Public Relations
Phone: 763-551-7000; Fax: 763-551-7826
E-mail: tamara.nystuen@selectcomfort.com
Web site: www.selectcomfort.com

Durrant
430 Oak Grove Street, Ste. 300
Minneapolis, MN 55403
Dennis L. Wallace, AIA, Managing Principal
Phone: 612-871-6864; Fax: 612-871-6868
E-mail: dwallace@durrant.com
Web site: www.durrant.com

DURRANT ®

Foreword

"It must be in the water."

This could certainly be an apt explanation for the success of Minneapolis and Minnesota, a city and a state whose histories have been shaped by their lakes and rivers. But geography alone can't account for the region's success.

Something more must lie behind the entrepreneurialism and drive to achieve that resulted in the founding and flourishing of so many legendary American businesses here—Weyerhaeuser, Greyhound, Cargill, Pillsbury, General Mills, Honeywell, Norwest (now Wells Fargo), Northwest Airlines, Target, Control Data, Best Buy, Digital River, and, dare I add to the list, Carlson Companies.

Why is it that the universal reply to "I'm from Minneapolis" is "Oh, that's a great city"? What is the magic ingredient?

Some say it's the cold winter that keeps our minds clear and focused on work during that season. Or the storybook cycle through a perfect spring, summer, and fall that keeps our spirits renewed and invigorated.

Some say the secret lies in the immigrant heritage of our community. Early waves of Germans and Scandinavians brought a zest for life and a demand for quality to the "new frontier" they built. Today's immigrants—Somalis, Hmong, and others—add their own new ideas to the mix, and new ideas equal innovation.

Still others—and I count myself among them—share the conviction that at the heart of our region's success is our belief in the value of education and culture. When a city the size of Minneapolis has more professional theater than anywhere between New York and Los Angeles; when it has internationally renowned art institutions and symphony, opera, and choral organizations; when its university is known around the world and linked closely with major local corporations—the result is an incredible vitality that is in the very nature of Minneapolis and its people and that will continue to shape and inspire Minneapolis.

You are about to experience that vitality for yourself through these pages. You will read about it and see it in the photographs. You will be inspired to journey here and feel the enthusiasm and excitement of one of the world's great cities.

Marilyn Carlson Nelson

Chairman and Chief Executive Officer
Carlson Companies

Third Avenue Bridge, downtown

Father of Waters statue (circa 1904) by Larkin Mead at the Minneapolis City Hall and Hennepin County Courthouse

Mayor's Message

Minneapolis
City of Lakes

Mr. Todd Klingel, President and CEO
Minneapolis Regional Chamber of Commerce

Dear Mr. Klingel,

Congratulations on the 125th anniversary of the Minneapolis Regional Chamber of Commerce and the publication of *Minneapolis: Currents of Change*, a unique history and economic overview of Greater Minneapolis.

Our city has a rich and impressive history and has retained a healthy economy and high quality of life for generations. Chronicling our successes with an eye towards the future is an important goal that this book accomplishes.

On behalf of the City of Minneapolis, I am pleased to extend my gratitude and thanks for everything that the Chamber does to promote the economic vitality of our city and region. Your rich history of service over the past 125 years is to be commended.

Sincerely,

Mayor R. T. Rybak
City of Minneapolis

Nicollet Avenue, looking north from Seventh Street, circa 1895

Champion of Business, Steward for the Region
Minneapolis Regional Chamber of Commerce History

The Minneapolis Regional Chamber of Commerce (MRCC), in various incarnations, has been integral to the area's development and success since 1868. The chamber voices the concerns of businesses and workers; champions art, education, and philanthropy; boosts the region; and encourages businesses to expand in and relocate to the area.

Although the Minneapolis Chamber name first appeared in 1881, today's MRCC most closely resembles its predecessors, the Minneapolis Board of Trade and the Minneapolis Commercial Club. Over the years, the chamber undertook a series of name and organizational changes to reflect the expanding scope of its work before adopting its present name and form in 2001. During the 19th century, it cleaned up waste and fraud in community charities, promoted public health and sanitation, and saw to the welfare of children, among many other useful pursuits. It was also instrumental in securing the location of the ninth Federal Reserve Bank of the United States in 1914, establishing Minneapolis as an important financial center.

Fortunes were made during World War I and the boom years that followed. Times were good. The chamber's seventh-annual Trade Tour in 1919, for instance, a three-day event, attracted some 200 prominent businessmen. But the war had also given rise to labor unrest and socialism. As early as 1903, the chamber had busied itself bolstering the rule of law, suppressing strikes, and countering threats to the free exercise of commerce, activities that it continued through the 1920s and into the 1930s.

Labor relations worsened during the Great Depression. However, in 1935 the chamber set up an Employer/Employee Committee to improve rapport between owners and workers. Later, in 1939, as businesses geared up to meet the looming challenges of World War II, the chamber allied with numerous civic organizations in helping manufacturers and distributors consolidate and expand operations, developing industrial growth in the area, and mitigating transportation problems, among other efforts.

Following World War II, the chamber sponsored goodwill tours, trade shows, and training programs for retail salespeople; looked for ways to fill gaps in faltering business districts; and set up a "Where to Buy" service. More importantly, it focused on urban renewal. In the face of the residential and retail exodus to the suburbs that began in the late 1940s, the chamber welcomed the Downtown Council as a way of making the inner city commercially competitive once more. The chamber also continued as a leader in the Lower Loop Redevelopment Project, which cleared 13 inner-city blocks that had fallen into severe disrepair. Recognizing the chamber's influence, Mayor Hubert H. Humphrey appointed five of its members to the city's first Housing and Redevelopment Authority in 1947.

During the unprecedented prosperity of the atomic age, the chamber became interested in seeing the region acquire major league sports franchises. The chamber played a key role in building Metropolitan Stadium, in Bloomington, in 1956; expanding the stadium in 1961 to welcome the Minnesota Twins and the Minnesota Vikings; building the Hubert H. Humphrey Metrodome in 1982; and opening the Target Center in 1990 as the home of the Minnesota Timberwolves.

Continued on next page

In the 1960s, the chamber created an Armed Forces Committee to support U.S. troops in Vietnam, set up the Women's Division to further the aims of business-women, and sought expanded air services and greater access to the St. Lawrence Seaway, among other projects. Associate members of the chamber included the Better Business Bureau and the Greater Minneapolis Traffic Association.

Although acquiring a downtown location for a new sports stadium took up much of the chamber's energy in the 1970s, it found time to establish the nation's first percentage-based corporate philanthropy program, now called the Minnesota Keystone Program, in 1976. This nationally influential program inspires and recognizes Minnesota businesses that donate 2 or 5 percent of their federally taxable income to philanthropic groups. The chamber honors Keystone members at an annual luncheon, a ceremony that has become one of the Twin Cities' most prestigious business events.

In the 1980s and 1990s, the chamber stepped up its efforts on behalf of education, workforce development, and economic advancement programs. Of note are its Voyager Program to help students with work-readiness training and the earning of postsecondary degrees, and Success Through Realization of Individual Development and Employability (STRIDE), an adult training and employment program.

The chamber took its present name when the Greater Minneapolis Chamber of Commerce merged with the Bloomington Chamber of Commerce in 2001. The Bloomington chamber, established in 1954, had led the charge in the critical fight to retain the international airport and helped pave the way for the Mall of America.

Today, the Minneapolis Regional Chamber of Commerce enjoys the membership of some 1,300 businesses in 68 communities. MRCC members are active in every type of business and social organization, from venture capital firms to youth centers. The chamber's name has changed through the years, but its mission remains the same: unite area businesses in mutual profitability, contribute civic leadership to the region, and increase the presence of the Twin Cities in the global economy.

Block E entertainment and dining district

At the Helm

Minneapolis Regional Chamber of Commerce Past Presidents/Chairpersons

Minneapolis Commercial and Athletic Club
Organized April 23, 1892

1892–93
Charles M. Harrington, Pres., Van Dusen-Harrington Company

Commercial Club of Minneapolis
Incorporated September 1893

1893–98
John F. Calderwood, Secty. and Auditor, Street Railway Co.

1898–99
Edmund J. Phelps Jr., Pres., Belt Line Elevator Company

1899–1900
Samuel H. Hall, S. H. & Company

1900–1901
Edwin C. Best, E. C. & Company

1901–03
Amasa C. Paul, Pres., Northwestern Mer. Company, and attorney, Paul & Hawley

1903–04
John Leslie, Pres., John Leslie Paper Company

1904–06
Fred R. Salisbury, Pres., Salisbury & Satterlee Company

1906–07
Charles W. Gardner, Pres., American Soap & Chemical Company

1907–09
Benjamin F. Nelson, Pres., B. F. Nelson Sons Company

1909–11
Harry A. Tuttle, VP and GM, N. A. Tel. Company

Minneapolis Civic and Commerce Association
Formally organized December 9, 1911
Incorporated December 1911

1911–12
Arthur R. Rogers, Rogers Lumber Company

1912–14
Douglas A. Fiske, Pres., Northwestern Terminal Company

1914–15
W. F. Decker, VP, St. Anthony Falls Bank

1915–16
Edgar J. Cooper, VP, North West Knitting Co.

1916–17
Albert M. Sheldon, Sheldon Bros.

1917–20
Cavour S. Langdon, Linton & Company

1920–21
E. J. Fairfield, VP, Lindsay Bros. Company

1921–22
F. T. Heffelfinger, Pres., Peavey & Co. and Monarch Elevator Company

1922–23
F. T. Heffelfinger, Pres., Peavey & Co. and Monarch Elevator Company

1923–24
A. E. Zonne, Pres., Conklin-Zonne-Loomis Company

1924–26
Karl De Laittre, Pres., John De Laittre Company

1926–28
Arthur R. Rogers, Rogers Lumber Co.

1928–30
David D. Tenney, Pres., Tenney Company

1930–34
B. B. Sheffield, Chairman of the Board, Commander-Larabee Corporation

1934–38
Herbert J. Miller, Manager, Taxpayers Association

1938–40
D. W. Onan, Pres., D. W. Onan & Sons

1940–41
Alfred D. Lindley, Partner, Kingman, Cross, Morley, Cant & Taylor

1941–43
Thomas J. Moore Sr., Pres., Coca-Cola Bottling Co.

1943–44
Lucien C. Sprague, Pres., Minneapolis & St. Louis Railway

1944–46
Emmett Salisbury, VP, Salisbury Company

Minneapolis Area Chamber of Commerce
Name change in 1946

1946–47
Emmett Salisbury, VP, Salisbury Company

1947–48
Emmett Salisbury, VP, Salisbury Company

1948–49
R. C. Duncan, Pres., R. C. Duncan Co.

1949–51
E. J. Grimes, VP, Cargill, Inc.

1951–52
Henry T. Rutledge, VP, Northwestern National Bank

1952–54
Gerald Moore, LaBelle Transfer & Storage

1954–55
Lyman Wakefield, Partner, Piper, Jaffray & Hopwood

1955–56
Curtis C. Coleman, First National Bank of Minneapolis

1956–58
Felton Colwell, Pres., The Colwell Press

1958–59
Joyce Swan, EVP/Publisher, *Rapid City Journal & Minneapolis Star Tribune*

1959–61
E. William Boyer, Partner, Bill Boyer Ford Company

1961–62
Jay Phillips, Ed Phillips & Sons Company

1962–63
Wayne Huffman, VP and GM, Northwestern Bell Telephone Company

Minneapolis Chamber of Commerce
Name change in 1963

1963–64
Philip B. Harris, VP, Northwestern National Bank of Minneapolis

1964–65
Alexander Query, VP, Prudential Insurance Co. of America

1965–66
Russell W. Laxson, Treasurer, Minneapolis-Honeywell Regulator Company

1966–67
William F. Foss, Pres., Minneapolis-Moline Inc.

1967–68
J. Roscoe Furber, VP and Manager, Minneapolis Division, Northern States Power Company

1968–69
Lawrence F. Haeg, GM, WCCO Radio and Midwest Radio-Television, Inc.

Greater Minneapolis Chamber of Commerce
Name change in 1969

1969–70
James G. Peterson, VP and Director, Dain Kalman Quail Company

1970–71
C. Dean McNeal, EVP, The Pillsbury Company

1971–72
Dennis W. Dunne, VP, Northwest Bancorporation

1972–73
Marshall Diebold, VP, Northrup King & Co.

1973–74
William G. Phillips, Chairman and CEO, International Multifoods

1974–75
Bruce G. Schwartz, VP, Northwestern Bell

1975–76
David Koch, Chairman and CEO, Graco, Inc.

1976–77
Bower Hawthorne, VP/Public Affairs, *Minneapolis Star and Tribune*

1977–78
Leonard Murray, Pres., Soo Line Railroad

1978–79
Harvey Mackay, Pres., Mackay Minnesota Envelope Company

1979–80
Arley Bjella, Chairman and CEO, Lutheran Brotherhood

1980–81
Howard Barnhill, Chairman and CEO, North American Life & Casualty Co.

1981–82
DeWalt Ankeny Jr., Chairman and CEO, First Bank System

1982–83
Merlin Dewing, Managing Partner, Peat Marwick, Mitchell & Co.

1984
Robert Krane, Vice Chairman of the Board, Northwest Bancorporation

1985
Gene Bier, VP and CEO, Minnesota Northwestern Bell

1986
Carl Pohlad, Pres., Marquette Bank Minneapolis/Minnesota Twins

1987
Glen Nelson, M.D., EVP, Medtronic, Inc.

1988
David Cox, CEO, Cowles Media Company

1989
H. William Lurton, CEO, Jostens

1990
Roger Scherer, Pres., Scherer Brothers Lumber Company

1991
James J. Howard, Chairman and CEO, Northern States Power Company

1992
Karen Bohn, Chief Administrative Officer, Piper Jaffray Companies, Inc.

1993
Daniel C. Rohr, EVP, Commercial Banking, U.S. Bancorp

1994
Paul Citron, VP, Science & Technology, Medtronic, Inc.

1995
John Grotting, EVP, Allina Health System

1996
Ty Thayer, Corporate VP, Cargill, Inc.

1997
Larry Newman, Region VP, AT&T

1998
David Abramson, Managing Partner, Grant Thornton LLP

1999
David Richard, CEO, Norstan

2000
David Mona, Chairman, Weber Shandwick

Minneapolis Regional Chamber of Commerce
Name change in 2001

2001
Rich Forschler, Partner, Faegre & Benson

2002
Lisa Bormaster, Publisher, *CityBusiness: The Business Journal*

2003
Jac Sperling, CEO, Minnesota Wild

2004
Jac Sperling, CEO, Minnesota Wild

2005
John Stanoch, Pres.–Minnesota, Qwest

Part One

Setting the Course

A Minneapolis Retrospective

by Mark Soderstrom

Stone Arch Bridge by Lloyd Hinton, painted in the early 20th century

St. Anthony Falls, painted by Henry Lewis, circa 1848

Forged by Rivers

Although Minneapolis calls itself the "City of Lakes," for most of its history this region has been defined by rivers: the Minnesota and the Mississippi. From the beginning, these rivers have dominated the city's geography, its visitors' attention, and its entrepreneurs' vision.

The geographic destiny of Minneapolis was shaped about 12,000 years ago at the end of the last ice age. As the ice pack receded, it left in its wake a great glacial lake whose drainage formed the channel of the Minnesota River and changed the shape of the Mississippi River. The ice pack also left behind a river bottom that made the Mississippi fall faster between Minneapolis and St. Paul than at any other point in its entire course. As a result, Minneapolis would be blessed with generous water-power to fuel its industry.

North America's earliest inhabitants used the Mississippi and Minnesota rivers as trade routes as long as 10,000 years ago. About 800 to 1,000 years ago, the Mississippian culture of indigenous Americans used the Mississippi as

Native American village near Fort Snelling, painted by Seth Eastman, circa 1846

part of an extensive trade network. It was the modern Dakota nation, however, who made this place their home. The Dakota, who controlled the Mississippi from its headwaters, south past St. Anthony Falls, used the river for travel, hunting, and warfare. They traveled the river in dugout canoes or buffalo skin boats and tapped sugar maples on Nicollet Island.

In the late 17th century, local Dakota began to come into contact with Ojibwe tribes that were being pushed west by other Native American nations displaced by European settlement. They also came into contact with French explorers who had discovered the region's lucrative fur trade.

One of the French explorers the Dakota encountered was Father Louis Hennepin, a Franciscan priest who was part of a group sent to explore the upper Mississippi River valley in 1680. During the expedition, a band of Dakota captured Hennepin and two companions near Lake Pepin in southern Minnesota and took them to a village near Mille Lacs Lake in the central part of the state.

Father Louis Hennepin at St. Anthony Falls

Native Americans trading goods, 1700s

Hennepin spent several months with the Dakota, who brought him to the great falls on the Mississippi that they called *minirara*, "curling water," and *owahmenah*, "falling water." Impressed by the falls' beauty, Hennepin decided to christen the formation St. Anthony Falls, after his patron saint, Anthony of Padua. In 1683, after Hennepin had returned to France, he wrote an account of his journeys that made the falls famous throughout Europe. The spectacular falls he described eventually became the heart of Minneapolis's development.

Life on the Frontier

French exploration and trade in Minnesota continued throughout the 1700s, but by the end of the century, French interest in the region began to decline. France had become embroiled in international disputes, and local French traders were coming under increasing pressure from encroaching British traders.

While the French battled other countries, tensions were high between local Dakota and Ojibwe tribes. Throughout the 18th century, the two nations struggled over

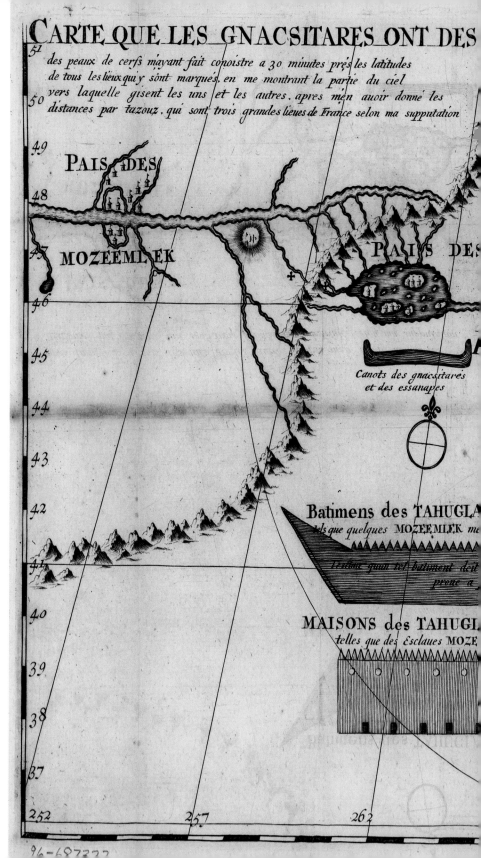

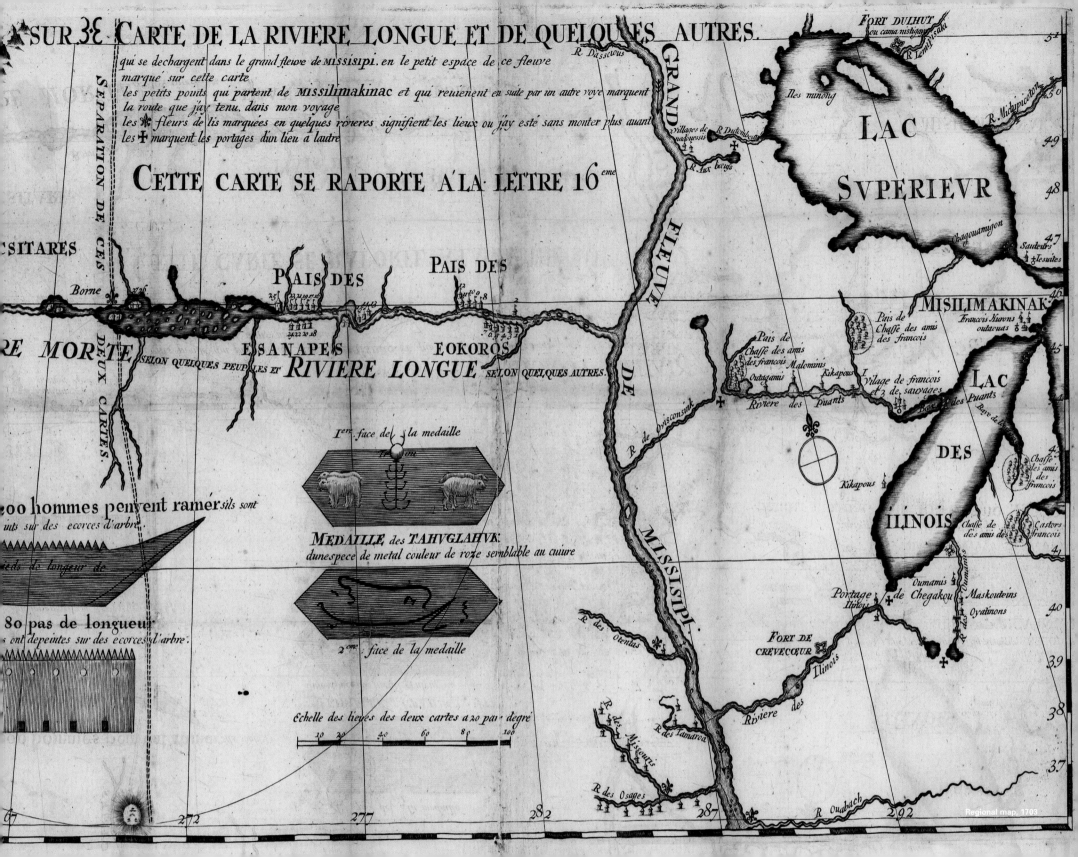

SUR ⅀ CARTE DE LA RIVIERE LONGUE ET DE QUELQUES AUTRES.

qui se dechargent dans le grand fleuve de MISSISIPI. en le petit espace de ce fleuve
marqué sur cette carte

les petits points qui partent de MISSILIMAKINAC et qui reuienent en suite par un autre voye marquent
la route que j'ay tenu, dans mon voyage

les ⚜ fleurs de lis marquées en quelques riuieres signifient les lieux ou j'ay esté sans monter plus auant

les ✝ marquent les portages d'un lieu a l'autre

CETTE CARTE SE RAPORTE A LA LETTRE 16ᵉᵐᵉ

SEPARATION DE CES DEUX CARTES.

CSITARES

Borne

RE MORTE

PAIS DES

PAIS DES

ESANAPES SELON QUELQUES PEUPLES ET RIVIERE LONGUE SELON QUELQUES AUTRES.

EOKOROS

1er face de la medaille

MEDAILLE des TAHUGLAHUK
dun espece de metal couleur de roze semblable au cuiure

00 hommes peuvent ramer s'ils sont
uts sur des ecorces d'arbre.

de longeur de

80 pas de longueur
s ont depeintes sur des ecorces d'arbre.

2eme fice de la medaille

Echelle des lieues des deux cartes a 20 par degré
10   20   40   60   80   100

FORT DULHUT
ou cama nistigaya

R. Dasscious

R. Lemisisaki

Iles minong

R. Midupicoton

LAC
SUPERIEUR

Villages de nadouessis

R. Dutonboan

R. Aux beuys

Chagouamigon

Sauteurs
Jesuites

MISILIMAKINAK

Francois Hurons
outaouas

Pais de
Chasse des amis
des francois

Pais de
Chasse des amis
des francois

Outagamis

Malominis

Kikapous

Vilage de francois
et 3 de sauuages

LAC

Riuiere des Puants

Baye des Puants

GRAND

FLEUVE

DE

MISSISIPI

R. de Ouisconsink

Kikapous

DES

Chasse
des amis
des
francois

ILINOIS

Chasse de
des amis des

Castors
francois

Oumamis
de Chegakou

Maskouteins

Portage
Ilinois

Oyatinons

R. des Otentas

FORT DE
CREVECOEUR

R. des
Ilinois

Riuiere des

R. des Missouris

R. des Tamaroa

R. des Osages

R. Ouabach

Colonel Josiah Snelling, 1820

territory. Ultimately, the Ojibwe gained the Mississippi headwaters and Mille Lacs in the late 1700s, restricting the Dakota to the territory from the Twin Cities area south to Wabasha.

France struggled to maintain its claim on the land as well, eventually losing all of its North American territories to the British in 1763, after the Seven Years' War. With the French no longer viable competition, the British began to dominate regional trade. The American Revolution, however, changed things again, and France regained its title to land west of the Mississippi. In 1803 Napoleon sold the land to the United States as the Louisiana Purchase.

Following the Louisiana Purchase, the U.S. government sent Lieutenant Zebulon Pike to secure land for military establishments in the northern part of the

Fort Snelling, painted by Edward K. Thomas, 1850

new territory. In 1805 Pike ascended the Mississippi and chose the area of modern-day Minneapolis as a good site for an outpost. On an island near the confluence of the Minnesota and Mississippi Rivers, Pike signed a treaty with local Dakota leaders for the purchase of land on both sides of the

Mississippi extending nine miles from the mouth of the Minnesota River, north to St. Anthony Falls. Pike valued the land at $200,000 but stipulated no price on the treaty itself. When Congress finally approved the treaty in 1808, it appropriated only $2,000 for the purchase.

In 1814, British forces captured Prairie du Chien, Wisconsin, during the War of 1812, and took control of the entire upper Mississippi River valley. At this point the U.S. government realized that it only nominally controlled the upper Mississippi and its valuable resources. Even so, it was not until

Farmhouse near Fort Snelling, illustrated by Rudolph Cronau, 1881

Blacksmith shop, 1885

constable to control the profitable local fur trade. Soldiers-turned-farmers cultivated significant acreage in the first large-scale, western-style agriculture in the region. Other soldiers took up civilian trades such as carpentry and blacksmithing to build and maintain the massive complex.

A Community Takes Hold

In 1837 the Dakota and Ojibwe ceded lands east of the Mississippi, opening the east bank of St. Anthony Falls for settlement. The first person to take advantage of the opportunity was Franklin Steele, a storekeeper from Fort Snelling. As soon as Steele heard the news that the land was open, he set off during the night to make his claim. When a commander from Fort Snelling went to claim the land the following day, he found 25-year-old Steele already there. Steele then set his sights on

1819 that Lieutenant Colonel Henry Leavenworth began construction of a fort on the land that Pike had secured 14 years before. Leavenworth envisioned a wooden fort some distance above the mouth of the Minnesota, but before he made much progress, he was replaced by Colonel Josiah Snelling. Snelling revised the plans, opting for a grander stone structure directly above the confluence.

One of Snelling's construction obstacles was the lack of sufficient wood in the surrounding region. To address this problem, soldiers made the first industrial use of St. Anthony Falls' immense power, building the first sawmill at the falls in 1821, nine miles upstream from the fort's construction site. Logs were floated down the Mississippi from a logging site 14 miles upstream and processed at a rate of 3,500 board feet a day. The fort

was completed in 1825, and it was named after its visionary colonel.

In Fort Snelling's first decade, operations were geared toward surviving the harsh Minnesota winter rather than surviving an attack. Indeed, in its long history there has never been a hostile shot fired from the fort, since it has never come under attack. Instead, the fort functioned as an agricultural colony and

Franklin Steele, 1875

harnessing the falls' power, and in 1848 he and Ard Godfrey, a Maine millwright, built the first civilian industry on the falls—a sawmill that would later provide the lumber to construct the town of St. Anthony.

When Minnesota became a territory in 1849, settlement began to boom and tensions rose as people tried to move to the Mississippi River's west bank. Congress finally opened the west bank to settlement in 1852, and a small community quickly formed.

Several names for the new settlement were suggested, including Lowell, Brooklyn, Addiesville, West St. Anthony, and All Saints. Finally, teacher Charles Hoag proposed Minnehapolis, a name that combined

Mills along St. Anthony Falls, 1840s–1850s

4th Street looking toward Jackson Street, 1850s–1860s

First bridge to span the Mississippi River, between Minneapolis and St. Anthony, 1868

East side of St. Anthony Falls and dam, 1867

the Dakota word for water, *minne*, and the Greek word for city, *polis*. The "h" was soon dropped, and the name Minneapolis was adopted in 1852.

By 1854 Minneapolis's population was 300. Most of the first settlers came from New England and the mid-Atlantic, and many were involved in the timber industry. Before long, Minneapolis began to resemble a small New England village, and by 1856 the population had risen to 1,555.

In 1855 Minneapolis and St. Anthony celebrated the opening of the first bridge to span the Mississippi River, a graceful suspension bridge that linked the two towns. From this point on, the interests of Minneapolis and St. Anthony merged in common competition with St. Paul, downstream.

In 1858 two local companies—the Minneapolis Mill Company and the St. Anthony Falls Water Power Company—completed a dam across St. Anthony Falls. Shaped like an inverted V, the dam channeled water from the middle of the river to both sides. The land around the river also began to change as people cut timber and plowed prairies. A new era was clearly on the horizon.

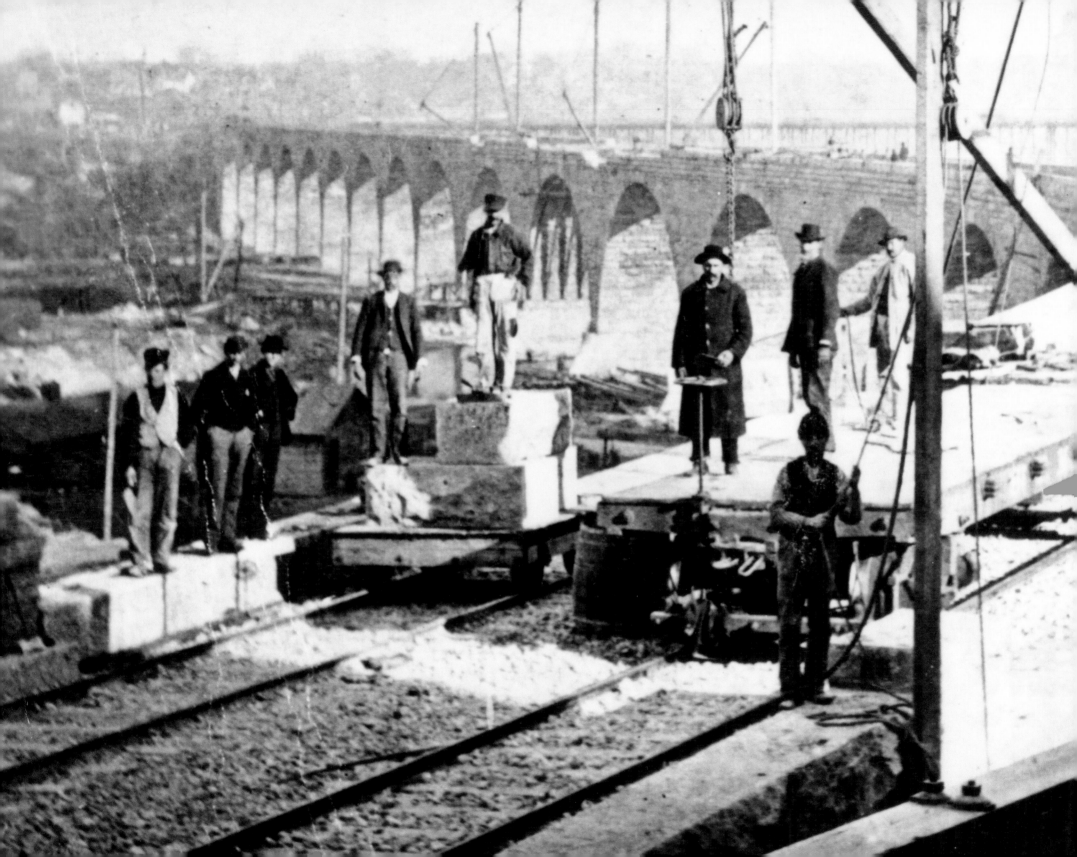

Construction of the Stone Arch Bridge, 1883

2

Dramatic Changes

Minneapolis expanded rapidly between 1860 and 1900. Industries were formed, infrastructure was established, and the population grew exponentially. In the span of 40 years, Minneapolis transformed from a small, quiet village into a bustling cosmopolitan center.

Industrial Might

Minneapolis's economy was built on a foundation of wood. By 1869, 18 mills processed lumber at or near St. Anthony Falls. In the 1870s and 1880s, however, concern about the effects of loose logs on the Mississippi River's limestone base caused many sawmills to relocate upstream to what is now North Minneapolis. The moves did nothing to stall the industry's growth; by the end of the 19th century, Minneapolis was the country's leading sawmill center.

The lumber industry inspired a host of satellite businesses, including paper and planing mills; furniture factories; sash, door, and blind factories; shingle manufacturers; wooden bucket makers; and barrel makers. It also

Logs accumulating at St. Anthony Falls, 1865

Lumber processing at a Minneapolis sawmill, 1885

Aftermath of the Washburn "A" mill explosion, 1878

gave birth to the local flour milling industry, as people who had made their fortunes in lumber used that money to finance flour mills.

During the Civil War, Minneapolis benefited from the increased demand for flour. By 1870 Minneapolis was producing 200,000 barrels of flour a year, and by 1884 it was the world's leading flour producer. In the late 1870s, 20 flour mills were in operation, including those owned by Cadwallader C. Washburn, Charles A. Pillsbury, John Sargent Pillsbury, George H. Christian, and George T. Smith. By

1890 the city's flour mills were producing seven million barrels per year, about a third of which were exported.

During this time, Minneapolis millers made revolutionary technological advances. Around 1873 the

Washburn mills began using an adapted purifier that captured the nutritious middle layer of wheat. This new process created fine white flour with higher nutritional and gluten content. Advances were also made in production capabilities. In 1881

Charles Pillsbury built his $1 million "A" mill, which could process up to 5,000 barrels per day.

This remarkable progress, however, did not come without setbacks. Washburn's "A" mill, one of the most important mills in the district, exploded and burned in 1878, killing 18 people and destroying several nearby mills, businesses, and residences. Undeterred, Washburn built a new, bigger "A" mill the next year.

All of this industry growth placed an increasing demand on St. Anthony Falls, with near-disastrous results. The "V" dam built by the Minneapolis Mill Company and the St. Anthony Falls Water Power Company in 1858 had placed a strain on the falls, exposing the center rock. Then in 1868 two local businessmen began work on a tunnel at the falls to provide power to Nicollet Island. It proved to be more than the rock could bear, and in 1869 the upper layer of limestone began to leak and then collapsed. Citizens rushed to plug the rapidly expanding gap, floating debris of all sorts into the river to stabilize the falls. Their efforts were only a temporary fix, and problems at the falls persisted. The federal government and the city of Minneapolis eventually stepped in, spending nearly $950,000 between 1870 and 1884 to create a system of dams and aprons to manage the water flow. The system they created ultimately preserved the falls as a source of power and beauty.

Minneapolis in Motion

As industrial production expanded in Minneapolis, the need for large-scale

Pillsbury "A" mill, 1879

Pillsbury employee with a cartload of flour, 1870s–early 1900s

Promotional poster in the *St. Paul Dispatch,* 1889

Workers repairing St. Anthony Falls, 1870

Break in the tunnel at St. Anthony Falls, 1869

Northern Pacific Railroad bridge near Bohemian Flats, 1880s–1910s

St. Paul and Pacific Railway, 1873

was completed in 1883, was the second mainline rail bridge to span the Mississippi.

By 1883 the Northern Pacific Railroad had reached the West Coast, and Minneapolis was connected to every part of the nation by railway. Minneapolis, like other cities on the rail lines, prospered and grew. To accommodate a growing number of passengers, the Chicago, Milwaukee, and St. Paul Railroad built a grand station at Third Street and Washington Avenue in 1889.

transportation became increasingly important. In 1862 the city got its first railroad access when the St. Paul and Pacific Railway added tracks between St. Paul and St. Anthony; in 1866 the railroad stretched as far as Nicollet Island. The first all-rail line linking

Minneapolis and Chicago opened in 1867, and a rail line to Duluth opened in 1872. In 1887 Minneapolis got unimpeded rail access to international markets with the Soo Line, which connected to the Canadian Pacific Railroad in Sault Ste. Marie, Michigan.

Though Minneapolis now had rail access, it still faced the challenge of transporting goods across the Mississippi River. In 1880 construction began on a rail bridge extending across the full width of the river, right below St. Anthony Falls. The Stone Arch Bridge, which

The sheer volume of activity in Minneapolis necessitated an effective transportation system within the city as well. Horse-drawn streetcars began serving the city in 1875, with lines radiating north and south from downtown along the

Old Union Station, 1887

Soo Line tracks under construction, 1892

Horse-drawn streetcar on Cedar Avenue, 1886

main commercial streets. In 1889 Minneapolis's first electric streetcar began operation, making the city a national leader in electric transportation. By the end of the century, the streetcars were carrying 175,000 passengers daily.

A Growing City

Minneapolis blossomed once the Minnesota legislature voted to upgrade it to city status in 1867. The fledgling city elected its first mayor, banker and mill owner Dorilus Morrison, to guide its growth. Five years later, St. Anthony was incorporated as part of Minneapolis, and the new charter provided for a mayor, comptroller, treasurer, and city council. Lawyer Eugene M. Wilson was elected the first mayor of the newly merged Minneapolis.

By 1880 Minneapolis was expanding at breakneck speed. Streets were paved, sidewalks were laid, water mains were built, and sewer systems were installed. Department stores such as Powers, Donaldson's, and Young Quinlan opened in the thriving commercial district along Nicollet Avenue.

Such massive growth demanded power, and as always, St. Anthony Falls provided a ready source. The nation's first hydroelectric station began operation at St. Anthony Falls in September 1882, less than a month before the next such station opened in Appleton, Wisconsin. Minneapolis

Nicollet Avenue, 1898

Electric streetcar, 1896

Crew working on a sewer, 1905

Lower Dam Hydroelectric Plant, 1895

Map of Minneapolis, 1874

quickly replaced its gas street lamps with electric ones.

In 1889 Minneapolis covered 53.5 square miles and included a limestone city hall, a lumber exchange building, a theater district, six hospitals, a baseball team, and many churches and schools.

Minneapolis's education system grew along with the city; its first high school, Central Union High, opened in 1857, and by 1874 the city had 10 school buildings with a combined enrollment of 3,807 students. Public education boomed after the Minnesota legislature mandated in 1885 that all Minnesota children between the ages of eight and 16 attend 12 weeks of school a year.

University of Minnesota, 1880

Higher education institutions also developed. In 1873 the University of Minnesota graduated its first class, which consisted of two students. Though the university was created in 1851, it struggled through a location change, an initial shortage

Central High School on 4th Avenue South, 1902

Danish immigrants, 1898

Swedish immigrant, 1870

of students, and the onset of the Civil War. Just seven years after it graduated its first class, the University of Minnesota had 300 students. By 1894 the campus consisted of several buildings, including a library, museum, and observatory. The university's departments ranged from agriculture and mining to law and medicine.

Private colleges were established in Minneapolis during this time as well. Augsburg College moved from Wisconsin to Minneapolis in 1872, and the Minneapolis College of

Art and Design opened its doors in 1886.

As Minneapolis flourished, it drew people from a variety of places and backgrounds. The post–Civil War era ushered in an age of migration and immigration, and Minneapolis experienced a great influx of people. The city, which had 13,066 residents in 1870, grew to 46,887 people in just 10 years. By 1900 the population had reached 202,718, making Minneapolis the 19th-largest city in the United States.

Many immigrants were from Scandinavian countries. This new population settled in developing urban centers such as the Cedar-Riverside neighborhood, creating a large and vibrant community. Other groups settling in Minneapolis included Britons, Germans, Bohemians, Russians, African-Americans, Jews, Canadians, and Poles.

The remarkable changes Minneapolis experienced between 1860 and 1900 propelled the city to prominence. These positive trends would continue in the 20th century.

Bohemian Flats neighborhood, 1885

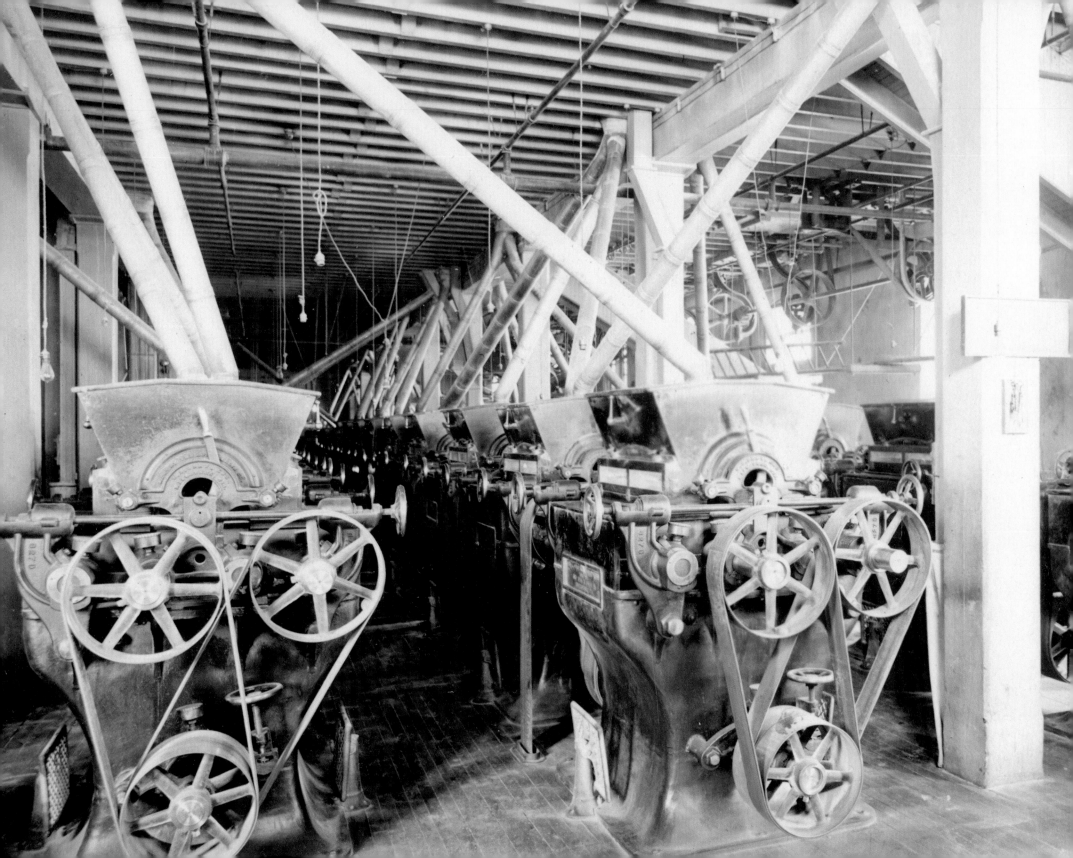

Pillsbury-Washburn mill, 1897

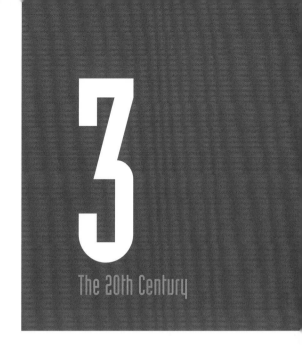

Prosperity and Possibilities

At the turn of the 20th century, Minneapolis was enjoying an unprecedented boom. The city was the top grain miller in the world, and that activity generated a furious level of development and diversification. The beautiful Chamber of Commerce/Grain Exchange building, designed by renowned architect Louis Sullivan and built in 1905, was one of many structures constructed during this time.

As grain production boomed, Minneapolis dedicated itself to art, education, and health. The Minneapolis Symphony Orchestra, later the world-renowned Minnesota Orchestra, played its first concert in 1903. Public schools blossomed: University High School opened in 1908, followed by West High School in 1909 and the second Central High School in 1913, which replaced the first building, which burned down in 1863. At the collegiate level, the University of Minnesota was growing steadily, both in size and prestige. The university established a relationship with the Mayo Clinic in 1915, developing the nation's first three-year, post-M.D. program for physicians in specialty practice. A number of health care facilities were

Construction of the Federal Reserve bank at Marquette Avenue and 5th Street, 1923

Chamber of Commerce/Grain Exchange building, 1900s–1920s

Federal Reserve bank, 1925

established as well, including Abbott Hospital for Women in 1902, and Hillcrest Surgical Hospital in 1910.

The city's financial industry was also gathering strength. In 1914 Minneapolis's importance as a financial center was enhanced when the Federal Reserve opened a district bank downtown. This bank, along with well-established local financial institutions such as Northwest Bank Corporation and First Bank Stock Corporation, kept the city relatively stable throughout the shocks of the Depression.

Minneapolis continued to thrive in the 1920s. The Minneapolis Public Library opened branches and expanded its collection. Enrollment in public schools grew; more than 70,000 students attended Minneapolis public schools in 1922.

New forms of transportation also developed. Air travel became possible when Northwest Airlines introduced passenger service in 1928. Founded in 1926, the airline operated out of a City of Minneapolis–owned airport that was renamed Minneapolis–St. Paul International Airport in 1948.

Meanwhile, local businesses thrived. In 1928 the Washburn Crosby Company combined with other regional millers to form General Mills. Three years later, General Mills introduced Bisquick baking mix, which quickly became popular in American households.

Public Hardship and Public Works

The good times, however, would not last. In 1929 Foshay Tower opened with a grand celebration. Built by public utilities speculator Wilbur B. Foshay, the 32-story building overextended Foshay's finances, as did the stock market crash two months after the tower opened.

Runway construction at Wold-Chamberlain Field, now Minneapolis–St. Paul International Airport, 1940

First Lady Eleanor Roosevelt (left) exiting Wold-Chamberlain Field, 1937

Passengers boarding a Northwest Airways plane piloted by Speed Holman, 1929

Foshay Tower under construction, 1928

Men working on a WPA project, 1938

World War II poster, 1943

"I've found the job where I fit best!"

FIND YOUR WAR JOB
In Industry – Agriculture – Business

Despite local banks' stability, the Depression assailed farming and other industries, and Minneapolis had its share of hardship. The Gateway District teemed with unemployed men. It was also during this time that Buffalo, New York, surpassed Minneapolis in grain production. Minneapolis never regained its distinction as the country's top grain miller.

Native Minneapolitan Floyd B. Olson, who was elected governor of Minnesota in 1930, worked to bring Franklin Delano Roosevelt's New Deal programs to Minnesota. One of

those programs, the WPA, helped turn Minneapolis's adversity into beauty. Otherwise unemployed tradesmen and workers built much of the city's current park system and public infrastructure under the aegis of this federal program.

The Tide Changes
The Great Depression finally came to an end when America entered World War II. Minneapolis's factories returned to full production, and more women entered the workforce as men left for battle. The war redefined Minneapolis life and business.

Launching of a U.S. Navy ship produced by Cargill, in Savage, 1943

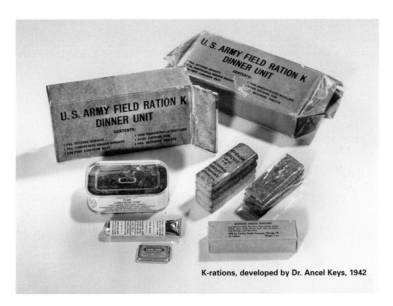

K-rations, developed by Dr. Ancel Keys, 1942

Earl Bakken's first wearable, battery-powered, transistorized pacemaker, 1957

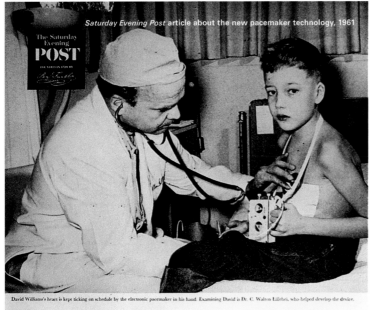

Saturday Evening Post article about the new pacemaker technology, 1961

The Saturday Evening POST

David Williams's heart is kept ticking on schedule by the electronic pacemaker in his hand. Examining David is Dr. C. Walton Lillehei, who helped develop the device.

Making a Heartbeat Behave

During the war, the milling industry expanded its technological innovation into other realms. In addition to providing food for the military, General Mills supplied gun sights and precision control instruments. Cargill, a grain trading company whose roots ran deep in the community, made ships for the U.S. Navy.

Honeywell was another local business that made technological contributions to the war. Founded in Minneapolis in 1886 as a maker of thermostats, Honeywell developed flight systems for Army aircraft and new types of bombs.

At the University of Minnesota, research for the war effort went into high gear, on everything from computers to food. In 1941 public health professor Dr. Ancel Keys developed K-rations to ensure a basic level of nutrition for U.S.

servicepeople. University researchers also worked on aerospace systems and missile guidance components.

Upward and Outward

The years following World War II were a time of innovation and expansion for Minneapolis, especially in the realms of health care and science. In 1951 the University of Minnesota opened the Variety Club Heart Hospital, the country's first hospital devoted to heart patients; in 1952 university doctors performed the first successful open-heart surgery. Another milestone in cardiac care was reached in 1957, when Earl Bakken, a University of Minnesota graduate and local businessman, developed a wearable, portable pacemaker system. Three years later, Bakken's company, Medtronic, acquired exclusive rights to build implantable pacemakers, lofting the firm to the top of its industry.

Southdale shopping mall, in Edina, 1956

Seymour Cray with his supercomputer, 1974

There were rapid changes within Minneapolis after the war as well. In 1950 the city's population reached its peak: 521,718. As automobiles became the preferred mode of transit, however, many people began moving to suburbs. In 1956, Southdale, the country's first enclosed shopping mall, opened in the suburb of Edina. The mall was developed by the Dayton Company, which later became Target Corporation.

In the 1960s and 1970s Minneapolis's industrial base continued to diversify. A strong computer manufacturing industry developed, and in 1976 Seymour Cray, who founded Cray Research in Minneapolis and graduated from the University of Minnesota, introduced the supercomputer. Strides were made in medical research as well. The first successful bone marrow transplant took place at the University of Minnesota Hospital in 1968, as did the first use of artificial blood in a patient, in 1979.

A downtown revitalization program was also launched. Minneapolis's first skyway, spanning Seventh Street South, was constructed in 1962, and a pedestrian boulevard along Nicollet Avenue was built in 1967. Landmark buildings were erected: a striking Federal Reserve building, in 1973; the city's tallest building, the IDS Center, also in 1973; and the street-spanning Hennepin County Government Center, in 1974.

Hitting Its Stride

Minneapolis claimed its place in the cultural limelight in the final decades of the 20th century. Musicians such as Prince, Morris Day and the Time,

Opening of the first skyway, 1962

IDS Center

Spoonbridge and Cherry sculpture at the Walker Art Center

Hubert H. Humphrey Metrodome

Minnesota Twins pitchers Les Straker (left), Bert Blyleven (center), and Frank Viola (right), 1987

Hüsker Dü, and the Replacements made the city's First Avenue club a world-class music venue, as immortalized in Prince's 1984 film, *Purple Rain*. Recording labels such as Flyte Tyme and Paisley Park Studios put Minneapolis firmly on the pop music map. In 1988 the Walker Art Center installed its Sculpture Garden, featuring the monumental *Spoonbridge and Cherry* sculpture by Claes Oldenburg and Coosje van Bruggen. The sculpture became a Minneapolis icon.

The tragedy of the Northwestern National Bank building fire in 1982 provided an impetus for Minneapolis to continue building. A great deal of the city's current skyline took shape during the next 10 years: City Center and Marriott Hotel City

Center, in 1983; the Norwest Center/ Wells Fargo Center, in 1987; and U.S. Bank Place, in 1992. Along with the construction boom came a system for funding Minneapolis neighborhood revitalization, which capitalized on the city's rich tradition of citizen participation.

One of the most significant structures built in this period was the Hubert H. Humphrey Metrodome, which brought professional sports into downtown Minneapolis. The American League Minnesota Twins and NFL Minnesota Vikings left Metropolitan Stadium, in Bloomington, to take residence at the Metrodome in 1982. The move paid off handsomely: in 1987 the Twins won the World Series in a Metrodome filled with adoring fans

Amusement rides at the Mall of America, in Bloomington, 1990s

waving Homer Hankies. (The team won another nail-biting World Series in 1991.) In 1989 the NBA Minnesota Timberwolves began playing at the Metrodome, but the team moved to its own downtown venue, the newly constructed Target Center, a year later. The Minnesota Lynx, of the Women's NBA, began playing at Target Center in 1999.

After the Twins and Vikings left Metropolitan Stadium, plans began for building the country's largest shopping and entertainment complex on the site. In 1992 the Mall of America opened to resounding success, and it quickly became one of the top tourist destinations in the country.

At the same time, the city turned back to its river. In the 1990s Minneapolis began transforming the city's riverfront, restoring and redeveloping the milling district into upscale residential areas and new cultural districts. The revitalized riverfront has reversed patterns of urban emigration and brought people back to live in the heart of the city. Today the Guthrie Theater's new site, the Frederick R. Weisman Art Museum's revolutionary architecture, and the Mill City Museum provide a cultural anchor for the riverfront. Minneapolis has entered the 21st century with its face toward the future and its heart, as always, focused on the river and the falls.

Frederick R. Weisman Art Museum at the University of Minnesota

Part Two

In the Flow of Success

Minneapolis Today

by Kristina Sauerwein and Penny Suess

The Local Brand

Minneapolis has catered to visitors since the 1800s, when sightseers made long treks to the city's unique natural attraction, St. Anthony Falls. Two centuries later, Minneapolis's hospitality, travel, and retail industries serve a far-flung clientele, host major conventions, and invite shoppers from around the world to delight in retail wonders.

A Tradition of Welcome

Father Louis Hennepin made St. Anthony Falls popular by describing the waterfall in a 1683 book that was widely read in Europe. By the mid 1800s sightseers regularly arrived at Fort Snelling by steamboat, traveling from there by carriage to St. Anthony Falls, Minnehaha Falls, and area lakes.

To accommodate early visitors, grand hotels such as the Winslow House (1857), Nicollet House (1858), and West Hotel (1884) were built. The Radisson Hotel, erected in 1909, quickly became the social center of Minneapolis. One of the first hotels in the country to have a telephone in each room, the Radisson was famous for its opulence.

Park Plaza Hotel, in Bloomington

In 1962 Minneapolis entrepreneur Curtis L. Carlson acquired the Radisson and built around it a chain that has spread throughout the world. Carlson started the Gold Bond Stamp Company in 1938, supplying Minneapolis grocery stores, gas stations, and other independent merchants with trading stamps to help draw customers. By the 1950s major supermarkets across the United States and Canada were offering the stamps. Following the Radisson purchase, the Minnetonka-based company changed its name to Carlson Companies and acquired dozens of restaurant and travel businesses. It is still family owned.

Carlson Companies currently operates 890 hotels in 70 countries under the Radisson Hotels & Resorts, Regent International Hotels, Park Plaza Hotels & Resorts, Country Inns & Suites By Carlson, and Park Inn brands. Other holdings include T.G.I. Friday's restaurants, Radisson Seven Seas Cruises, and a half interest in Carlson Wagonlit Travel, a corporate travel agency that has branches in more than 140 countries. With 2004 sales of $26.1 billion, Carlson Companies is one of the largest privately held corporations in the United States.

A relative newcomer to the lodging business, Chanhassen-based AmericInn was founded in 1984. The franchise has more than 220 locations nationwide and is already making a name for itself as upscale yet affordable. AmericInn's motto, "Quiet Nights, Rest Assured," is backed up by the soundproof construction of its properties.

Meet Me in Minneapolis

Sometimes a restful retreat is the last thing conventioneers are looking for. This was certainly the case at the 1892 Republican Convention in Minneapolis. "Until morning the

Country Inns & Suites Hotel, in Bloomington

political boomers made pandemo-
nium in the hotels," proclaimed
the *Brooklyn Daily Eagle* during the
convention. The city's Exposition
Building, site of Minnesota's only
national political convention, was
just six years old at the time.

Later conventions were held in two
Minneapolis Auditoriums, built in 1905
and 1927, and in the 1965 Convention
Hall. By 1989 the city had become so

popular with meeting organizers that
a larger venue, the Minneapolis
Convention Center, was begun. An
expansion that nearly doubled the
center's size was completed in 2002,
resulting in more than 700,000 square
feet of meeting and exhibition space.

Unique Retail
Local attractions, including theaters
and renowned museums, are a big
part of Minneapolis's appeal for

conventioneers, and a pilgrimage
to the country's largest shopping
center, the Mall of America, in
Bloomington, is a must for visitors
of all kinds. Every year more than
42 million people browse the
complex, famous the world over
for its sheer size (4.2 million square
feet), variety (500-plus stores,
50 restaurants), and unique attractions (among them a seven-acre
amusement park, a 1.2 million-

gallon aquarium, and a four-story
LEGO showplace).

What some people may not
know is that the enclosed mall
was born in a Minneapolis suburb
in 1956, with the opening of
Southdale Shopping Center, in
Edina. Designed to complement
the new suburban lifestyle, the
center borrowed elements of the
village green, European city square,

Singer Nick Carter signing autographs at the Mall of America, 2002

Mall of America's West Market

and elegant shopping arcade. The visionary yet practical idea was to unite commerce and sociability in one compact, temperature-controlled location—with plenty of free parking. Southdale remains a premier regional center, featuring more than 130 retailers.

The Dayton Company, which developed Southdale, got its start in 1902 with the opening of Goodfellows—later known as Dayton's—in downtown Minneapolis. Generations of Minneapolitans shopped in the big department store, and it was in front of Dayton's on Nicollet Mall that Mary Tyler Moore tossed her hat during the opening credits of the 1970s television classic *The Mary Tyler Moore Show*.

In 1962 the Dayton Company opened the first Target discount store.

Underwater Adventures Aquarium at the Mall of America, in Bloomington

Target Corporation headquarters

Wireless telephone display at Best Buy

The popular chain eventually assumed central importance for the company, which changed its name to Target in 2000. Target now has more than 1,300 Target stores in 47 states and employs more than 275,000 people. In 2004 the retailer sold its other holdings, Marshall Field's and Mervyn's. Revenues reached $45.6 billion that year.

National retailers Best Buy and the Musicland Group, like Target Corporation, also came of age in Minneapolis. The first Musicland record store opened in Minneapolis in 1956, and in 1978 the company acquired the Sam Goody music store chain. Headquartered in Minnetonka, the Musicland Group sells music, movies, movie memorabilia, and video games at more than 900 Sam Goody, Suncoast, and Media Play stores in the United States, Puerto Rico, and the Virgin Islands. The Musicland Group had sales of $1.4 billion in fiscal 2004.

Best Buy, the Richfield-based retailer of consumer electronics, entertainment software, computers, and more, also has made the move from selling strictly audio products. The company was founded as Sound of Music in St. Paul in 1966 and changed its name to Best Buy in the early 1980s when it expanded into video products and appliances. In 2004 the National Retail Federation rated Best Buy the top-earning specialty retailer in the nation, with 2004 revenues of $27.4 billion, and *Forbes* named it Company of the Year. The corporation operates more than 800 stores under the names Best Buy, Magnolia Audio Video, and Future Shop in the United States and Canada.

Local Flavor

Food is another category in which Minneapolis retailers have enjoyed generations of success. Nash Finch Company, which began in the 1800s as a few small stores in North Dakota, moved its food packing and shipping businesses to Minneapolis in 1918. Today it is one

Family dinner at a Buca di Beppo kitchen table

of the nation's leading food retail and distribution companies, with fiscal 2004 revenues of $3.8 billion. Nash Finch owns and operates 110 supermarkets in the upper Midwest under various banners such as Econofoods, Sun Mart, and Family Thrift Center. It supplies independent markets and military commissaries around the world as well.

Supervalu, a Fortune 100 company, built its first grocery warehouse in Minneapolis in 1924. The Eden Prairie–based company operates more than 1,500 grocery stores in 40 states, including well-known supermarkets such as Cub Foods and Save a Lot. One of Minnesota's top five public companies, Supervalu employs 55,000 people and had revenues of $19.5 billion in fiscal 2005.

Minneapolis retailers also know how to tempt people away from their own kitchens. The secret is plentiful, down-home cooking. The Buca di Beppo chain of eateries, known for family-size tables, big platters of hearty Southern Italian fare, and tongue-in-cheek decor, began with a single restaurant in Minneapolis in 1993. Owned by Buca Inc., of Minneapolis, Buca di Beppo now has 95 locations coast to coast.

HomeTown Buffet and Old Country Buffet, owned by Eagan-based Buffets Inc., celebrate traditional American home cooking. Food is prepared with fresh ingredients and made from scratch in small quantities. Begun in 1983, Buffets Inc. has extended its friendly, family-oriented restaurants into 380 company-owned and franchised locations in 38 states.

Sweet treats from Minneapolis's International Dairy Queen have been around longer than many Minneapolis food purveyors. The opening of the first Dairy Queen, in Joliet, Illinois, in 1940, also laid the foundation for franchising as a business model; today most of the company's 5,900-plus stores are independently owned and operated. A subsidiary of Omaha, Nebraska–based Berkshire Hathaway, International Dairy Queen also franchises Karmelkorn and Orange Julius stores.

Dairy Queen, 1955

Minneapolis has grown up impressing visitors with scenic wonders and charming them with homegrown hospitality. And while the city didn't invent retail, it certainly has added a few new twists.

5

Education

Leading in Learning

Excellence in education, especially higher education, has been a point of pride for Minnesotans since territorial days. Nowhere is this truer than in Minneapolis, home of the University of Minnesota, strong private and community colleges, and academically superior primary and secondary schools. Fine schools contribute to the city's outstanding quality of life and create the workforce Minneapolis needs to stay competitive in a changing economy.

The first school in Minnesota was established in 1834 in a log building on the western shore of Lake Harriet. The teachers were Christian missionaries; the students were drawn from both the Native American community and from military families posted to Fort Snelling. In 1849 the first private schools opened in St. Anthony, a village on the east side of the Mississippi River that was incorporated as part of Minneapolis in 1872. By 1874 some 3,800 students were enrolled in 10 schools in Minneapolis.

Education was highly esteemed in this frontier state. A generous land grant system, established during the first state legislative session in 1858, provided

Students gathering in front of Northrop Auditorium at the University of Minnesota

income from valuable timber and iron ore royalties to operate primary and secondary schools as well as teachers' colleges. By the 1930s, Minnesota was known for the number of children who completed eighth grade—84 percent, compared to half, on average, for the rest of the country.

Today Minnesota receives top grades when it comes to preparing students for college and enrolling them, according to the National Center for Public Policy and Higher Education, an independent, nonprofit organization. *Measuring Up 2004*, the center's report card on higher education, finds that consequently a very high proportion of the state's students complete certificates and degrees relative to the number enrolled.

The Minneapolis Public Schools district has played a part in this success

through a 2002 decision to transform district high schools into small learning communities. In order to boost achievement and motivate students to stay in school, the district encourages students to take an active role in their education. Students can choose which community to join and can help design the curriculum. Areas of study include business, liberal arts, health, and more. Small class sizes create better connections with teachers, who take on the challenge of relating the classroom experience to the real world. Developing a personalized postgraduation plan for each student is an essential part of the process.

A University to Be Proud Of

A likely college of choice for Minneapolis high school students is the University of Minnesota. In fall 2004 more than 50,900 students

University of Minnesota's Gophers football game

Students walking by the Frederick R. Weisman Art Museum at the University of Minnesota

Coffman Memorial Union at the University of Minnesota

Quad at Augsburg College

were enrolled in degree programs at the university. One of the most comprehensive and prestigious universities in the country, the University of Minnesota was named one of America's Best Colleges by *U.S. News & World Report* in 2004. It also was ranked among the top public research universities nationwide from 2001 to 2004, as measured by an annual University of Florida study. According to the 2004 study, the university was 11th in the country for the number of Ph.D. degrees awarded.

Throughout the years, research at the university has resulted in many accomplishments, from the development of the frequently used Minnesota Multiphasic Personality Inventory (the MMPI), in 1942, to the first bone marrow transplant (at University of Minnesota Hospital), in 1968, to the development of Gopher, the first successful Internet document retrieval system, in 1991. The University of Minnesota is also a leader in agricultural research, especially in food crops and natural resource conservation.

This prominence is the culmination of more than 150 years of growth. Though the university was incorporated in 1851, it operated as a preparatory school at first, in a single two-story frame building, then temporarily closed during the Civil War. Its first bachelor's degrees were

James G. Lindell Library at Augsburg College

Students walking through Augsburg College's quad

awarded in 1873 and its first doctorate in 1888. Today the university offers more than 290 undergraduate and graduate degree programs and is Minnesota's fourth-largest employer, with around 18,000 employees. Its sprawling campus comprises more than 250 buildings in Minneapolis and St. Paul.

Private Colleges Inspire

With religious zeal equal to hunger for learning in the new state, Minneapolis became fertile ground for church-based educational institutions. The oldest private college in the city, Augsburg College, moved from Wisconsin to Minneapolis in 1872. Founded in 1869 by

Norwegian Lutherans who had immigrated to America, it was the nation's first seminary for Norwegian Lutheran pastors. After relocating to Minneapolis, Augsburg articulated its purpose as training future ministers and providing practical education to farmers, workers, and businessmen.

Today the college offers undergraduate degrees in more than 50 areas of study, as well as six graduate degrees. It is the only college in the state to offer a master of science in physician assistant studies. More than 3,300 students were enrolled at Augsburg in fall 2004.

Exhibit at the Minneapolis College of Art and Design

Minneapolis College of Art and Design

Minneapolitans embraced art education early as well. The first session of the Minneapolis School of Fine Art was held in 1886, with 28 students attending. Now known as the Minneapolis College of Art and Design (MCAD), the school was affiliated with the Minneapolis Institute of Arts until 1988. MCAD offers bachelor of fine arts degrees in 14 major fields, from advertising design to filmmaking to painting, plus a bachelor of science in visualization and a master of fine arts degree. The only art and design school on *The Princeton Review*'s 2005 list of Best Midwestern Colleges, MCAD had more than 650 students enrolled in fall 2004.

Community Colleges Build Skills

Two-year colleges are also part of the educational mix in Minneapolis. More than 11,000 students attend Minneapolis Community and Technical College (MCTC), which was formed in 1996 when Minneapolis Technical College, founded in 1914, and Metropolitan State Junior College, founded in 1965, consolidated. MCTC's credit-based programs lead to associate in arts, associate in science, or associate in applied science degrees. The college offers 47 liberal arts programs and more than 50 career or technical programs that include screenwriting, nursing, computer technology, air traffic control, law enforcement, and urban teaching. Some 80 languages and dialects are spoken on campus, mirroring Minneapolis's ethnic diversity.

MCTC is a member of the Minnesota State Colleges & Universities System (MnSCU), which consists of 32 institutions located in 46 communities. One of these schools is Normandale Community College, in Bloomington, whose annual enrollment of around 13,000 makes it one of Minnesota's largest two-year colleges. Established in 1968, Normandale offers academic and professional programs in 40 subjects, including anthropology, art, computer technology, hospitality management, nursing, and law enforcement.

Another MnSCU school is Inver Hills Community College, in Inver Grove Heights, which has approximately 7,400 students. Inver Hills offers 25 two-year degree programs in fields ranging from liberal arts to accounting, construction management, aviation, and paralegal services.

Normandale Community College, in Bloomington

Education for the New Century

Minneapolis is home to virtual as well as bricks-and-mortar educational institutions, and even students who have never been to the city can claim a degree from a local school. Online Capella University, based downtown, has served adult learners since 1993. In 2004 more than 10,000 people representing all 50 states and more than 50 countries were enrolled at the university. With statistics like these, it's no wonder that Capella was named one of America's fastest growing private companies by *Inc.* magazine from 1998 to 2004. Accredited since 1997, Capella grants bachelor's,

master's, and doctoral degrees through more than 80 programs and specializations in five schools: technology, business, education, psychology, and human services. The university employs approximately 550 people.

For more than 170 years, Minneapolis's educational institutions have enriched the community. Public schools are preparing students for college and are moving with the times to make education more accessible for all. A top public university, respected private colleges, strong community-based colleges, and non-traditional learning environments are also keeping Minneapolis at the head of the class.

Stock

Buy

Sell

Hold

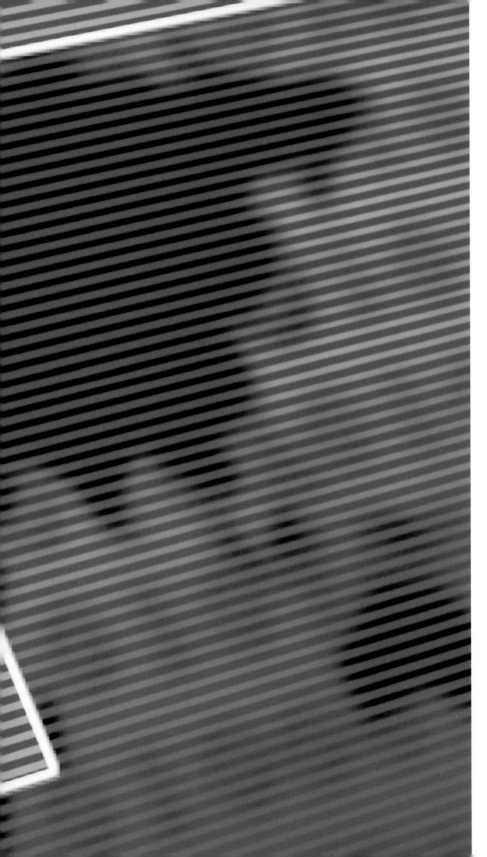

A Pillar of Strength

Minneapolis's financial portfolio is one of success. With the Ninth Federal Reserve District and some of the country's top financial institutions headquartered in the city, Minneapolis dominates as the financial pillar of the upper Midwest. Insurance and real estate firms also flourish in Minneapolis, a place committed to regional and personal growth.

Increasing Wealth

Minneapolis's banking sector tethered itself to the growth of the lumber and flour milling industries during the mid 19th century. In 1914 the city was saluted as one of the nation's important financial centers when it became the headquarters for the Ninth Federal Reserve District. Nearly a century later, Minneapolis maintains its distinction as a leader in finance.

Minnesota's oldest and largest independent mortgage company, Bell Mortgage, has had success since it issued its first mortgage bond in 1888 for $3,500. Founded in Minneapolis in 1880 as the David C. Bell Investment Company, Bell Mortgage now has more than 500,000 family

Piper Jaffray Tower

mortgages and 22 offices across the country.

Another longtime Minneapolis financial company is Ameriprise Financial, formerly American Express Financial Advisors, which was established in Minneapolis in 1894 as Investors Syndicate. Ameriprise now ranks as one of the country's top financial planning, asset management, and insurance companies, with revenues of more than $7 billion in 2004.

Its 12,000 financial advisors provide mutual funds, retirement accounts, insurance, and annuities to more than 2.5 million customers nationwide. In 2005 Amerprise's parent company, American Express, announced plans to spin it off. The firm will maintain its Minneapolis headquarters.

Established in Minneapolis as a commercial paper brokerage in 1914, Piper Jaffray & Company has strong historical ties to Minneapolis as well.

U.S. Bank Tower (center)

Blue Cross and Blue Shield of Minnesota headquarters, in Eagan

The company gained a seat on the New York Stock Exchange in 1929 and in 1971 was the first regional brokerage company to sell the public its own stock. U.S. Bancorp purchased Piper Jaffray in 1997 but spun it off into an independent company in 2003. Piper Jaffray offers financial products such as asset management, online trading, and underwriting services. The company, which employs approximately 3,000 people in more than 100 offices nationwide, had net sales of $797.5 million in 2004.

TCF Financial Corporation, a financial holding company for TCF National Bank, distinguished itself as a prominent Minneapolis institution when it was founded in 1923 as Twin City Federal. Now based in Wayzata, TCF Financial provides customers with multiple banking options as well as investments, insurance, mortgage services, and securities brokerage. A top issuer of Visa debit cards, TCF Financial had assets of $12.3 billion in 2004. The company operates 430 banking locations in six states and employs about 8,500 people.

Six years after TCF Financial was founded, another major banking institution formed in Minneapolis.

In 1929, the year of the great stock market collapse, the First National Banks of Minneapolis and St. Paul founded the First Bank Stock Corporation. That corporation eventually became U.S. Bancorp, the country's sixth-largest bank holding company. With $195 billion in assets in 2005, Minneapolis-based U.S. Bancorp is the parent company of several successful business units, including U.S. Bank, which has nearly 2,400 locations; NOVA Information Systems, a leading processor of merchant credit card transactions; and U.S. Bancorp Asset Management, a financial services company that handles more than $120 billion in assets.

A Policy of Protection

Minneapolis has long had a policy of protecting residents. Whether safeguarding a life or one's health, local insurance companies have a history of success. Founded in Minneapolis in 1896 as North American Casualty, Allianz Life Insurance Company of North America is the continent's second-largest provider of fixed annuities and a major insurer of health maintenance organizations (HMOs). The Minneapolis company provides insurance and investment services such as universal life insurance, long-term care insurance, and annuity reinsurance. A subsidiary of Allianz Group in Germany, Allianz Life has more than 200,000 representatives across the country.

The state's first health plan, Blue Cross and Blue Shield of Minnesota, began servicing Minneapolis in 1935, two years after it was chartered in St. Paul. The health organization is

now the state's largest health plan, with more than 2.6 million members. Headquartered in Eagan since 1970, the nonprofit insurer and its affiliates offer products such as health coverage for employees and individuals, pharmacy benefits management, managed care services for workers' compensation, and health and wellness programs. The

company offers its members access to 96 percent of Minnesota's health care providers. An employer of about 4,000 people, Blue Cross and Blue Shield of Minnesota reported revenues of more than $5 billion in 2003.

The metro is also home to United Healthcare Corporation, founded in

Minneapolis in 1977 by a group of physicians who formed a nonprofit health plan based on the business model of an HMO. By 1984, the year the company went public, it was running 11 HMOs in 10 states. Today the Minnetonka-based company and its affiliates offer health care plans and services to approximately 55 million customers. United

Healthcare employs about 40,500 professionals nationwide and had revenues of $37.2 billion in 2004.

The nation's largest consumer-governed nonprofit health care group, HealthPartners, has been headquartered in Bloomington since 1992. Founded in 1957 in St. Paul, the organization offers integrated services such as disease management and prevention, research, inpatient and outpatient services, and medical education. In 2005 the group served more than 630,000 members in Minnesota and western Wisconsin, covering nearly one in four residents in the Twin Cities metro. HealthPartners is the state's ninth-largest employer, with about 9,600 workers at more than 50 locations.

Thrivent Financial for Lutherans established its corporate center in Minneapolis when it formed as the world's largest fraternal benefit society in 2002. The financial services group emerged when the Aid Association for Lutherans, founded in 1902, joined with the Lutheran Brotherhood, established in 1917. Thrivent manages $155 billion in life insurance in force and boasts $65 billion in assets through its bank, mutual fund, and trust services, among other offerings. With some 2,900 employees, the group serves nearly 2.8 million members nationwide.

Dayton's department store, built by Kraus-Anderson Companies, 1910s–1920s

Building Communities

Since it was first settled in 1852, Minneapolis has grown exponentially. Prosperous industries helped attract people to the economically vibrant region, which in turn boosted the real estate and construction sector. Kraus-Anderson Companies, which was established in Minneapolis in 1897, seized upon that growth. The construction company made its mark with several high-profile projects, including the original Dayton's department store in downtown Minneapolis, completed in 1902. Now one of the nation's top builders, Kraus-Anderson undertakes projects nationwide that range from building and designing schools, hotels, and conference centers to overseeing historic renovations. In 2004 Kraus-Anderson tackled 596 projects that generated $792 million in construction volume. The company, which has 11 offices in the United States, also operates subsidiaries in property management, insurance, equipment financing, facilities management, and advertising.

Another notable local real estate firm is The Opus Group, based in Minnetonka, which began in 1953 as Rauenhorst Construction Company, in Richfield. Since its founding, the company has built more than 2,200 industrial, retail, office, and institutional projects in the United States and Canada. It provides a full-service menu that includes development,

American Express Financial Center, in Minneapolis, constructed by Opus Corporation, designed by RSP Architects

architecture, engineering, construction, property management, leasing, and financing options. With 28 offices and approximately 1,400 employees in North America, Opus has helped shape many city skylines, including Minneapolis's. In 1992 one of the company's divisions, Opus Northwest, helped develop 225 South Sixth, a landmark high-rise in downtown Minneapolis.

Family-owned since its establishment in Minneapolis in 1954, M. A. Mortenson Company is one of the nation's largest builders. The company offers general contracting, planning, construction management, and design and construction, among other services. It has had projects in nearly every U.S. state, as well as other countries. Ranging from less than $1 million to more than $300 million, projects include corporate offices, sports and hospitality venues, high-tech manufacturing plants, educational institutions, and industrial facilities. Some of its well-known projects are the FedEx Forum, a stadium for the NBA's Memphis Grizzlies, and the Walt Disney Concert Hall, home to the Los Angeles Philharmonic Orchestra. M. A. Mortenson has satellite offices in five states and Australia.

Headquartered in Minneapolis since 1991, Ryan Companies US is involved in multimillion-dollar ventures for businesses such as Ford Motor Company, Target Corporation, and U.S. Bancorp. The company's history dates back to 1938, when it started as a small lumber company in Hibbing, Minnesota. To date the commercial development and property management company has participated in more than 400 design-build projects in more than 150 cities nationwide. Family-owned, it also currently manages more than 9.5 million square feet of property valued at more than $700 million. Ryan Companies has six U.S. offices.

Together, Minneapolis's finance, insurance, and real estate industries will continue to build prosperity among Minneapolis businesses and residents.

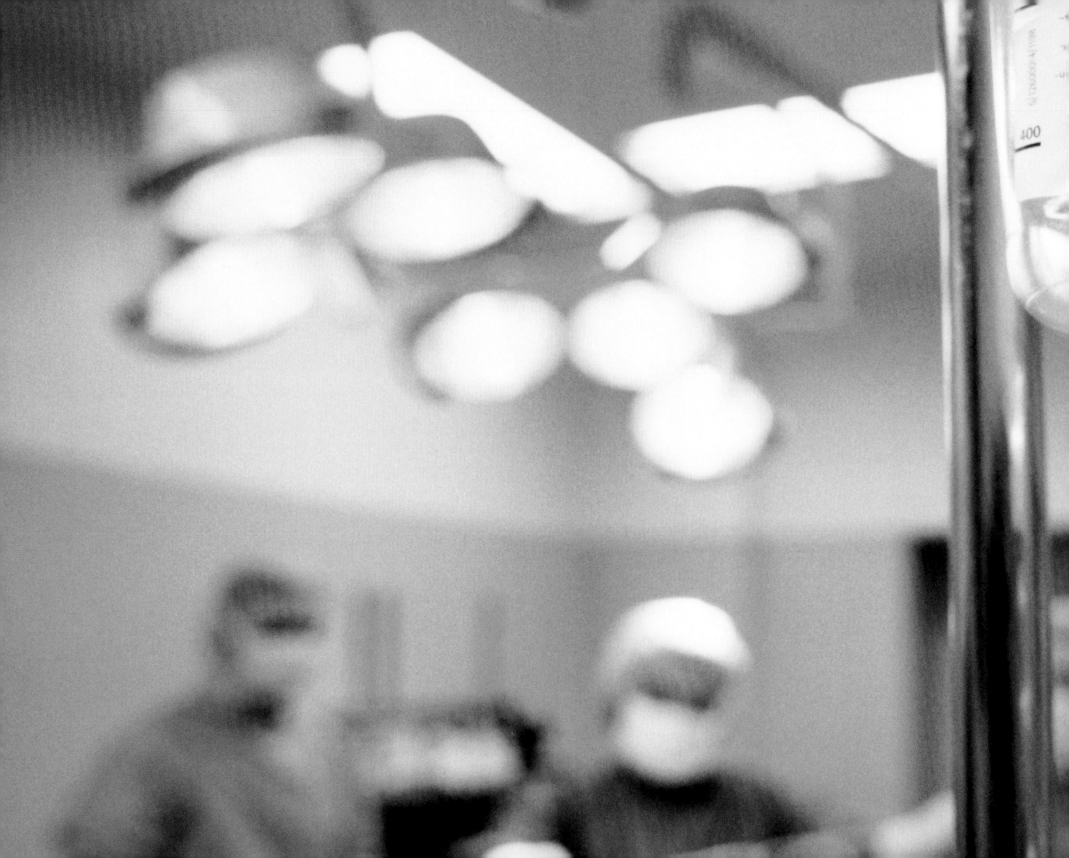

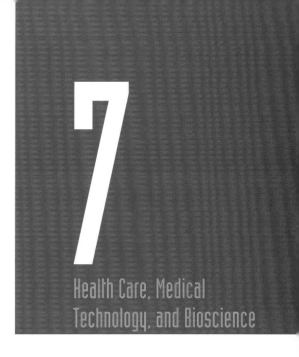

Science for Life

Minneapolis is the jewel in the crown of a state renowned for the health of its people, fine medical care, and groundbreaking biological research. Hospitals and physicians in the region are providing care that takes full advantage of the latest medical innovations. On another front, medical device companies are working to improve health and reduce the effects of debilitating illnesses. Meanwhile, the local bioscience industry is transforming new discoveries into everything from gene therapies to consumer products.

The Best of Health

In 2004 Minnesota was named the healthiest state in the nation for the ninth time in the last 15 years by Minnetonka-based United Health Foundation. (The state was rated number two in the other six years.) Factors cited, from a low rate of cardiovascular deaths to high support for public health, reflect well on health care in the Minneapolis metro, one of the state's largest population centers.

Good hospitals are a cornerstone of good health, and a number of local medical centers can claim more than a century in the service of that ideal. Abbott

Hennepin County Medical Center

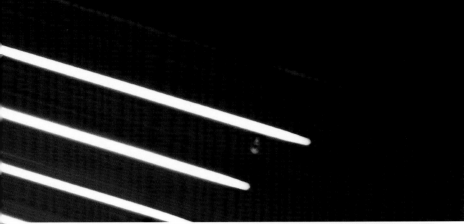

Abbott Northwestern Hospital

Northwestern Hospital, a 627-bed facility that provides medical, surgical, and critical care to more than 200,000 patients every year, opened in 1882 as Northwestern Hospital for Women and Children. In 1970 the hospital merged with Abbott Hospital for Women, which was founded in 1902. Today Abbott Northwestern is a member of nonprofit, Minneapolis-based Allina Hospitals & Clinics, a network of 11 hospitals and 42 clinics in Minnesota and western Wisconsin.

In 1887, five years after Northwestern Hospital for Women and Children was founded, Minneapolis City Hospital opened in downtown Minneapolis. The hospital dedicated itself to medical excellence, and in the 1960s the upper Midwest's first kidney transplants were performed here. Now known as Hennepin County Medical Center, the 910-bed hospital is a major teaching facility. More than 90,000 patients are treated at its busy emergency and urgent care departments each year.

Another venerable Minneapolis hospital, Fairview-University Medical Center, traces its roots to the early 20th century. The medical center was formed in 1997 by the merger of University Hospital, founded at the University of Minnesota in 1911, and Fairview Health Services, started in 1916. When the two hospitals merged, acute and high-technology

Fairview-University Medical Center

care were consolidated on the university campus, while ambulatory, short stay, and outpatient care were centered at Fairview Health Services. Fairview-University Medical Center,

which has 1,700 licensed beds, is the largest hospital in the state.

By the mid 20th century Minneapolis's health care community

was becoming more comprehensive than ever. In 1942 the Sister Kenny Institute, a hospital devoted exclusively to polio patients, opened in Minneapolis. The institute was founded by Elizabeth Kenny, an Australian nurse whose revolutionary use of hot packs and "muscle re-education" laid the groundwork for the practice of physical therapy. When polio vaccination became widespread, in 1955, the institute's focus shifted to other maladies. In 1975 it merged with Abbott Northwestern as Sister Kenny Rehabilitation Services, which today treats arthritis, spinal cord and brain injuries, chronic pain, sports injuries, and more.

Devised to Help

In their quest to extend the frontiers of medicine, local medical device companies have impacted the health of people around the globe. This is certainly true of Medtronic, one of the world's top medical device companies. Founded in Minneapolis in 1949, the company first focused on medical equipment repair. Eight years later, at the request of a University of Minnesota doctor, Medtronic developed a portable, battery-powered pacemaker that could be strapped to a patient's chest. Medtronic went on to market the first implantable pacemaker in 1960. During the next four decades the company continued to innovate with pacemakers while developing devices for noncardiac-related conditions. Today Medtronic's medical devices address everything from cardiac arrest and vascular blockage to diabetes, acid reflux, and degenerative disc disease. The Fridley-based firm employs nearly 32,000 people worldwide and had sales of more than $10 billion in fiscal 2005.

After Medtronic, a cluster of medical device companies formed in Minneapolis. SciMed Life Systems, founded in Maple Grove in 1980, came to dominate the worldwide angioplasty market with its catheters by the decade's end. In 1995 SciMed was acquired by Boston Scientific, a medical technology company based in Natick, Massachusetts. Boston

Elizabeth Kenny celebrating the Sister Kenny Institute's first anniversary with polio patients, 1943

Medtronic's InSync® device for heart failure

Medtronic headquarters, in Fridley

Scientific moved its Cardiovascular Group headquarters to Maple Grove, and the firm is currently expanding facilities in the Minneapolis area to produce its recently approved drug-delivering coronary stent. Up to 600 people will be hired, bringing the total number of employees in Boston Scientific's Maple Grove and Plymouth plants to 3,500.

The continuum of medical device businesses in Minneapolis also includes the largest manufacturer of hearing instruments in the world, Starkey Laboratories. Starkey got its start in 1967 as Professional Hearing Aid Service in St. Louis Park. The company furthered its mission of enabling better hearing in 1971 when it acquired Starkey Laboratories, a maker of ear molds. From manufacturing custom hearing aids to aids that fit entirely within the ear canal, Eden Prairie–based Starkey has progressed to programmable and digital instruments that offer superior audibility, fidelity, and comfort. The

company now has more than 800 distributors in 18 countries.

In Minnetonka, American Medical Systems (AMS) is dedicated to producing devices for incontinence, erectile dysfunction, prostate disease, and other urological conditions. Founded in 1972, AMS was first to introduce an artificial urinary sphincter, an inflatable penile prosthesis, and a permanent urethral stent. The company estimates that more than 130,000 patients benefited from its

products in 2004, when its sales exceeded $208.7 million.

The Next Level

With its successful medical device industry and research base, Minneapolis is making the logical move into bioscience. Bioscience is the application of cellular, molecular, or genetic technologies to create products and services for life sciences and for agricultural, commercial manufacturing, and industrial use.

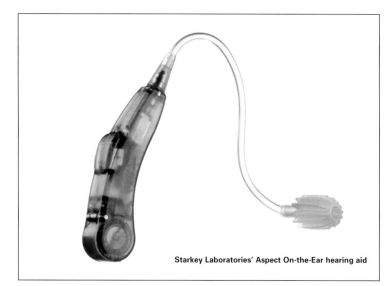

Starkey Laboratories' Aspect On-the-Ear hearing aid

Utensils made from biodegradable plastic polymer

One specialty is medical genomics, which identifies and uses the functions of individual genes to diagnose and treat disease. At the forefront of medical genomics are companies such as Discovery Genomics and Protein Design Labs (PDL).

Discovery Genomics was founded in 2000 to develop gene therapies for diseases of the blood and to identify disease gene targets for drug therapies. The Minneapolis company, which is in the early stages of development, has an exclusive license to technologies discovered at the University of Minnesota. Discovery Genomics' promising system of gene delivery inserts a corrective gene directly into the chromosomes of a patient's cells, which can then manufacture proteins to correct genetic disorders or diseases such as cancer.

PDL, which is headquartered in Fremont, California, is currently developing antibodies for use against Crohn's disease, ulcerative colitis, asthma, and other conditions. Currently, the firm is bringing online a 214,000-square-foot, commercial-scale manufacturing facility of its own in Brooklyn Park, which will produce its first commercial antibodies by 2007.

Food-processing giant Cargill, associated with Minneapolis since the 1870s, joined the bioscience ranks early with functional food products such as phytosterols that lower cholesterol and soy isoflavones for bone health. In 1997 Cargill partnered with Dow Chemical to form Cargill Dow in Minnetonka, which today produces a proprietary plastic polymer made from renewable resources such as corn. So far, the biodegradable material has been used for food packaging, disposable tableware, and fibers for clothing, bedding, and carpets.

Start-up company Biorefining, of Golden Valley, also aims at transforming basic plant materials into value-added products. The company's patented milling, extraction, and conversion processes can turn byproducts such as dried grains left over from ethanol production into low-calorie sweeteners for sports drinks, foods for diabetics, and even pharmaceuticals. Incorporated in 2000, Biorefining has several other patents pending.

Over the last 150 years, Minneapolis has helped set the standard for health. By all indications, that pace will continue as local hospitals consolidate their strengths, entrepreneurial firms create the next generation of medical devices, and researchers focus on the very building blocks of life.

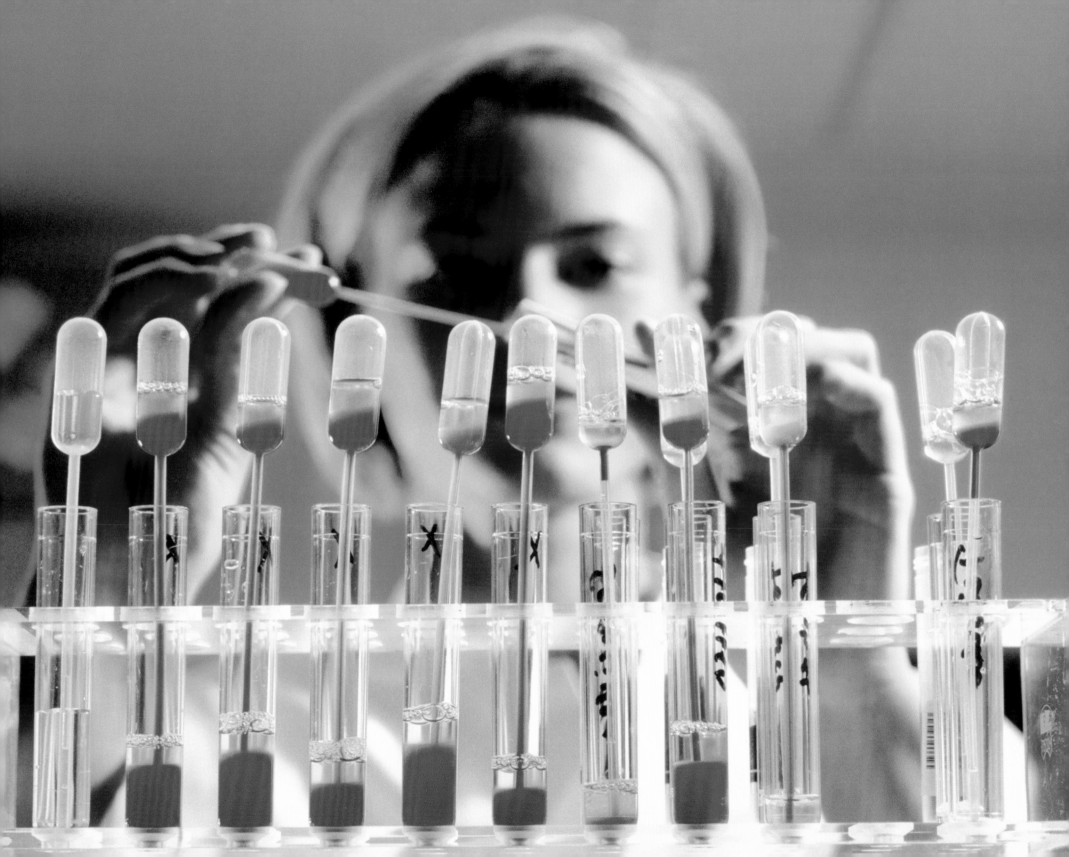

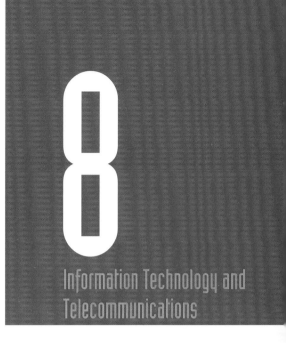

Hooked on Technology

Minneapolis residents are wired. Their fondness for technology was demonstrated in a 2004 survey conducted by Intel, which ranked the Twin Cities 15th among 100 U.S. cities offering high-speed, wireless Internet connections. Minneapolitans are also using, or benefiting from, information technology developed by local companies. As a result, Minneapolis's IT and telecommunications businesses are thriving.

Plugged In

Information technology is a young business, and Minneapolis has been at the forefront of the industry from its start. In 1950 Engineering Research Associates in Minneapolis developed the first digital computer in Minnesota. During the 1960s and 1970s Minneapolis's computer sector expanded, getting a boost in 1976 when Seymour Cray, a University of Minnesota graduate, invented the supercomputer. While major strides in computer design were taking place, related businesses, such as software and IT services companies, were emerging.

MTS Systems Corporation road simulator

Minneapolis-based business offers services that range from network analysis to custom programming to project management. With 35 locations in the United States, Canada, and England, Analysts International employs approximately 3,000 people. The firm had sales of $341.6 million in fiscal 2004, with IBM accounting for roughly 13 percent.

Datacard Group made its mark in 1969 when its founders invented high volume and economical systems for personalizing plastic credit cards—and forever altered consumer transactions. In 1991 the company again revolutionized the identity card market by introducing the world's first digital photo ID system. Headquartered in Minnetonka, Datacard Group is now a worldwide powerhouse in secure-identity cards and card personalization. Each day millions of financial cards and identification documents, including credit cards, corporate employee badges, passports, and ID cards, are issued using Datacard equipment. Datacard also has installed about 30,000 photo ID systems worldwide. More than 1,400 employees work on implementing and developing hardware, software, and custom integration services in more than 120 countries.

Like Datacard Group, Retek has changed the way retailers operate and consumers shop. Founded in 1986 by three Australian retailers, the Minneapolis company offers

One of the most experienced IT companies in the region is MTS Systems Corporation, in Eden Prairie, which was founded in 1966. Originally established to analyze the safety of mechanical materials, structures, and products, MTS Systems has since become an international leader in computer-based testing and simulation equipment. Following the deadly Hanshin earthquake in 1995, the Japanese government turned to

MTS Systems and purchased a $23 million seismic simulator from the company. MTS Systems' reputation has lured other clients such as The Boeing Company and the Korean Aerospace Research Institute, as well as government agencies, industrial businesses, and university laboratories worldwide. The firm employs more than 1,600 people and had sales of $366.9 million in fiscal 2004.

Analysts International, a global technology provider with more than 1,000 corporate and government clients, was founded in 1966 as well. It started small, in a Minneapolis carriage house, but by 1970 had nabbed its first national client, General Motors. Around this time Analysts International also helped develop programs for the U.S. Army's anti-intercontinental ballistic missile (ICBM) systems. Today the

Datacard security laminate for Datacard desktop card printers

software that helps retail firms manage sales and, via the Internet, access suppliers, wholesalers, and others in the supply chain. Retek boasts more than 200 customers worldwide, a staff of 550 people, and 2004 sales of $174.2 million. Oracle Corporation, of Redwood Shores, California, one of the largest enterprise software companies in the world, acquired Retek in 2005.

Minneapolis also nurtures young IT companies. In 1994 Digital River dove into e-commerce, supplying

clients with the technology and services needed to sell products on the Internet. The Eden Prairie company uses its exclusive server technology to provide more than 40,000 customers with Web development and hosting, transaction processing, and fraud screening, among other services. Digital River's core business comes from software publishers and online software retailers; its clients include Symantec, 3M, Motorola, and Staples.com. Digital River's revenues were $154.1 million in 2004, up more than 52 percent from the previous year.

Stellent, of Eden Prairie, started in 1995, just as technology was switching from electronic publishing to Internet applications. The company seized on that change by offering content management software. Today Stellent has more than 4,300 clients worldwide, including Coca-Cola, The Home Depot, Procter & Gamble, Los Angeles County, and British Aerospace Airbus. Its software helps users manage documents and publish information on the Internet and corporate networks, as well as organize data such as digital images and Web content. In 2004 Stellent

had nearly 400 employees and revenues of $75.8 million.

Innovations in Telecommunications

Minneapolis's telecommunications industry started ringing in shortly after the telephone was invented in 1876. By 1909 the Minnesota Telephone Association formed to represent industry workers, some of whom lived in Minneapolis. In 2003 the group changed its name to the Minnesota Telecom Alliance to reflect the diversity of the telecommunications sector. Today many of the state's leading telecommunications companies are based in the Minneapolis metro.

A veteran in the industry is Midcontinent Media, which began in 1933 as a small movie theater in Minneapolis. The company acquired other theaters in Minnesota, South

Dakota, and North Dakota until 1952, when its focus turned to radio and television. That shift set the stage for the company's foray into telecommunications, and now the Edina-based firm provides data network services, cable TV, local and long distance phone service, and broadband Internet access to approximately 200 communities in Minnesota, the Dakotas, and northern Nebraska.

ADC Telecommunications, an industry powerhouse, started in a South Minneapolis basement. It was 1935 when Ralph Allison, a young engineer, invented the audiometer, which tests hearing. Two years later, Allison teamed with another engineer, Walt Lehnert, to build a product line by offering transformers and

amplifiers for the broadcast industry. The company, then called ADC, continued to expand, providing sophisticated audio components during the 1940s to the University of Minnesota. After Allison left the company in 1949, ADC concentrated on transformers and filters for telephone jacks and plugs, military electronics, and power lines. During the 1960s, the company developed the bantam jack, a small device crucial to the emerging telecommunications industry. ADC persisted with its products and changed its name to ADC Telecommunications in 1984 to reflect the industry's technological shift from analog to digital. Since then it has become a global leader in telecommunications software and equipment, with net sales reaching

One of ADC's first facilities, 1940s

ADC assembly line, 1940s

ADC Telecommunications headquarters, in Eden Prairie

during the late 1980s—Minnesota Regional Network (MRNet) and Minnesota Equal Access Network Services (MEANS Telcom). In 1997 the two companies merged to form Onvoy in Minneapolis. Onvoy offers video, voice, and private data network services and runs a statewide fiber-optic network traversing roughly 2,000 miles.

Eschelon Telecom, one of the nation's fastest growing telecommunications companies, started in 1996 by supplying phone systems to other businesses. Within a few years the Minneapolis-based company switched to providing Internet, voice, and data services. Eschelon Telecom now has more than 60,000 customers in eight states. Sales reached $158 million in 2004.

$784.3 million in fiscal 2004. Headquartered in Eden Prairie, ADC employs approximately 7,500 professionals worldwide.

Norstan entered the Minneapolis telecommunications scene in 1973 as a distributor of phone equipment. For three decades Norstan expanded its geographic territory in the United States and Canada and its intellectual capital by acquiring companies and partnering with industry players such as Cisco Systems. Today the Minnetonka-based firm offers network management, installation, and maintenance services and sells refurbished telecommunications equipment. Norstan, which posted sales of $225.8 million in 2004, was purchased by Lawrence, Pennsylvania–based Black Box Corporation in 2005.

The state's first Internet service provider, Onvoy, traces its roots to two Minneapolis companies formed

With people hooked on technology, Minneapolis's IT and telecommunications companies are poised to continue prospering.

9
Manufacturing and Food Processing

Making It in Minneapolis

Major transportation hubs, a healthy economy, and a prime location halfway between the East and West coasts attract manufacturers to Minneapolis, while rivers, lakes, and lush land sustain local food processors. Together, these industries shine international distinction on the metro area.

Minneapolis Productions

Manufacturing helped make Minneapolis. During the mid to late 1800s, wood-crafters harnessed the power of St. Anthony Falls and established more than a dozen sawmills. By the end of the 19th century, Minneapolis's status as the nation's leading lumber mill center beckoned manufacturers of wood-related items such as furniture, shingles, paper, and barrels. In the 1900s the sector expanded further, and Minneapolis became known for making everything from packaging and paints to lawn mowers and defense weapons.

One of Minneapolis's success stories is Honeywell Automation and Control Solutions (ACS), whose history dates back to 1885, when Albert Butz patented the furnace regulator and alarm. The following year he

Honeywell ACS's VisionPro touch screen thermostat

Residential HVAC equipment produced by Honeywell ACS

opened Butz Thermo-Electric Regulator Company in Minneapolis, which eventually progressed into Honeywell, a multibillion-dollar company with global reach. Although Honeywell moved its headquarters from Minneapolis to Morristown, New Jersey, in 1999, it based its $7.5 billion business unit, Honeywell ACS, in Minneapolis.

Today Honeywell ACS makes security, fire, and safety devices, as well as systems that control and automate humidity and temperature. Its products are found worldwide, in more than 105 million homes, buildings, planes, trains, and automobiles. The company, which has a manufacturing center in Golden Valley, employs 2,500 people locally and 42,500 more people worldwide.

Another longtime Minneapolis-area manufacturer is The Toro Company, which revels in the outdoors with its lawn mowers, irrigation equipment, electrical trimmers, and other landscaping products. Founded in 1914 as a tractor engine company, Toro quickly bloomed. In 1921 it created the first mechanical maintenance equipment for a golf course by mounting five lawn mowers behind a Toro tractor. Toro equipment is now used at golf courses nationwide as well as at Super Bowl venues, the Indianapolis Motor Speedway, and other major sports sites. In the Minneapolis metro, the company operates manufacturing facilities in Shakopee and Windom and employs about 1,000 people at its headquarters in Bloomington. Toro has 11 manufacturing locations in all and employs more than 5,000 people

worldwide. Revenues reached $1.6 billion in 2004.

In 1956, Bemis Company, a global manufacturer of flexible packaging materials, moved its headquarters to Minneapolis. The company began in 1858 as a bag factory in St. Louis, Missouri, catering to milling companies that shipped cargo on the Mississippi River. Today Bemis produces paper bags, polymer films,

and barrier laminates. With net sales of $2.8 billion in 2004, Bemis employs 300 people at its facilities in Minneapolis, Hopkins, and Mankato, and another 15,200 people worldwide. The company has 62 manufacturing plants across the globe.

Tyco Plastics, a division of Tyco International in Princeton, New Jersey, has had a presence in Minneapolis since the early 1960s.

The Minneapolis-based company is the world's largest producer of items made with polyethylene film and is a national leader in trash bag production. A maker of disposable dinnerware, bags of all kinds, shrink film, custom-packaging film, and more, Tyco Plastics operates 23 manufacturing facilities in North America and employs 4,300 people. Locally, the firm has manufacturing facilities in Minneapolis, Lakeville, and Coon Rapids, and employs 575 people.

Based in Minneapolis since 1970, the Valspar Corporation has focused on appearances for nearly 200 years. Founded in Boston in 1806, Valspar is the world's sixth-largest paint and coating company, offering decorative paints, protective coatings, inks, and other products for exteriors and interiors, as well as for vehicles, floors, furniture, commercial packaging, and industrial surfaces. Its goods are marketed to mass merchandisers such as Wal-Mart and Lowe's. Valspar employs more than 7,000 professionals—about 500 in Minneapolis—at more than 80 locations worldwide. The company recorded $2.4 billion in revenues in 2004.

Alliant Techsystems (ATK), of Edina, rocketed into manufacturing when Honeywell ceded its defense units to shareholders in 1990; however, the company's history began 50 years prior. During World War II the United States and its allies relied on

ProCore® 648 aerator manufactured by The Toro Company

Toro's 5xi tractor

Honeywell's defense equipment, such as an electronic autopilot for pinpoint bombing missions. As an independent company, ATK launched into aerospace through major acquisitions that positioned it as the world's largest supplier of solid propellant rocket motors and the nation's top ammunition manufacturer. The company also offers aircraft weapons systems, antitank mines, and high-tech weapon components. In 2004 ATK's sales soared to $2.4 billion, with approximately 75 percent coming from the federal government and its prime contractors. ATK, which has more than 50 facilities in 23 states, has

operations in Plymouth, Anoka, and Elk River. It employs about 14,000 people, including 1,800 in Minnesota.

A Taste of Minneapolis

With trademarked names such as Betty Crocker, Cheerios, and Malt-O-Meal, Minneapolis's food processing companies are known worldwide. Like manufacturing, the industry dates back to the 19th century, when millers discovered the power of St. Anthony Falls.

General Mills, one of the world's largest food companies, evolved from flour mills stationed along the riverbanks near St. Anthony Falls in

the 1860s. Two of those mills belonged to Cadwallader C. Washburn, who built his first mill in 1866 and his second in 1874. By 1928 Washburn's company merged with other regional millers to form General Mills.

Success has followed General Mills throughout its existence. The company introduced premade

Conventional munitions manufacturing (20-gage shotgun shells)

Happy 60th Birthday Cheerios

General Mills employees celebrating Cheerios' 60th anniversary at the Mall of America, in Bloomington, 2001

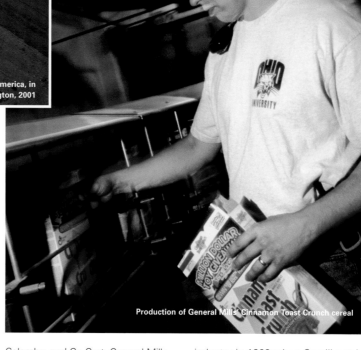

Production of General Mills' Cinnamon Toast Crunch cereal

Bisquick baking mix to rave reviews in 1931; in 1937 it unveiled Kix, the first puffed-corn cereal; and four years later it introduced Cheerioats, the first ready-to-eat oat cereal. Other innovative food products followed, including Sugar Jets presweetened cereal, in 1953; Hamburger Helper dinner mixes, in 1971; Fruit Roll-Ups, in 1983; and Pop Secret popcorn, in 1985. In 2001 General Mills expanded its empire when it acquired its historic hometown rival, Pillsbury, which was founded across the Mississippi River in 1869.

Today General Mills boasts more than 100 brands, such as Pillsbury, Betty Crocker, Green Giant, Gold Medal, Häagen-Dazs, and Old El Paso. Cheerios, Wheaties, Chex, and Lucky Charms contribute to the company's portfolio, making it one of the world's largest cereal makers. With Yoplait,

Colombo, and Go-Gurt, General Mills is also a leading U.S. yogurt producer. The multifaceted business employs about 27,500 people worldwide, including 7,000 in Minnesota, and had revenues of $11 billion in 2004. Two of General Mills' manufacturing facilities are located in Minnesota.

Minneapolis gained another powerhouse in the food processing

industry in 1909 when Cargill established headquarters in the city. Founded in Illinois in 1865, Cargill is the nation's largest private corporation, providing food and agricultural products such as sugar, cotton, and feed and fertilizer supplies to countries worldwide. The company is the nation's top grain producer as well and is a leading meatpacker, with Honeysuckle White poultry,

General Mills headquarters, in Golden Valley

Sterling Silver meats, Gerkens cocoa, and Diamond Crystal salt among its brands. Now based in Wayzata, Cargill employs 101,000 people worldwide, including more than 4,700 in Minnesota. With six manufacturing facilities in the state and another 1,000 worldwide, the company had sales totaling $62.9 billion in fiscal 2004.

Malt-O-Meal Company, the nation's fifth-largest cereal maker, introduced the first hot wheat cereal when it was founded in Owatonna in 1919. The growing company moved its headquarters to Minneapolis in 1963. Today Malt-O-Meal continues to offer the product that launched the company, along with more than 20 private-label cold cereals that are distributed to grocery stores nationwide. Malt-O-Meal employs about 1,100 people, the majority of whom work in Minnesota. It has two production facilities in Northfield and one in Utah.

A leading producer of egg and refrigerated potato products, Michael Foods was formed through a series of mergers and

CHS soybean crushing oil plant in Fairmont, Minnesota

acquisitions. Based in Minnetonka, the company's history dates back to 1926 with the establishment of Crystal Farms, which today produces everything from eggs and cheese to butter and margarine. Michael Foods' egg divisions, Papetti's and M. G. Waldbaum, combined are the world's largest supplier of processed eggs. Michael Foods employs about 3,800 people, 1,000 of whom work in Minnesota. It has facilities in Minneapolis, Gaylord, and Le Sueur, as well as 28 other locations across North America.

Established in 1998, CHS represents about 2,200 U.S. ranchers, farmers, and cooperatives that supply food, grain, and energy products. Though the Inver Grove Heights company has existed for less than a decade, its roots go back to the 1920s with the formation of regional cooperatives. CHS is now one of the nation's top exporters of grain and is the world's largest confection sunflower processor, supplying companies such as Frito Lay and ConAgra. Its oilseed division processes nearly two million acres of soybeans each year, creating ingredients that are used in Lipton and Campbell's products, among others. This diversified company employs 1,650 Minnesotans and another 6,000 people worldwide. CHS has approximately 500 manufacturing facilities, four of which are in Minnesota. In 2004 it posted net sales of $10.9 billion.

The manufacturing and food processing sectors played a major role in building Minneapolis into the thriving city it is today. More than a century later these industries still add richness to the community.

10

Philanthropy

A Tradition of Giving

Minneapolis's strong philanthropic tradition is ingrained. For generations, people in the area have embraced the idea that individual well-being depends on the welfare of the community. Such public-mindedness has resulted in charitable foundations that serve as a national template for generosity.

A Philanthropic Model

Minneapolis is a national leader in corporate giving. During the late 1960s and early 1970s, as some American companies grappled with public distrust, Minneapolis businesses turned toward philanthropy. Major companies such as Honeywell, Dayton Hudson Corporation, and General Mills invested in local neighborhood revitalization programs.

During this time, Minneapolis companies also pursued other philanthropic efforts. First Bank Minneapolis created a task force to combat Dutch Elm disease in trees, while Control Data Corporation, a Minneapolis computer manufacturer, focused on the then-revolutionary idea of placing computers in classrooms.

Writers gathering at the Loft's Literary Center

The Loft, in the Open Book literary center

In 1975 the Greater Minneapolis Chamber of Commerce (GMCC) created the nation's first 5% Club, a breakthrough movement that encouraged corporations to donate five percent of federally taxable income to philanthropic groups. GMCC is credited with inspiring American businesses to donate billions of dollars annually to charitable causes.

Target Corporation, which started donating five percent of its profits to charities in 1946, was the model for and a founding member of the 5% Club. Today the Minneapolis-based retailer is one of the state's leading charitable contributors. In fiscal 2004 the Target Foundation gave $96.3 million to local organizations that support the arts and social services. The foundation continued its giving mission in 2005, distributing grants to organizations such as the Emergency Food Shelf Network, in New Hope; the Loft, a literary center in Minneapolis; the Ragamala Music and Dance Theater, in Minneapolis; and Dakota Woodlands, a shelter for homeless women and children in Eagan. Target also donates more than $2 million each week to communities throughout the United States.

Another major employer in Minneapolis, food processing giant General Mills has a distinguished history of giving. Whether supporting the Washburn Orphanage in the 1880s or collecting $6 million for the Greater Twin Cities United Way in 2004, General Mills has improved the lives of many Minneapolis residents. The company established a foundation in 1954 with an investment of $18,500 in educational and community organizations. Since then it has donated more than $330 million for scholarships and groups focusing on youth nutrition and fitness, education, literacy, arts and culture, and social services. In fiscal 2004 the General Mills Foundation distributed $86 million to communities nationwide; some $22 million in food products was

Volunteers making teddy bears for the Greater Twin Cities United Way

Emergency Food Shelf Network staff collecting food from a donor

Schools district for updated laboratory equipment, lab materials, and professional development for science teachers.

A Giving Community

Community philanthropic organizations have established roots in Minneapolis as well. The Minneapolis Foundation, one of the nation's oldest and largest community foundations, has served Minnesotans since it was established in 1915. Its staff offers philanthropic consulting services, manages endowments, and sponsors community initiatives on issues such as child homelessness, education, and affordable housing. Some of the foundation's partners in grant making are the Piper Family Fund, the Emma B. Howe Memorial Foundation, and Community Loan Technologies. In fiscal 2004, The Minneapolis Foundation awarded 770 charitable funds approximately $40.9 million. Beneficiaries included Mount Olivet Rolling Acres, a nonprofit organization in Victoria

donated to America's Second Harvest, the country's largest hunger relief group. In the Twin Cities, 50 nonprofits that celebrate ethnic diversity received grants from the foundation. Other local programs that General Mills sponsors include the Presidential Active Lifestyle Award challenge at Minneapolis Public Schools and the Hawthorne Huddle, a lauded

initiative begun in 1997 to reduce crime in North Minneapolis's Hawthorne neighborhood.

Since its founding in 1949, Medtronic, a top maker of medical devices, has given more than $220 million to causes worldwide. Medtronic honed its philanthropic goals in 1978, when it established a foundation to improve health,

communities, and science education. In fiscal 2004 the Fridley company gave more than $40.2 million, which equaled roughly two percent of its domestic pretax profits, to organizations such as the Minneapolis Heart Institute Foundation, Minneapolis Community and Technical College Fund, and Minneapolis Institute of Arts. Medtronic also donated $550,000 to the Minneapolis Public

Achieve!Minneapolis students from Edison High School

dedicated to people with developmental disabilities, and Achieve!Minneapolis, a nonprofit that supports Minneapolis Public Schools arts programs.

Since it received federal recognition in 1969, the Shakopee Mdewakanton (Dakota) Sioux Community, located in Prior Lake and Shakopee, has donated millions of dollars from gaming and nongaming resources to help Native Americans. Since 1998 the tribe has contributed more than $42 million to other tribes, to schools, and to charities. Its philanthropic goal is to help tribes with economic development through grants for land purchases, equipment, construction, and other community improvements. In fiscal 2004 the community donated $10.2 million, primarily to Native American organizations and tribes in the Northern Plains region. Donations included $1 million each to the Lower Sioux and Upper Sioux communities in Minnesota. In 2005 the Shakopee Mdewakanton (Dakota) Sioux Community increased its philanthropic funding to $14.5 million.

Minneapolis is also home to a public charity, the Minnesota Partnership for Action Against Tobacco (MPAAT).

The independent nonprofit started in 1998, the result of a court decision that required tobacco companies to pay $202 million for smoking cessation programs and tobacco research. Since 2000, MPAAT has funded 61 antitobacco projects such as tobacco counseling, help lines, and academic research.

A Generous Foundation

The generosity of Minneapolis residents is evident in the city's established private foundations. For decades such groups have improved the quality of life in metro Minneapolis with grants geared toward economic development, social services, education, the arts, and more.

A personal history of giving inspired The Jay and Rose Phillips Family Foundation, established in Minneapolis in 1944 by Jay and Rose Phillips. The children of Russian immigrants, the Phillipses believed in the Jewish values of charity and social justice. They created the foundation to fund organizations that promote self-sufficiency among the disadvantaged, the disabled, and the young. In 2003 the foundation funded more than 316 organizations ranging from the Minnesota AIDS Project, in Minneapolis, to the Sholom Community Alliance, in St. Louis Park, to the Minneapolis Adult Basic Education program.

As one of the top charitable contributors in Minnesota, The McKnight Foundation in Minneapolis influences the metro as well as the state, the nation, and the world. In 1953 the private philanthropic group was endowed by William McKnight (once the president and CEO of 3M Company) and his wife, Maude. Since its inception The McKnight Foundation has mirrored its founders' belief in civic responsibility, grassroots action, and policy reform. In 2004 the foundation granted about $85 million to organizations supporting children and families, the arts, and other causes. Additionally, the group funds research on the environment and neuroscience as well as economic and social service programs in Southeast Asia and Africa.

Together Minneapolis's corporate, community, public, and private foundations have made the city a national role model in philanthropy, influencing the welfare of people across the country and the world.

Business Matters

With global businesses and some of the country's largest companies headquartered in Minneapolis, the city demands—and gets—esteemed firms specializing in professional and business-to-business services. Together, these industries rev up the metro's economic engine, ensuring business success and a high quality of life.

Getting Down to Business

Minneapolis's professional services sector sprang to life at the turn of the 20th century, when the city was becoming a vital economic center. One of Minneapolis's oldest enduring law firms, Faegre & Benson, got its start this way when it was founded in 1886. The firm's historical ties to Minneapolis are evident in its client list, which includes local companies such as General Mills, Target Corporation, and Land O' Lakes. Specializing in transactions and litigation, Faegre & Benson serves a wide range of industries. With five additional offices in the United States, Europe, and Asia, Faegre & Benson employs more than 450 lawyers, about 300 of whom work in Minneapolis.

More than 50 years later, Robins, Kaplan, Miller & Ciresi won another high profile case when it secured a $7.1 billion settlement against tobacco companies in 1998. The firm's 250 lawyers litigate in areas such as intellectual property, business, insurance, and mass tort. Robins, Kaplan, Miller & Ciresi has five other U.S. offices.

As Minneapolis's businesses and population grew, so did the need for accounting firms. McGladrey & Pullen, which was established in Cedar Rapids, Iowa, in 1926, has been headquartered in the Minneapolis metro since 1946. Today the national certified public accounting firm is based in Bloomington. With its tailored accounting methodology, McGladrey & Pullen provides audit and attest services to midsized businesses in industries such as health care, financial services, manufacturing, and real estate. Additionally, it is the nation's largest auditor of credit unions. McGladrey & Pullen works with RSM McGladrey, a separate company owned by H&R Block, to offer business services such as tax consulting, IT, and business planning.

Architecture firms also prospered in Minneapolis during the 20th century. Based in Minneapolis since 1981, Hammel, Green and Abrahamson (HGA) began in a St. Paul basement in 1953. Its

Minneapolis law firm Dorsey & Whitney, one of the largest in the world, started in 1912 when two esteemed Minneapolis lawyers began providing counsel to the First National Bank of Minneapolis (now U.S. Bancorp and still a client). Over the years, the firm's distinguished reputation has attracted top litigators, including U.S. Supreme Court justice

Harry Blackmun and former U.S. vice president Walter Mondale. With approximately 650 lawyers, Dorsey & Whitney offers expertise in corporate finance, litigation, international trademark issues, mergers and acquisitions, and more. Its customers include Cargill, Northwest Airlines, and the Mayo Clinic. Dorsey & Whitney has 19 offices around the world.

Another prominent local law firm, Robins, Kaplan, Miller & Ciresi was formed by two University of Minnesota Law School graduates in 1938. The firm had almost immediate success when it won *Hayward v. State Farm* in 1942 and set a legal precedent that secured an insurance company's right to recoup payment from a liable party.

Coffman Memorial Union at the University of Minnesota, renovated by Ellerbe Becket

founding architects appreciated modern design, which they applied to one of the company's first major projects, Highland Park Junior High School in St. Paul. During the 1960s and 1970s, the firm expanded its designs to medical centers, universities, concert halls, and other venues. Today HGA's clients include schools, colleges, and churches, as well as major businesses such as 3M, IBM, General Mills, and Kaiser Permanente. The company employs more than 450 professionals in six U.S. offices; 270 people work at its Minneapolis headquarters.

Like HGA, Ellerbe Becket began as a St. Paul–based architecture firm. Founded in 1909 and head-quartered in Minneapolis since 1991, Ellerbe Becket is one of the nation's leading architecture, engineering, construction, interiors, and environmental graphics companies. From medical centers to sports arenas to high-rises, the firm has created structures in all 50 states and in 20 countries. Some of its notable projects include the Mayo Clinic in Rochester, built in 1913, and Bank One Ballpark in Phoenix, built in 1998. Through its six domestic

and international offices, Ellerbe Becket employs 350 professionals, including 200 in Minneapolis.

Attuned to Business

Like the professional services industry, the business-to-business services sector burgeoned with Minneapolis's growth. The demand for services inspired companies that specialized in a wide range of practices, from garment care to commercial printing to advertising. One local business-to-business services company, AmeriPride Services, planted roots in the community in 1896 to provide towel service to Minneapolis businesses. Founded in Lincoln, Nebraska, in 1889 and today based in Minnetonka, AmeriPride has grown into one of North America's largest garment services and linen supplies companies. Still owned by

the founding family, AmeriPride rents, sells, and maintains work apparel. Its 200,000 weekly customers are in the food service, maintenance, health care, and technology industries. AmeriPride employs about 6,000 people in more than 190 locations in the United States and Canada. Approximately 370 people work for the company in the Minneapolis metro.

Clothing is also the focus of another local company. The nation's third-largest uniform rental agency, G&K Services started as a small dyeing and dry cleaning company in 1902 when it opened stores in Minneapolis and St. Paul. In the 1950s, G&K entered the uniform rental market; today it provides uniforms to more than 160,000 North American customers in the manufacturing, hospitality, technology, and automotive industries. Now based in Minnetonka, the company processes more than five million garments each week at some 130

locations in the United States and Canada. G&K employs more than 9,000 people.

As printing technology advanced, businesses started turning to firms such as the Japs-Olson Company. One of the nation's largest commercial printers and direct mail production firms, the company started in Minneapolis in 1907 by manufacturing business forms. Japs-Olson soon became a pioneer in the field of lithography, creating ledgers with patented binders that people could add sheets to. Now based in St. Louis Park, Japs-Olson has a state-of-the-art facility with a full digital prepress, web presses, flexography printing, a bindery, and data processing. Its on-site post office processes names and addresses for mailings. Unlike some printing houses, Japs-Olson is a one-stop shop, operating seven days a week, 24 hours a day. With more than 650 employees, the printer has clients that include national banking and financial institutions, food and retail businesses, and insurance and credit card companies.

The advertising industry also mirrored the city's growth at the turn of the 20th century. In 1891 the *Minneapolis City Directory* listed four advertising agencies; by 1925 that number had climbed to 60. Part of this new wave of advertising companies was Campbell Mithun, which opened its doors in 1933. Today the nation's 22nd-largest advertising and communications company, the agency has a long history of representing big-name clients. Andersen Windows and Land O' Lakes, for example, have both been with Campbell Mithun since its founding. The agency also builds brands for major companies such as Burger King, Verizon Wireless, The Coca-Cola Company, H&R Block, and General Mills. Campbell Mithun employs approximately 370 people,

including 300 at its Minneapolis headquarters. Part of the Interpublic Group of Companies in New York City, Campbell Mithun has offices in New York City and Irvine, California, as well.

As the field of psychology developed in the 20th century, a local company formed to apply its principles to business. Founded in Minneapolis in 1967, Personnel Decisions International (PDI) consults with Fortune 500 and Global 1000 companies, government agencies, and other employers to develop talent

and leadership. PDI employs more than 250 organizational and counseling psychologists who use behavioral science methods to measure work-based performance and success. The company operates 27 offices in the United States and abroad.

Ceridian Corporation harnessed the power of computer technology to help businesses run more efficiently. The Minneapolis company is a leader in providing information services in human resources, including benefits administration and payroll and tax processing.

Though Ceridian formed in 1992, its history dates back to 1957, with the founding of Control Data Corporation, a Minneapolis computer services and manufacturing company. Ceridian employs 9,300 people in more than 70 offices worldwide, including 530 people in the Twin Cities metro.

With a history of top quality support, Minneapolis's professional and business-to-business services companies will help keep Minneapolis at the forefront of the American economy in the years to come.

Minnesota Vikings playing the Dallas Cowboys at the Hubert H. Humphrey Metrodome, 2004

Model Sportsmanship

Minneapolis is steeped in a historic sporting tradition. Its professional baseball, football, and basketball teams, past and present, have commanded national attention for their championship wins and talented players. Minneapolis's teams have also inspired loyalty among fans, who time and again have broken attendance records. It is for these reasons that *The Sporting News* has named the Twin Cities among the nation's 20 best sports cities since 1999.

The Big Leagues

Baseball is a celebrated institution in Minneapolis that dates back to 1884, when the city's first professional team, the Minneapolis Millers, began playing at Athletic Park downtown. Twelve years later, the Millers won their first professional baseball championship, the Western League flag, and moved to Nicollet Park in South Minneapolis.

In 1902 the Millers became a charter member of the American Association, a leading minor league franchise that was one notch below the major leagues. The Millers eventually became one of the association's top teams, attracting

Minneapolis Millers, 1896

Willie Mays at the Millers' clubhouse, 1951

Enthusiasm for the Twins compelled civic leaders to bring sports back to downtown Minneapolis. The result was the Hubert H. Humphrey Metrodome, an enclosed sports stadium that opened in 1982. On a cold April night, the Twins played their first game at the Metrodome, and first baseman Kent Hrbek christened the stadium with two home runs.

In 1987 and 1991 the Twins won the American League pennant, which allowed the team to advance to the World Series. The Twins won both series, beating the St. Louis Cardinals in 1987 and the Atlanta Braves in 1991.

In the 1990s individual Twins players earned special accolades of their own. In 1993 Dave Winfield got his 3,000th career hit, as did

talented players such as Ted Williams and Willie Mays. When the Millers moved into Metropolitan Stadium, in Bloomington, in 1956, a record crowd of more than 18,000 people showed up for the opening game—in 45-degree weather.

Despite their devoted fan base, the Millers folded in 1960. In the

59 seasons the Millers belonged to the American Association, the team achieved the association's best win-loss record. The Millers also won nine pennants, tying it with cross-river competitor, the St. Paul Saints.

The end of the Millers era was marked by the entrance of a Major League Baseball team, the

Washington Senators from Washington, D.C., in 1960. Renamed the Minnesota Twins, the American League team moved into Metropolitan Stadium. Just two years later the Twins finished second to the legendary New York Yankees. In 1965 the Twins attracted attention again by hosting the All-Star Game and capturing the American League pennant.

Outfielder Kirby Puckett and teammates celebrating the Minnesota Twins' World Series victory, 1991

Twins pitcher Terry Mulholland

Minnesota Twins Plaza at the Metrodome

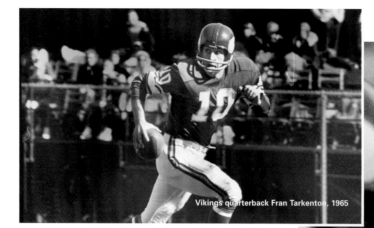
Vikings quarterback Fran Tarkenton, 1965

Coach Bud Grant, 1977

Paul Molitor in 1996. Both of them were inducted into the Baseball Hall of Fame.

With a history of success behind them, the Twins entered the new millennium strong, winning Central Division Titles in 2002, 2003, and 2004.

Hitting the Gridiron

Professional football arrived in Minneapolis with the American Professional Football Association's Minneapolis Marines team, which began playing at Nicollet Park in 1921. The team was short-lived, however, folding in 1924. Five years later, the National Football League (NFL) revived the team with a new name, the Minneapolis Red Jackets. Like the Marines, the Red Jackets played at Nicollet Park and had a brief history, folding during the 1930–31 season.

Minneapolis got its third professional football team in 1960, when the NFL created its 14th expansion team, the Minnesota Vikings. Named to reflect Minnesota's Scandinavian heritage, the Vikings took residence at Metropolitan Stadium and kicked off their first season by defeating the Chicago Bears 37 to 13.

The Vikings made it to the Super Bowl for the first time in 1969—and again in 1973, 1974, and 1976.

Enthusiastic fans at the Metrodome

Although the Vikings did not win the championships, they retained their tough-team status throughout the 1970s, primarily due to the skills and talents of coach Bud Grant and star quarterback Fran Tarkenton.

In 1982 the Vikings moved to the Metrodome. When the team played its first game there, it defeated the Tampa Bay Buccaneers 17 to 10. In 1987 the Vikings vied for the National Football Conference (NFC) title. Two years later, the Vikings won the division championship—a victory that was repeated in 1992, 1994, 1998, and 2000.

In the late 1990s, quarterback Daunte Culpepper emerged as one

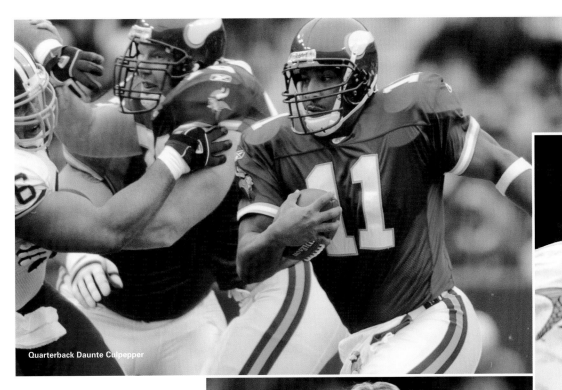

Quarterback Daunte Culpepper

Vikings cheerleaders

Defensive tackle Steve Martin

of the Vikings' stars, earning two of the Vikings' three all-time single-season passer ratings, in 2000 and 2003. With players such as Culpepper, the team is bound to make sports history.

A Slam Dunk for Minneapolis

Basketball is another favorite pastime in Minneapolis. The city's first professional basketball team, the Minneapolis Lakers, arrived on the sports scene in 1947 and played at the Minneapolis Auditorium. Thanks to six-foot-ten star player George Mikan, the Lakers won the National

Basketball League championships for the 1947–48 season. During the 1949–50 season the Lakers became part of the National Basketball Association (NBA) and won that year's championship. Although the Lakers did not regain the title during the 1950–51 season, the team rebounded the following three seasons, winning consecutive

championships. Sports critics raved that the Lakers had become the NBA's first dynasty.

Much to the disappointment of local fans, the Lakers moved to Los Angeles in 1960. Afterward, Minneapolis flirted with two short-lived professional teams, the American Basketball Association's Minnesota Muskies, in 1967–68, and Minnesota Pipers, in 1968–69.

Minneapolis Lakers, 1953

Minnesota Timberwolves playing the San Antonio Spurs at the Target Center, 2005

Minnesota Lynx celebrating Katie Smith's 5,000th point, 2005

It wasn't until 1989 that the NBA revisited Minneapolis, this time with the creation of the Minnesota Timberwolves, part of the league's expansion efforts. More than a million fans cheered the Timberwolves on during the team's inaugural season at the Metrodome, setting an all-time-high NBA attendance record. When the Timberwolves moved to the new Target Center in 1990, fans followed.

Tapping into the skills of star players such as Kevin Garnett, the Timberwolves became formidable competitors during the mid to late 1990s, advancing to the NBA play-offs for the first time during the 1996–97 season. The team has since appeared in eight playoffs.

Still strong, the Timberwolves ended the 2003–04 season by winning their first Midwest Division Championship and being named the top team in the Western Conference.

On the Ball

While men's professional basketball was on hiatus in Minneapolis during the 1970s, women's professional basketball took off with the 1978 debut of the Minnesota Fillies, which played for three seasons during the brief existence of the Women's Professional Basketball League. The team played at both the Metropolitan Sports Center in Bloomington and Williams Arena in Minneapolis.

In 1999 the Minnesota Lynx of the Women's NBA (WNBA) brought women's basketball back to Minneapolis. Local fans greeted the team with enthusiasm. In the Lynx's first regular season game at the Target

Center, 12,000 people watched the team pounce the Detroit Shock. In 2003 the Lynx finished the season with a franchise-best record and advanced to the WNBA playoffs for the first time. Contributing to the team's success are star players such

as Katie Smith, a top scorer and record breaker in the league.

With a diverse range of professional teams and a solid fan base, Minneapolis has an enviable sporting tradition.

Timberwolves' Latrell Sprewell

Power and Go

At a crossroads of major air, highway, inland waterway, and rail networks, Minneapolis is an important force in U.S. transportation. One of the country's busiest airports, the Minneapolis–St. Paul International Airport, is located here, along with large airline companies, thriving transport businesses, and a Mississippi River port that handled more than 1.2 million tons of cargo in 2004. Dependable, affordable sources of energy, from petroleum products to natural gas and electricity, have helped make such success possible.

Making Tracks

The earliest chapters of Minneapolis history center on the transport of people and commodities on the Mississippi River. As the area diversified and expanded beyond its early dependence on the river, it did so along streetcar routes. Minneapolis's first horse-drawn streetcar began operation in 1875, and by the 1880s streetcar lines extended outward from Minneapolis's downtown commercial core. In 1889 the streetcars were electrified, and in 1920 ridership peaked at 140 million passengers.

Electric streetcars on Hennepin Avenue, 1906

City bus in downtown Minneapolis, 1958

Metro Transit bus at Nicollet Mall

SkyWeb Express prototype

Illustration of a SkyWeb Express guideway

As automobiles gained popularity, however, streetcar ridership waned. By 1954 the streetcars were scrapped and replaced with buses. The city's bus system, now known as Metro Transit, grew into one of the country's largest. Today Metro Transit comprises more than 900 buses on 137 routes, serving about 69 million passengers each year. It also includes the Hiawatha Line, Minnesota's first light-rail line. Opened in 2004, the line runs from downtown Minneapolis to Minneapolis–St. Paul International Airport and the Mall of America, in Bloomington, 12 miles to the south. A second light-rail line, which will connect downtown Minneapolis and St. Paul, is expected by 2010.

What Goes Around, Comes Around

The growth of Minneapolis and its suburbs has prompted new local transit solutions—some based on historical models, some on revolutionary paradigms. Half a century after streetcars were retired in Minneapolis, residents are hoping to bring them back into service. In 2004 the Minneapolis City Council passed a resolution to study the feasibility of a streetcar system. A likely site for the first line is the Midtown Greenway, a below-grade pedestrian and bicycle path following an abandoned railroad right-of-way that spans South Minneapolis.

At the other end of the people-moving spectrum is SkyWeb Express, a personalized rapid transit system prototype that features computer-automated "pods." Developed by Taxi 2000 Corporation, in Fridley, the prototype was introduced at the 2003 Minnesota State Fair in St. Paul. SkyWeb Express pods are designed to carry passengers along elevated steel guideways directly to their destinations. As with a taxi ride, there are no set schedules and no intermediate stops to board or discharge riders. Clients currently interested in the system include the cities of Minneapolis and Duluth.

In It for the Long Haul

Goods are on the move in Minneapolis, too. C. H. Robinson Worldwide (CHRW), a century-old company headquartered in Eden Prairie, has built a business focusing on over-the-road freight hauling. One of North America's largest third-party logistics companies, CHRW contracts with truck, rail, ocean, and air carriers to transport cargo for more than 16,000 clients. Located in the Minneapolis area since 1919 and with more than 160 offices around the world, CHRW earned revenues of $4.3 billion in 2004.

Eagan-based Transport Corporation of America serves mostly Fortune 500 department store, grocery, industrial, consumer, and paper products customers in the United States

Passenger drop-off at MSP

Lindbergh Terminal at the Minneapolis–St. Paul International Airport (MSP)

Deicing of a plane at MSP

and Canada. In business since 1984, the company employs about 1,300 people and had revenues of $258.4 million in 2004.

Flying Like Eagles

Air transport first came to Minneapolis in 1911, when a New Orleans–bound hydroplane took off from Lake Calhoun on an experimental airmail run. By 1921 a former auto speedway in Bloomington had been acquired for an airport, and two landing strips and a number of wooden hangars were built to accommodate regular mail flights. Passenger service began in 1928, and in 1948 what had been called Speedway Field and then Wold-Chamberlain Field finally acquired its present name, Minneapolis–St. Paul International Airport (MSP).

In 2004 MSP accommodated more than 36.7 million passengers and

more than 541,000 landings and takeoffs. Over the years, many passengers have expressed their satisfaction with MSP in annual surveys conducted by the International Air Transport Association, which ranked MSP the Best Large Airport in the Americas from 2000 to 2004. To meet regional growth demands, MSP has opened new concourses and cargo facilities. A fourth runway is scheduled for completion in 2005.

Northwest Airlines (NWA), MSP's largest tenant, accounted for 78 percent of takeoffs and landings at the airport in 2004. NWA began operations in 1926 by flying the Twin Cities–Chicago mail route using two rented, open-cockpit biplanes. In 1927 the airline carried its first ticketed passengers, a total of 106 that year. Much has changed since then—NWA is now the

Christening of a Northwest Airways airmail plane, 1926

Northwest Airlines aircraft at MSP

world's fourth-largest airline and flies to approximately 750 destinations in 120 countries.

NWA commuter affiliate Mesaba Airlines is the country's oldest regional airline, serving 110 U.S. and Canadian cities from hubs at MSP, Detroit Metropolitan Wayne County Airport, and Memphis International Airport. In 2004 Mesaba carried more than 5.4 million passengers. Founded in Coleraine, Minnesota, in 1944, Mesaba took its name from a Native American word meaning "soaring eagle." A subsidiary of MAIR Holdings, of Minneapolis, Mesaba established headquarters at MSP in 1985 and moved them to Eagan in 2003.

Sun Country Airlines, headquartered in Mendota Heights, is another tenant at MSP. Sun Country operates both regularly scheduled and charter flights out of the airport, with nearly 30 routes to popular tourist destinations in the United States, Mexico, and the Caribbean.

Dependable Energy

The region's first settlers discovered a tremendous source of power in St. Anthony Falls. The falls fueled Minneapolis's earliest industries, including the giant lumber and flour mills that ultimately shaped the city's destiny. By the end of the 1800s, however, the falls could no longer withstand the pressure of supplying all

that energy, and Minneapolitans began turning to other sources of power.

Today residents benefit from the presence of two powerful energy providers with roots deep in the community—CenterPoint Energy Minnegasco and Xcel Energy. More than a century ago Minnegasco was lighting Minneapolis streets with natural gas. Now a Minneapolis-based subsidiary of Houston's CenterPoint Energy, Minnegasco serves 745,000 residential and business customers in more than 240 Minnesota communities, with the largest concentration in Minneapolis and its suburbs.

Xcel Energy, headquartered in Minneapolis, serves the gas and electricity needs of 11 states, including dozens of communities in the west metro. The 130-year-old company is a major generating utility whose plants produce more than 15,000 megawatts of power. In the Minneapolis metro area, Xcel operates six generating plants that burn coal and gas and one nuclear-powered plant.

Power to the People

In the 1930s electric distribution cooperatives were organized to serve farmers without access to affordable power. Two such co-ops,

Northwest Airlines cargo plane

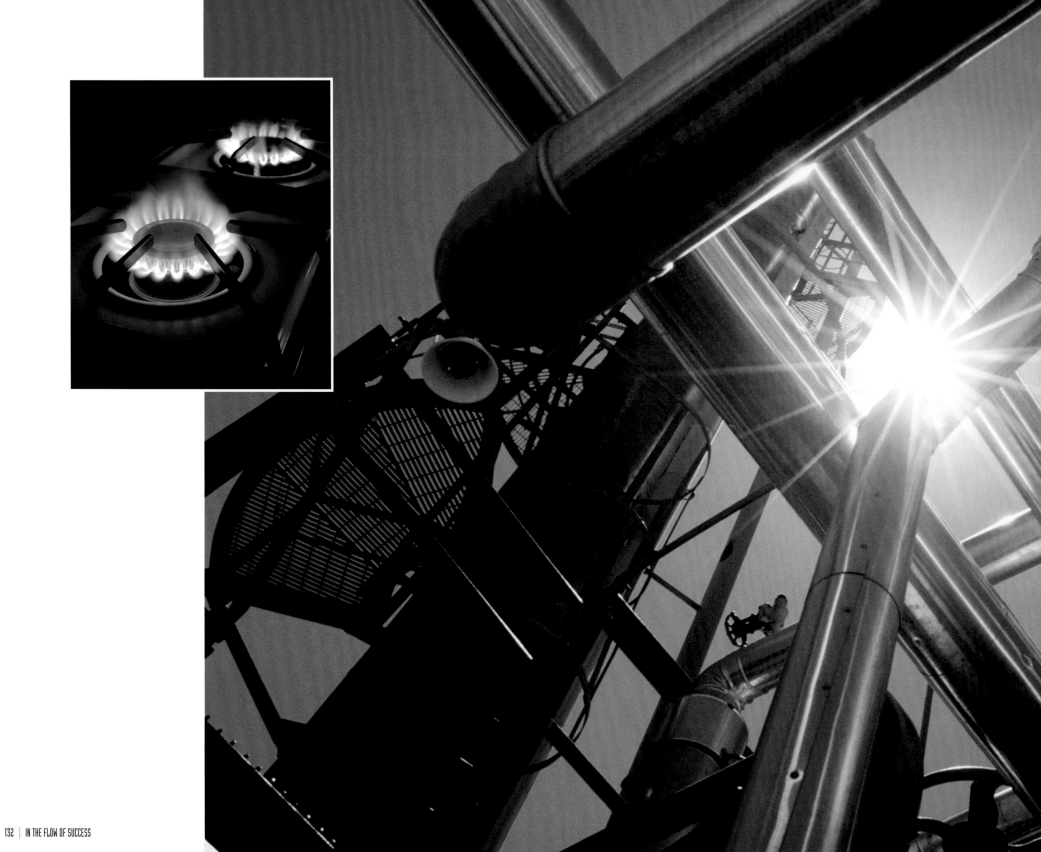

Branches being cleared from a Dakota Electric Association power line

Dakota Electric worker placing insulated cover-ups on a 7,200-volt line

members of the Touchstone Energy alliance, serve parts of the Minneapolis area today.

Dakota Electric Association, based in Farmington, supplies more than 94,000 commercial and residential customers over a territory that includes Dakota County and parts of Scott, Rice, and Goodhue counties. Founded in 1937, Dakota Electric is among the nation's 20 largest electric distribution cooperatives. Wright-Hennepin Cooperative Electric Association, headquartered in Rockford, provides power to Wright County and the western portion of Hennepin County. Also founded in 1937, Wright-Hennepin serves 35,000 retail accounts.

Fueling the Economy

Some Minneapolis businesses provide energy to customers throughout the country. CHS, of Inver Grove Heights, is the largest cooperative refiner in the United States. The Fortune 500 company, whose diverse products range from energy to grains, annually markets more than 3 billion gallons of gasoline, diesel, ethanol blends, and alternative fuels. CHS owns two refineries, in Montana and Kansas, and operates eight terminals, 1,200 miles of pipeline, and one of the largest truck fleets in the country to handle its output. Cenex-branded fuels are sold through CHS's 800-plus gas stations and through more than 700 other petroleum outlets. The company, which traces its roots to 1929, earned $10.9 billion in net sales in 2004.

Innovative solutions to energy and transportation needs, from power cooperatives to personalized rapid transit, are business-as-usual in Minneapolis.

Part Three

Portraits of Success

Profiles of Companies and Organizations

Historic Houses of Worship

Profiles of Corporations and Organizations

Minneapolis Historic Houses of Worship

Historic houses of worship in Minneapolis are architectural marvels, symbolic windows to the past, places for prayer, venues for music and art, and social and cultural community centers, and they are integral to the vitality of the city.

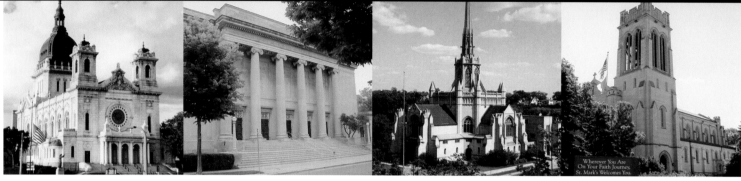

Basilica of Saint Mary

Anchoring the downtown skyline, the Basilica of Saint Mary is a dynamic community center where visitors experience art exhibits, superb concerts, life-changing social justice programs, and rich celebrations of Catholic faith. Warm and hospitable, the Basilica of Saint Mary welcomes a great diversity of people of all ages, ethnicities, races, and social and economic backgrounds. Designed by French architect Emanuel Masqueray and completed in 1915, it was designated the first basilica in the United States by Pope Pius XI in 1926. The Basilica of Saint Mary is one of the finest examples of beaux arts architecture in the country and is listed on the National Register of Historic Places. For more information, visit www.mary.org.

Temple Israel

Established in 1878, Temple Israel is the oldest Reform Jewish synagogue in Minneapolis and one of the largest Reform synagogues in North America. Life cycle events, Jewish text, and Jewish living are at the center of spiritual life at Temple Israel. A variety of worship styles, innovative teaching techniques geared toward lifelong Jewish education, a culturally diverse congregation, and a legacy of engaging with its neighbors and the larger community make the temple a vibrant presence in its urban location.

Temple Israel has a strong tradition of community involvement and philanthropy. For additional information, visit www.templeisrael.com.

Hennepin Avenue United Methodist Church

Hennepin Avenue United Methodist Church invites all people on a spiritual journey. Founded in 1875, Hennepin has been open for worship in its current building since 1916. The eight-sided sanctuary is modeled after the Ely Cathedral in Ely, England. The Border Memorial Chapel commemorates Hennepin's historic 1957 merger with Border Methodist Church, a predominantly African-American congregation. Hennepin's rich tradition of sacred music and art is exemplified by its 4,000-pipe organ, numerous choirs, stained-glass windows, and an outstanding collection of religious art. For additional information, visit www.haumc.org.

Saint Mark's Episcopal Cathedral

Saint Mark's Episcopal Cathedral, founded in 1858, is an artistic and architectural testament to the spiritual life that takes place within a house of God. The building was completed in 1910. Among its decorative treasures are stained glass, textiles, banners, needlepoint, mosaics, tiles, and sculptures—many of which represent biblical figures as well as early American and Minnesotan church leaders. Elaborate carvings in the white oak pulpit depict the evangelization of the world by teachers, preachers, and missionaries, and beautiful wood carvings adorn the altar area. For additional information, visit www.st-marks-cathedral.org.

Plymouth Congregational Church

Plymouth Congregational Church was organized nearly 150 years ago, in 1857. The church was first built at Fourth Street and Nicollet in 1858 and moved to Eighth Street and Nicollet in 1875. In 1909, it dedicated its present location at 19th Street and Nicollet. Plymouth embraces liberal Christian theology that affirms all people as beloved children of God—without regard to ability, age, economic status, ethnicity, gender, race, or sexual orientation—and celebrates music and the arts as religious expressions. The community pledges to walk with one another on faith journeys, respecting differences in belief and theology. For additional information, visit www.plymouth.org.

Mount Olivet Lutheran Church—Minneapolis

Mount Olivet Lutheran Church has grown to be one of the largest active Lutheran churches in the world. Senior Pastor Paul Youngdahl leads this servant congregation, responding with compassion and excellence in Christian ministries and embracing persons in all seasons and situations in life. The church is expanding throughout the Twin Cities region and making a positive impact throughout the United States and around the world. The mission center for Mount Olivet's eight affiliated ministries is one dynamic congregation located on two campuses in southwest Minneapolis and Victoria, Minnesota. For additional information, visit www.mtolivet.org.

Westminster Presbyterian Church

Westminster Presbyterian Church's mission is to gather as an open community to worship God and to be a telling presence in the city. For 150 years, Westminster and the city of Minneapolis have shared a common history. Westminster was founded in 1857, and the current sanctuary was built on Nicollet and 12th Street in 1897. Westminster's commitments to the Gospel and to the city include partnerships with Habitat for Humanity and support for transitional and affordable housing. Uplifting music and quality programs for children and youths are hallmarks of Westminster. For additional information, visit www.ewestminster.org.

Our Lady of Lourdes

Overlooking the Mississippi River, Our Lady of Lourdes Catholic church holds key positions in Minneapolis geography and history. It is the city's oldest continuously operational church. In 1877, French-Canadian Catholics purchased the building—built in 1855 for use as a Universalist church—and expanded it. These French-Canadian roots are distinctly reflected in the church's architecture and decoration. The church offers a warm welcome to visitors and to those who consider it their spiritual home. The church's steeple lights up the city skyline every night as a symbol of hope and prayer. For additional information, visit www.ourladyoflourdesmn.com.

This page, left to right: Plymouth Congregational Church, designed by St. Paul architect Monroe Sheire, was built with native blue limestone and is modeled inside and out after a typical New England church. Mount Olivet Lutheran Church—housed in a native Mankato-stone building—serves people throughout the Minneapolis and St. Paul metropolitan areas and is one of the world's largest active Lutheran congregations. Westminster Presbyterian Church is listed on the National Register of Historic Places, and after extensive renovation it received the 1999 Heritage Preservation Award from the Minneapolis Heritage Preservation Commission and the Minnesota Chapter of the American Institute of Architects. Our Lady of Lourdes Catholic church, which shares a rich history with the city of Minneapolis, is recognized by its majestic wooden steeple, characteristic of French provincial churches.

Conventions, Hospitality, and Tourism

Profiles of Corporations and Organizations

Sofitel Minneapolis

This award-winning hotel, conveniently located for business and holiday travelers in the Twin Cities, is designed throughout with Parisian flair, offering guests well-appointed accommodations, French cuisine, live musical entertainment, and gracious service.

Sofitel Minneapolis is a world-class luxury hotel that embodies the French art of living in its elegant interiors, fine cuisine, well-appointed guest quarters, and impeccable service. Located in Bloomington, just 15 minutes from the Minneapolis–St. Paul International Airport and 10 minutes from the Mall of America, the hotel offers business and holiday travelers a convenient setting with Parisian ambience.

The hotel's decor has been updated with a redesign that maintains the French atmosphere. Guests are welcomed into an interior atrium lobby with sparkling chandeliers. In the hotel's lounge are jewel-toned furnishings, including comfortable chairs and sofas arranged for conversation and leather booths for enjoying the music of a pianist or jazz trio.

Accommodations include 277 spacious guest rooms and five suites, with amenities such as featherbeds and down comforters and pillows. In the Executive Deluxe guest rooms are luxurious furnishings and artwork, spa-style baths, soft robes, and flat-screen television sets. Services in all guest rooms include Internet connectivity and Wi-Fi wireless Internet access. A business center is located on the grounds, as is a fitness center; concierge services are available, and there is 24-hour room service.

For entertaining and meetings, the hotel offers a variety of venues. The garden court seats up to 180 guests banquet-style. The grand ballroom can be set up to seat 360 guests for a banquet or 500 people theater-style. Other meeting rooms are available for smaller groups.

In the hotel are two award-winning restaurants that have a following of local customers and share the hotel's reputation for excellence. Chez Colette is a 1920s-style brasserie featuring typical dishes of French cuisine. The Chez Colette Lounge provides an intimate atmosphere for cocktails, snacks, and live musical entertainment. La Fougasse is designed in the French Provençal style, with colorful tilework, fireplaces, an outdoor terrace in summer, and an open demonstration kitchen. Its menu features Mediterranean cuisine from the Provence region of France. The La Fougasse Bar offers appetizers and aperitifs in a vibrant setting.

Since its opening in 1975, Sofitel Minneapolis has upheld a reputation for excellent service, restful nights, and fine dining in surroundings of understated elegance, and for 22 years it has earned the hospitality industry's AAA Four Diamond rating. Part of Accor hotels, Sofitel includes 190 hotels in worldwide business and resorts destinations. Sofitel Minneapolis's premier accommodations and services make it an ideal place for exploring the Twin Cities while also experiencing the French "Art de Vivre."

Bloomington Convention & Visitors Bureau

Bloomington—home of *the* mall, the world-famous Mall of America—is celebrated as the 'Center of It All' for its ideal location (central to all U.S. states, just minutes from the Twin Cities), its man-made splendors (the range of dining, shopping, and entertainment venues), and its natural wonders (acres of parks, refuges, and more).

Bloomington is known the world over for its unique attractions, ideal location, and year-round warm welcome for visitors—both from city residents and the Bloomington Convention & Visitors Bureau. As one of Minnesota's largest cities, Bloomington is home to the nation's number one visited retail/ entertainment attraction—the magnificent Mall of America.

Developed by the visionary Ghermezian brothers of the Triple Five Group, in cooperation with the Bloomington Port Authority, the mall made history—as the nation's largest enclosed retail complex—when it opened in 1992. Today, this singular mall attracts more than 40 million shoppers annually, including 2.5 million international travelers; employs more than 10,000 dedicated personnel; and is located less than five minutes from most Bloomington hotels. All area hotels offer free shuttle service to and from the mall.

Certainly, Bloomington is number one when it comes to its convenient location, world-class amenities, and human-scale neighborhoods. With the downtowns of Minneapolis and St. Paul just 10 miles away, Bloomington sits in the heart of one of the most culturally dynamic metropolitan areas in the United States. Yet Bloomington's urban excitement is balanced with its serene parks and out-door recreation areas—in fact, more than one-third of the city is designated as parkland and recreation space.

The Minneapolis–St. Paul International Airport is located just five minutes from Bloomington, and no U.S. city is more than three-and-a-half hours away by air. Ranked among the five safest in the world, the airport is served by 19 airlines and handles up to 1,000 arrivals and departures every day. Again, courtesy shuttle service to and from the airport is offered by all Bloomington hotels.

Visitors who arrive in Bloomington by car enjoy free parking throughout the city. Direct access to the airport, the Mall of America, and downtown Minneapolis is available on the new Hiawatha Light Rail Transit Line. A fare of $2.00 takes visitors anywhere on the route, and a ticket is valid for two-and-a-half hours.

Remarkably, Bloomington's 33 hotels offer more than 6,900 guest rooms—more than either St. Paul or Minneapolis—and ample meeting facilities for 10 to 2,000 people. More than 100 restaurants offer a range of dining options, and there are many entertainment choices as well, from sports bars and dinner theater to comedy clubs and jazz spots. Bloomington's three golf courses, the Minnesota Valley National Wildlife Refuge, and 123 parks offer visitors ample recreation opportunities for all seasons.

The Bloomington Convention & Visitors Bureau is dedicated to helping visitors get the most out of their stay in the city, providing maps, information on activities and accommodations, and tour itineraries. As an ambassador of goodwill and service, the Bloomington Convention & Visitors Bureau is an integral part of Bloomington's vibrant social, cultural, and economic life. For more information, call 866-435-7425, e-mail sales@bloomingtonmn.org, or visit the Bloomington Convention & Visitors Bureau's Web site at www.bloomingtonmn.org.

Left: Among Bloomington's many one-of-a-kind attractions is the Mall of America, a 78-acre shopping, dining, and entertainment complex that includes more than 520 stores, four national department stores, more than 50 restaurants, the always-popular carousel (shown), the huge Underwater Adventures aquarium, and the seven-acre Camp Snoopy amusement park. As an added bonus, no sales tax on clothing or shoes is charged at the Mall of America or by any retailer in Minnesota.

Carlson Companies

With a tradition of superior service in hospitality, business and leisure travel, and marketing, this family-owned company is a global leader in the hotel, resort, restaurant, and cruise line industries, catering to leisure and corporate customers worldwide.

A family of companies with operations in more than 140 countries, Carlson Companies is a global leader in the hospitality, business and leisure travel, and marketing industries.

Carlson hotel operations are dedicated to providing "great hospitality built on great relationships." Carlson brands encompass the Regent International Hotels®, the Radisson Hotels & Resorts®, the Park Plaza® Hotels & Resorts, the Country Inns & Suites By Carlson℠, and the Park Inn® hotels.

Carlson is also a leader in the casual-dining industry and the emerging fast-casual segment. Carlson's restaurant brands are T.G.I. Friday's®, Friday's Front Row® Sports Grill, Friday's American Bar®, and Pick Up Stix®.

In the travel segment, Carlson serves corporate and leisure clients through its owned and franchised operations. Travel brands and services include Carlson Wagonlit Travel; Carlson Destination Marketing Services; Carlson Leisure Travel Services; Carlson Vacation & Business Travel; CW Government Travel;

Results Travel®; Cruise Holidays℠; America's Vacation Store®; Cruise Specialists, Inc.; Fly4less.com℠; SinglesCruise.com℠; and SeaMaster Cruises℠.

Radisson Seven Seas Cruises® is Carlson's cruise line division, which has four small to midsize ships in its six-star fleet—the new all-suite, all-balcony *Seven Seas Voyager*; her sister ship, the *Seven Seas Mariner*®; the all-suite *Seven Seas Navigator*®; and the French Polynesian *Paul Gauguin*.

Carlson Marketing Group® helps companies build better relationships with their customers, employees, and channel partners. Ranked by *Advertising Age* magazine as the number one marketing services agency in the United States, Carlson Marketing provides the complete range of services—including incentive travel, events, performance improvement, training programs, prepaid card services, merchandise, and fulfillment—as well as integrated, loyalty, and interactive marketing. The Peppers & Rogers Group® and the Gold Points Reward Network℠ are part of this organization.

Carlson's history is a classic success story. In 1938, with an idea and $55 of borrowed capital, entrepreneur Curtis L. Carlson founded the Gold Bond Stamp Company in his home city of Minneapolis. Designed to help store operators build relationships with customers, trading stamps swept the nation. Diversification into hotels, travel, and other related businesses

in the 1960s and 1970s established the foundation of Carlson Companies.

Today, Carlson strives to cross-market the strengths of all of its brands to meet its customers' needs. Carlson also is a great place to work. *Working Mother* magazine has recognized Carlson Companies for four consecutive years as one of the 100 Best Companies for Working Mothers.

Left: The Carlson Companies' headquarters is located in Minnetonka, Minnesota. In 2004, Carlson's systemwide sales, including franchised-operations sales, totaled $26.1 billion; sales from Carlson-owned-and-managed operations reached $8.4 billion. Above: Carlson chairman and CEO Marilyn Carlson Nelson (left) and Carlson president and COO Curtis C. Nelson (right) are pictured with a portrait of the company's founder, the late Curtis L. Carlson.

Retail

Profiles of Corporations and Organizations

Target

With Minnesota roots and a national reach, the iconic Target—offering quality merchandise with superior service since 1902—aims for solid business, inclusive employment practices, and strong community leadership.

Proudly headquartered in Minneapolis, Minnesota, Target is the nation's fifth-largest retailer. As a growth company focused on general merchandise retailing, Target provides exceptional value to its guests through multiple formats, ranging from upscale discount stores to online shopping. As the corporation has grown, so, too, has its workforce—more than 50,000 jobs have been created since 1998 and retention rates are comparable to or exceed the retail industry average. In fact, Target is among America's top 20 private-sector employers and was ranked 27th on the 2005 Fortune 500 list.

As a retailer, Target delights its guests by delivering well-designed products at an exceptional value in clean, bright, comfortable stores. As a corporation, Target is committed to upholding the highest standards of business practices and continuing its ambitious philanthropic efforts. Target was founded upon, and continues to foster, a positive community spirit. Its guests place a high priority on doing business with an ethical

This impressive two-story Target store, located on Ninth Street and the Nicollet Mall in downtown Minneapolis, opened with great success in 2001. Such convenient store locations, welcoming curb appeal, well-organized layouts, attractive merchandising, and premium guest service make the shopping experience easier, quicker, and more satisfying. And always, Target stores deliver on the brand promise of "Expect More. Pay Less."

company that is supportive of programs they consider meaningful, including those focused on education, the arts, social services, and other vital community partnerships. Target's goal is to exceed these expectations as both a business and civic leader.

While Target is known for its catchy, innovative advertising for its stores, the company's scope is much greater, comprising several operations. These operations include Target Sourcing Services/AMC, a leading global sourcing organization; Target Financial Services, which operates the corporation's credit card services; Target.com, which focuses on electronic retailing; and Target Commercial Interiors, a provider of office interiors in the Upper Midwest.

A Proud Heritage
Target was founded in Minneapolis in 1902 by businessman George Draper Dayton. His Dayton Dry Goods Company consisted of a single department store in the heart of downtown Minneapolis. In 1956, the

renamed Dayton Company opened Southdale Center—the world's first fully enclosed two-level shopping mall—in suburban Minneapolis.

In 1962, The Dayton Company entered the discount merchandising arena with the opening of the first Target store, in Roseville, a suburb of St. Paul, Minnesota. The company publicly offered stock for the first time in 1967 and merged with the J. L. Hudson Company, a leading Detroit retailer, in 1971.

In 2000, acknowledging the prominent position of the Target brand, the company changed its name from Dayton Hudson Corporation to Target Corporation. Today there are more than 1,300 Target stores, employing more

than 275,000 team members in 47 states.

'Value Creation— It's Good for Business'
Target's commitment to delight its guests is at the heart of the company's mission. Every day, value is created by delivering on the Target brand promise—"Expect More. Pay Less."—by offering guests unique, quality products at competitive prices. Convenient store locations, well-organized layouts, attractive merchandising, and premium guest service help make guests' shopping

experiences easier, quicker, and more satisfying. Guests, communities, shareholders, and team members have responded to Target's successful formula with resounding approval, helping the company grow by a rate of 8 to 10 percent of new square footage each year in new stores.

SuperTarget, introduced in 1995, is a full grocery store combined with a Target store. With fresh produce, premium meats and seafood, gourmet and imported products, a selection of natural and organic foods,

Above: SuperTarget stores, which combine the exceptional value and high quality of general-merchandise Target stores with a full grocery store, provide guests with an enjoyable, convenient one-stop shopping experience. Above left: SuperTarget stores enable guests to "Expect More. Pay Less." on the company's most popular grocery items. Market Pantry is one of the affordable SuperTarget grocery brands that deliver quality at prices lower than those of traditional brands.

and top regional and national brands, SuperTarget offers the same high quality differentiated products, competitive prices, and convenient shopping experience that consumers have come to expect from Target. SuperTarget stores are successfully providing guests with greater convenience and will remain a primary growth vehicle for the company. SuperTarget represents approximately one-quarter of new square-footage growth annually.

A Philanthropic Leader

Target is a nationally recognized leader in many areas, including corporate philanthropy, corporate governance, employment practices, and global quality assurance. For nearly six decades, the company has contributed 5 percent of its federally taxable income—more than $2 million each week in 2004— to support nonprofit programs across the country. Target has been recognized by *Forbes* magazine as one of America's most philanthropic companies and is unique in making this kind of financial commitment to its communities.

Target is deeply committed to community involvement through financial support, volunteerism, and the contribution of relevant expertise and best practices. Target's nationwide network of volunteers annually donates more than 300,000 hours to more than 7,000 community-based projects—demonstrating Target's spirit of giving and personal community support.

Among the philanthropic initiatives sponsored by Target are Take Charge of Education, a program through which Target stores have donated over $138 million to more than 110,000 schools since 1997; and Start Something, Target stores' character-education program in partnership with the Tiger Woods Foundation. With nearly 2 million children enrolled, Start Something helps kids ages eight to 17 pursue their dreams. In 2003, Target extended its philanthropy beyond U.S. borders as its Associated Merchandising Corporation division committed $200,000 to international charitable giving.

Another initiative, Target House, serves as a home-away-from-home for the families of patients receiving treatment at St. Jude Children's Research Hospital in Memphis, Tennessee. With 96 fully furnished apartment suites, Target House meets the long-term housing needs of these families, free of charge. Other areas of philanthropic focus include early childhood reading programs, family cultural events, and art education programs.

The Strength of Many. The Power of One

Target's team members are a key factor in the company's performance. The company's ability to recruit and hire people from diverse backgrounds to create a team with a rich variety of strengths, perspectives, and lifestyles is essential to the business. Additionally, the ability of store team members to "know their guests" is greatly dependent upon having team members who reflect the diversity of the communities served by Target.

Diversity is reflected at the highest levels of the organization, up to and including the board of directors. Target consistently strives to create an inclusive work environment that provides opportunities for success and performance in every area of the corporation.

This inclusive environment has been recognized by numerous publications and organizations every year. In 2005, for just two examples,

Target was named as one of the 100 Best Companies for Working Mothers by *Working Mother* magazine and as one of the Top 30 Companies for Executive Women by the National Association for Female Executives. Among other awards and distinctions, Target was honored for its consistent commitment to diversity and community with The King Center's Salute to Greatness award.

Positioned for a Bright Future

Target is committed to continued growth and to delivering upon its promise of providing greater value to its guests, greater opportunities for its team members, greater growth

for its shareholders, and greater vitality for its communities. Target is pleased to call Minneapolis home and looks forward to growing with the city for many years to come. This area offers a superior quality of

life. Home to many large corporations, nationally recognized cultural institutions, vibrant urban areas, top colleges, and a healthy environment, the area is rich in economic substance and is well-positioned for continued growth.

Additional information is available on Target's Web site at www.target.com.

This page, all photos: The Target dog greets children at a Target community relations event. Opposite page: With its headquarters located in downtown Minneapolis, Target is an enduring partner in progress with the Twin Cities and its home state of Minnesota.

Lupient Automotive Group

The award-winning Lupient Automotive Group—encompassing more than 35 franchises in Minneapolis and Wisconsin—is recognized nationally for its total yearly sales, its winning and comprehensive customer service, and its contributions to the communities in which it does business.

Above: The national award–winning car dealerships of the Lupient Automotive Group extend across the Twin Cities from Bloomington to Brooklyn Park. The company succeeds by following its founding principle of making the ownership experience first-rate for its customers.

Company founder Jim Lupient established his first car dealership, Lupient Oldsmobile, in 1969. Today, his Lupient Automotive Group operates more than 35 franchises in Minnesota and Wisconsin. Its Twin Cities locations extend from Bloomington to Brooklyn Park, and include major manufacturers such as Buick, Chevrolet, GMC, Infiniti, Isuzu, Kia, Oldsmobile, Pontiac, Saturn, and Suzuki. The Lupient Automotive Group is also recognized as one of the nation's leading dealerships in fleet sales, with title and license administration services and nationwide delivery.

Driven to Succeed

Jim Lupient has always been driven to succeed. A self-made man and entrepreneur in the complete and best sense of the terms, Lupient has been in the automotive business since 1950. He started out at the age of 16 as a lot person washing cars part-time for the Schmelz brothers, who owned a Kaiser-Fraser dealership in northeast Minneapolis. After his father's death in 1952, it was up to Lupient, a senior in high school, to provide for his mother and three sisters. He began working full-time for the Schmelz brothers' dealership, and before long, he was promoted to salesperson.

Lupient went on to join Central Hudson, and within 90 days he was their number one new-car salesperson. In 1964, Lupient became sales manager at Iten Chevrolet, which at the time was Minnesota's largest Chevrolet dealership. He remained at Iten until he opened his own dealership in 1969. Since its founding, Lupient Oldsmobile has ranked with the top Oldsmobile dealers in the nation and has achieved the Olds Elite status.

Focused on the Customer

Following in the tradition of Lupient Oldsmobile, the Lupient Automotive Group succeeds on the same principle that ensured the success of its founding company—namely, to make the ownership experience first-rate, so that satisfied and loyal customers will keep coming back for all their automotive needs.

Overall, the Lupient Automotive Group prides itself on delivering exceptional service and on building customer satisfaction and trust. The company's employees are both experienced and committed to their customers. For example, the service technicians and service consultants at the Lupient Auto Mall in Golden Valley have a combined 917 years of experience. The sales consultants, support staff, and management team also have impressive credentials and extensive experience.

The Lupient Automotive Group creates a comfortable, convenient environment for its customers. Courtesy shuttles run between the dealerships and downtown Minneapolis at regular intervals. Dealerships also offer workstations with computer ports, play areas for children, spacious lounges for waiting, and complimentary refreshments.

'Dealer of the Year' Awards and Accolades

The Lupient Automotive Group's commitment to its customers has

been recognized with numerous national awards over its long history in business. For example, in 1988 Lupient was awarded the prestigious Isuzu President's Cup. In 1989 Lupient was honored as the top dealer in total sales for both Oldsmobile and Buick automobiles— a double honor that has never, to date, been achieved by another single dealer. That same year, Lupient was also the number seven Chevrolet dealer in the country.

In 1990 Lupient was awarded the Quality Dealer of the Year honor by *Time* magazine. It was a high honor considering that Lupient was chosen to be first among 33,000 auto dealers across the country. During that year, Jim Lupient also served as an official national spokesman for auto dealers. Then in 1992 his company received *Sports Illustrated* magazine's American Dealer of the Year award as well as the Top Foreign-Car Sales designation. Impressively, this company

was the only dealer to have received both awards in the same year.

Community and Philanthropy Matters

The Lupient Automotive Group's commitment to service goes beyond its showrooms to the communities it serves. This company gives back to its communities through a wide variety of efforts, including sponsoring neighborhood sports teams, building playgrounds, and supporting

local charities. The Jim and Barbara Lupient Foundation is devoted to supporting a variety of programs, including the stewardship of Minneapolis parks.

The Lupient Automotive Group's long history of success can be attributed to its clear corporate philosophy, which stresses first-rate customer service and giving back to the community.

"Once we get to know a person and he or she gets to know us, that person will want to come back to Lupient time and again," states Jim Lupient, who currently serves as chairman of the board of the dynamic Lupient Automotive Group.

This page: The Lupient Automotive Group's Twin Cities locations include Infiniti, Buick, Chevrolet, GMC, Isuzu, Kia, Oldsmobile, Pontiac, Saturn, and Suzuki dealerships. Serving customers well at every stage of ownership is a main focus of the Lupient Automotive Group and its expert, experienced team of managers, sales consultants, support staff, service technicians, and service consultants. The company's high level of professionalism in all aspects of its business—from the sales floors to the service bays— has earned the Lupient Automotive Group numerous industry and mainstream awards and accolades.

Select Comfort Corporation, creator of the Sleep Number® bed and one of the nation's leading bed retailers, is committed to its mission of improving people's lives by improving their sleep. With more than 365 retail locations and 2,500 employees nationwide, the company has grown well beyond its humble beginnings to deliver personalized comfort, innovative sleep technology, and high quality products to more than 3.5 million people.

Sleep Number® Bed Technology

The original technology of what is now called the Sleep Number bed was invented by a former innerspring mattress maker in 1979, when the idea of an advanced sleep system using air technology became a reality in his garage workshop. In 1987, Select Comfort Corporation was founded from those efforts. The company immediately began investing in sleep research to improve its bed

design, ensuring that every customer could find individualized comfort and support with a variety of options and price points. Today, Select Comfort holds 32 U.S.–issued or pending patents for its products.

Because no two sleepers are alike in what makes them comfortable, the company identified the need for an adjustable sleep surface in a world of one-size-fits-all, fixed-firmness

mattresses. Each sleeper's preference is distinguished by a Sleep Number, which can be changed whenever the sleeper wishes. A Sleep Number is a setting between zero and 100 that represents each person's ideal combination of mattress comfort, firmness, and support, based on variations in weight, body shape, sleep position, and sleep surface preference.

The Sleep Number bed's air-chamber design conforms to the unique shape of each sleeper, reducing painful pressure points and distributing weight more evenly, while giving the sleeper more proper spinal support. The air chambers can be regulated within seconds by a Firmness Control™ System ("the brains behind the bed") that includes a discreet forced-air pump and handheld digital remote control. Dual air chambers can be adjusted individually, much to the pleasure of the many couples who disagree on mattress firmness.

More than 50,000 company testimonials speak to the satisfaction of Sleep Number bed owners who regularly report improved sleep quality, back-pain relief, and more energy. Select Comfort's chairman and CEO, Bill McLaughlin, attests to the buzz around his company's product, noting: "When I first joined the company five years ago, I was impressed by the persistence of its employees and the passion of Sleep Number bed owners. They believe that this product can and does improve people's lives by improving their sleep. When I discovered my Sleep Number was 55, I knew I had found the key to a perfect night's sleep."

The Science of Sleep

Independent clinical studies support the technology behind the Sleep Number bed. In a study conducted at Stanford University's Sleep Disorders Center, researchers found that 87 percent of those who slept on a Sleep Number bed experienced a greater percentage of REM sleep, with fewer sleep disturbances. In a study conducted by the Sister Kenny Institute at Abbott Northwestern Hospital and The Marsh health center in conjunction with Sleep Fitness Center, 93 percent of respondents said they experienced back-pain relief,

and 90 percent reported reduced aches and pains.

Select Comfort seeks to establish itself as an industry expert in most matters related to better sleep. The company's Sleep Innovation Group supports that mission through its dedication to developing solid, science-based sleep expertise, credible sleep solutions, and educational tools for communicating the science of sleep. In 2003, Select Comfort founded its Sleep Advisory Board℠, an inter-disciplinary group of leading clinicians and scientists that provides guidance

on issues related to the science and practice of better sleep. The board supports Select Comfort's commitment to integrity and objectivity in the appli-cation of sleep science to promote sound sleep and productive wakefulness.

Leading the Industry

The specialty sleep category is the fastest growing segment of the mattress industry, and Select Comfort's net sales totaled more than $558 million in 2004. In 2005—for the sixth consecutive year—the company was ranked the number one bedding retailer in the United States by *Furniture/Today*, a

leading trade publication. Select Comfort also boasts an award-winning, multi-million-dollar integrated marketing campaign for the Sleep Number brand, featuring Emmy-winning actress Lindsay Wagner as spokesperson. In 2004, Select Comfort and Minnesota-based Carlson Companies, Inc. part-nered to make the Sleep Number bed exclusively available at Radisson Hotels & Resorts in the United States, Canada, and the Caribbean. By the end of 2006, up to 90,000 traditional mat-tresses in Radisson properties may be replaced with the Sleep Number bed.

Select Comfort is also proud to be the Official Bed Provider for Ronald McDonald House Charities and supplies Sleep Number beds for the 150 Ronald McDonald Houses in the United States. Since 2001, thousands of families have experi-enced a better night's sleep while their children receive medical treat-ment at nearby hospitals. Select Comfort and its employees have donated more than $250,000 and 5,000 volunteer hours to the charity in fulfilling their mission to improve people's lives by improving their sleep.

Above: Select Comfort spokesperson Lindsay Wagner appears in print and television advertisements and is one of more than 3.5 million people who own a Sleep Number bed.

The Nash Finch Company

A Minneapolis fixture for nearly 90 years, this Fortune 500 company is one of the nation's leaders in food distribution, serving independent retailers and military commissaries in 28 states and the District of Columbia, Europe, Cuba, Puerto Rico, Iceland, the Azores, and Honduras.

Above: The Nash Finch Company traces its beginning to the late 1800s. This image, circa 1889, is the oldest known photograph of the Nash Brothers building in Grand Forks, North Dakota. Above right: Under CEO Ron Marshall, Nash Finch has reemphasized its focus on food distribution and significantly improved its operational efficiency, customer service, and shareholder return.

The footprints of the Nash Finch Company, an innovative, Minnesota-based firm, can be traced back to a small candy and tobacco store in Devils Lake, North Dakota, in 1885. Founded by the oldest Nash brother, Fred—who was soon assisted by brothers Edgar and Willis—this tiny enterprise gave rise to the Nash Finch Company, which built its reputation as a premier food distributor and is now a multibillion-dollar firm.

The Nash brothers' methodology for success was simple: they listened to their customers and matched product offerings to customer needs —and did so efficiently and at a fair price. While the business is certainly larger and more complex today, the Nash Finch Company, headquartered in Minneapolis since 1918, has grown to industry leadership using that same philosophy for over 120 years.

Creating an Industry

From 1885 to 1889, the Nash brothers expanded their operation to include fruit and moved to Grand Forks, North Dakota. During that time, the upper Midwest, particularly the Minneapolis area, was quickly becoming an important food center. The agricultural strength of the region, manifest in the number of successful farms, was increasing. As a result, the brothers had ready access to abundant and varied crops, especially fruits such as cherries and peaches, to sell. At first occasionally and then quite often, the brothers found that their retail operation could not sell the entire product volume available to them on a given day. The situation became inefficient

and wasteful and, worst of all for merchants, unprofitable.

To correct the problem, in 1889 the Nash brothers began to job fruit, gathering products in large quantities for other retailers in the region to sell, and within two years they were immersed in the wholesale fruit business. In the same year, the brothers hired the firm's first nonfamily member, Harry B. Finch. Just 14 years old at the time, Finch would grow in experience and go on to make contributions to the company in many capacities over a distinguished 50-year career.

As customer demand increased, the firm kept pace within the distribution industry, expanding through the acquisition of several small distributors called "fruit houses." Between 1904 and 1912, it opened or purchased more than 20 fruit houses, increasing its storage capacity in numerous locations and strengthening its already growing reputation for quality, service, and efficiency.

In 1915 Fred and Willis Nash moved their personal offices to Minneapolis to

be closer to that thriving city's financial institutions. (Edgar had passed away in 1896.) Harry Finch remained in North Dakota to manage general operations. By 1918 the company owned 31 fruit houses and that year moved its general operating offices to Minneapolis. Through the years, the Nash Finch Company occupied five locations in Minneapolis, including its present headquarters building at 7600 France Avenue South.

A Modern-Day Leader

Today the Nash Finch Company is on the Fortune 500 list and is one of the leading food distributors in the United States. Nash Finch's core business, food distribution, serves independent retailers and military commissaries in 28 states, the District of Columbia, Europe, Cuba, Puerto Rico, Iceland, the Azores, and Honduras. The company also owns and operates retail stores, primarily in the upper Midwest.

Nash Finch employs approximately 10,000 associates, and by using metrics to determine efficiency in the procurement, storage, handling, and transportation of products, the company enjoys industry-leading levels of performance. Nash Finch is strategically focused and demands consistent, ever-improving performance from company associates, a philosophy not all that different from the practices of Fred, Edgar, and Willis Nash. In fact, the wording of the modern company's promise, mission, and values statements would probably have fit right into the brothers' plans a century ago.

Continuing Success

The Nash Finch Company has been part of Minneapolis for more than 90 years. Over that time, the company has distinguished itself by its continued growth, financial success, efficiency, and overall return generated for its shareholders. Nash Finch takes great pride in its record, its many customers and associates, and the city and state it calls home: Minneapolis, Minnesota.

The Nash Finch Company

Promise
- Our associates have superior skills
- Our associates demonstrate strong values
- Our associates are passionate
- Our associates are competitive

Mission

We are a performance-driven culture that uses metrics to ensure continuous improvement. Through our distribution and marketing competencies, we provide creative, customized solutions for our grocery customers. As a result, we achieve superior profit growth as the grocery distribution company of choice.

Values
- We exceed our customers' expectations
- We continually improve
- We demand excellence
- We reward performance
- We act with urgency
- We value our supplier relationships
- We honor the communities we serve
- We demand integrity

Left: A Nash Finch advertisement features a historic photograph of the company's founders and early associates; standing, from left, are Mr. Maynard, Willis K. Nash, N. Frank Felton, Fred P. Nash, and, seated, Edgar W. Nash; and a modern-day photograph of six grandsons of the founding Nash brothers.

Best Buy

This innovative retailer of consumer electronics, personal computers, entertainment software, and home appliances is focused on providing customers with great products and retail experiences that complement their priorities and lifestyles.

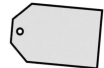

Through more than 800 retail stores across the United States and Canada, Best Buy, headquartered in Richfield, Minnesota, provides its customers with the latest in consumer electronics, home-office products, entertainment software, and home appliances designed to make life fun and easy.

At every store, knowledgeable, well-trained staff members are on hand to assist customers. Best Buy also makes round-the-clock shopping convenient with online sites that offer even more products. With its customer-centric philosophy of "putting the customer at the core of all that we do," Best Buy is increasingly focused on services to help customers make the most advantageous use of their purchases. Along with standard product and installation services and subscriptions, it offers, for example, the services of its Geek Squad, a rapid-response task force of experts that brings computer support to a customer's home or office or provides service by telephone. Efficiency is key to the company's global operations and a prime ingredient of its customer-service strategies.

In 2004, Best Buy—with revenues of $27.4 billion—was ranked by *Fortune* magazine as 77th among the nation's 500 largest corporations and named by *Forbes* magazine as its "Company of the Year."

By living up to its name, Best Buy has earned a major share of the consumer electronics market, while also making a name for itself as a company with heart. In fiscal year 2005, Best Buy and the Best Buy Children's Foundation infused local communities with more than $19 million in several forms, including charitable gifts, scholarships, and volunteerism. "Giving back to the community is central to the way we do business," explains Best Buy vice chairman and CEO Bradbury H. Anderson. "As a company that understands the importance of learning and innovation, we believe it is our responsibility to create opportunities for others."

One of Best Buy's many philanthropic efforts is the te@ch program, available to nonprofit public, private, and parochial K–12 schools located near a Best Buy store. The program awards

$2,500 to schools that make learning fun by creatively integrating interactive technology into classrooms. In 2005, te@ch will provide more than $3 million to 1,200 schools across the nation.

For Best Buy, being active in the community also means being environmentally responsible. A drop box in the entryway of each store allows for the daily collection of old cell phones, ink-jet cartridges, and rechargeable batteries, while larger recycling events are held to collect used appliances and other electronics. The company also

annually recycles 35 million pounds of the shipping materials and office paper it discards.

Making the world a better place is a deeply ingrained fundamental at Best Buy, whether accomplished by offering products that entertain and inform; by giving donations, awards, and scholarships; or by reducing waste to help the environment. Best Buy distinguishes itself as an innovative company that strives to create superior customer experiences and to be a partner in the neighborhoods it serves.

BEST BUY™

Above left: Best Buy, which is proudly headquartered in Richfield, Minnesota, runs more than 800 retail stores across the United States and Canada. Left and above right: Best Buy's excellent staff members are encouraged to contribute as community and school volunteers, imparting their knowledge to the next generation. In addition to such personal and corporate volunteerism, Best Buy contributes to its communities with charitable gifts, scholarships, and other donations. In 2005, for one example, Best Buy and the Best Buy Children's Foundation infused local communities with more than $19 million.

Education

Profiles of Corporations and Organizations

The Blake School

More than 100 years of educational excellence distinguish this independent prekindergarten through grade 12 school, which is renowned nationally for its students' success and for the outstanding quality of its faculty, curriculum, and facilities.

Above: The Blake School's students come from more than 50 communities located throughout the Minneapolis metropolitan area. Here, an all-school group gathers on the playground. Above right: Blake's teachers, students, parents, and alumni are dynamic, caring, motivated, and involved.

The Blake School—recognized as one of the finest independent college preparatory day schools in the nation—has nurtured notable alumni such as entrepreneur Ray Plank (class of 1940), U.S. Senator Mark Dayton (1965), producer Sarah Pillsbury (1969), and geophysicist Marcia McNutt (1970). Contributing to the success of these and other graduates is this liberal arts institution's emphasis on a student-centered curriculum that is taught by educators who possess the highest standards of academic excellence, independent thinking, character development, and social responsibility.

Today's Blake is the result of a 1974 merger of three highly regarded independent schools: Northrop Collegiate School, a girls' school founded in 1900; the Blake School for boys, founded in 1907; and Highcroft Country Day School, a coeducational school founded in 1958. Blake was established on the egalitarian principle to provide an education "not only for the wealthy, but for the worthy." This principle was set forth by the institution's founding families, many of whom—including the Crosbys, Pillsburys, and Boveys—were also leaders within the Twin Cities community.

Challenging the Mind, Engaging the Heart

Blake's philosophy and approach to education are holistic and grounded in a belief in the value of a liberal arts education—an education that is broad and deep, cumulative, synergistic, and self-sustaining; one that moves students to passionate, active learning and personal growth. "Challenging the mind and engaging the heart" is the school's motto and the core of its work and campus life.

Blake's multifaceted curriculum, which provides an integrated mix of arts, academics, and athletics, is designed to incorporate leading-edge technologies that enhance learning, develop the individual student as a whole, nurture

a multicultural perspective, and foster community and world involvement. High expectations, which are matched to each student's unique gifts and abilities, are established in the earliest grades and follow students through their years at Blake and beyond. Students' impressive SAT and ACT scores and the school's matriculation list are objective indicators of the excellence of the Blake program. Blake students go on to success at prestigious universities around the country and around the world, such as Carleton, Harvard, Northwestern, Stanford, and Yale.

These high standards extend to Blake's faculty as well. This school recruits teachers and administrators from throughout the country and is enormously proud of its outstanding staff members, who bring to the classroom an average of 18 years of experience, innovative teaching strategies, and a deep commitment to their students. More than 80 percent have advanced degrees. A student-to-teacher ratio of eight to one ensures that each student is known by teachers, coaches, and staff throughout the school and across multiple divisions and disciplines.

Honoring Character, Community, and Diversity

Developing the character of its students, instilling a sense of world community, and honoring diversity are also integral to the Blake experience. As it was at the school's founding, it is also today: Blake believes that a sound education is inextricably linked to the development of character founded on the values of respect for self and others, a love of learning, academic and personal integrity, and intellectual and ethical courage.

In keeping with these values, the school's service curriculum includes community work that is often student-driven and expected of every student from the earliest grades. From planting trees to entertaining seniors to tutoring in cross-cultural classrooms, Blake students are actively involved with and taught by individuals from all walks of life, throughout the Twin Cities and beyond.

Blake believes that a sound education makes life a part of learning and learning a part of life, bringing the

world and its many dimensions into the classroom. As such, the school celebrates diversity in its many aspects and forms. It is Blake's steadfast belief that pluralism immeasurably enhances educational excellence by having students (and adults) experience the richness of different perspectives and backgrounds coming together in one community. Blake recognizes that, in light of today's increasingly multicultural society, fostering connections among diverse people is critical to helping students become informed, productive, lifelong learners.

"For more than 100 years, The Blake School has been bringing intelligent, dedicated, passionate teachers, coaches, and artists together with eager, talented, inquisitive students with impressive results," states Head of School John C. Gulla. "For our second 100 years of work as a school, we remain committed to providing a

rigorous, well-rounded education in a diverse, supportive school community. We work to nurture and to graduate valuable members of society and fully engaged world citizens." In doing so, Blake continues to help shape the future and success of its students and of Minneapolis.

Large enough to provide a breadth of academic, athletic, artistic, and social opportunities, Blake also offers the intimacy of a campus where every student is known by the faculty and staff. Committed to attracting and retaining the best educators and administrators, informed by its belief in the importance of character in its work with young people, thoughtful in the design of a dynamic course of study, resolute in its efforts to create a pluralistic community, and fortunate in having magnificent facilities, The Blake School (www.blakeschool.org) is a very special place.

Above left: Blake students—who enjoy and benefit from Minnesota's four seasons—are interviewed by the middle school's video news crew. Above: Dedicated spaces at each of the school's three campuses (Minneapolis, Hopkins, and Wayzata) support strong music and visual arts programs. Recent renovations and expansions at the upper school (above) and Wayzata lower school created a number of spacious studios for Blake's multitalented students.

Augsburg College

This liberal arts college in the heart of the Twin Cities offers undergraduate degrees in over 50 major areas of study and six graduate degrees and provides a fully rounded education shaped by the values of the Christian faith to prepare students as leaders for service in a global society.

Above: Augsburg College's Old Main, built in 1900 and listed in the National Register of Historic Places, also features modern energy efficiency. It houses the departments of modern languages and art.

Providing its students with a first-rate, transforming education and imbuing them with the spirit of service shaped by the values of the Lutheran Church has been the cornerstone of Augsburg College's mission for more than 135 years.

Augsburg is a residential liberal arts college of the Evangelical Lutheran Church in America (ELCA). The college was founded by Norwegian immigrants in 1869 in Marshall, Wisconsin. It is widely respected throughout the United States for its undergraduate programs and distinctive graduate studies.

Located in the heart of the Twin Cities of Minneapolis and St. Paul since 1872—at the crossroads of some of the most culturally rich neighborhoods of Minneapolis—Augsburg serves some 3,000 students from a variety of religious, cultural, and ethnic backgrounds. Its students come from more than 40 states, more than 30 countries, and numerous Native American tribes. The college also is nationally recognized as a leader in providing services to students who have physical or learning disabilities.

As the ELCA's most diverse urban institution, Augsburg provides education to serve students with traditional schedules as well as those with nontraditional schedules by offering both a day school and a Weekend College. There are bachelor's degree programs in more than 50 major areas of study, and at the graduate level Augsburg offers a master of business administration as well as master's degrees in education, leadership, nursing, social work, and physician assistant studies.

Augsburg is the only institution of higher learning in Minnesota that offers a master's degree in physician assistant studies.

In the field of education, Augsburg has been preparing teachers of kindergarten through grade 12 since 1923. In the field of science, Augsburg's critically acclaimed programs have produced a Nobel Prize winner in chemistry and hundreds of other scientists making an impact nationally.

In the field of business, Augsburg is the only private college in the state to offer a degree in management information systems, and it is one of only a few private colleges in the area to offer marketing as a major subject. Augsburg is also one of just two colleges in the state to offer business students the opportunity to specialize in international business, a reflection of its commitment to diversity and global perspective. Augsburg is the only private college in Minnesota to offer three degrees in accounting—general, public, and managerial. And because of its location in the heart of the thriving Twin Cities business community,

Augsburg is able to provide its business students with a variety of internship possibilities with firms ranging from entrepreneurial start-ups to Fortune 500 companies.

What students find soon after enrolling at Augsburg is a close-knit learning community where small classes and personal attention from faculty and staff members are a way of life. It is a place where all people are accepted and respected, where lifelong friendships are made, and where exciting new experiences are shared. And while matters of faith and spiritual inquiry are an integral part of an education at Augsburg, no one tells a student what to believe; instead, students are challenged to grow and search for their own answers.

Among private colleges, Augsburg is exceptional in helping to bridge the gap between the level of support parents and students can provide and the cost of education for the year. More than 85 percent of the students enrolled receive financial assistance in some form.

Accommodations for students living on campus include comfortable residence halls for freshmen and apartments, suites, and town houses for upperclassmen, all with around-the-clock security features.

Fine arts courses and programs are an important component of student life at Augsburg, and those who participate in music, theater, and art gain superb resources available in the greater Twin

Cities community. Athletics also are a big part of campus activities, and nearly half of all entering students participate. Augsburg offers intercollegiate competition at the junior varsity and varsity levels in various sports and provides numerous intramural and recreational sports as well as up-to-date athletic and fitness facilities.

What truly distinguishes Augsburg among comparable institutions of higher

learning, however, is its dedication to nurturing future leaders to perform service for the world. It offers outstanding educational programs and the opportunity for students to participate in community service and internship experiences. "Education for Service" is Augsburg's motto, and this is exactly what Augsburg College does—preparing its students for not only successful, fulfilling careers but also a lifetime of service in a global, multicultural society.

Above: Augsburg offers the state's only physician assistant studies program. Above left: Service-learning is a hallmark of Augsburg's transforming education. Students volunteer at dozens of community programs, such as the Campus Kitchens Project, a groundbreaking national initiative launched in 2003 to reduce hunger and improve nutrition.

Pearson Education

A global media company and educational publisher, Pearson Education established itself in the Twin Cities' business and greater community with its acquisition of the Minneapolis-based National Computer Systems, a prominent provider of educational and psychological assessment and scoring solutions used worldwide.

Although Pearson Education is a relatively new name among Minneapolis companies, it joined the local business community with its 2000 acquisition of National Computer Systems (NCS), a company founded in Minneapolis in 1961.

NCS was started by Harlan Ward, with the idea that there needed to be a better way to score psychological tests. That is how the scanner was born, which enabled NCS to expand

and offer data processing and management, which led to different types of scanners and related software and services. As the company evolved, it moved into acquisitions in educational software and test processing. NCS eventually became a leader in K–12 assessment. This success attracted the attention of Pearson, a global media company and educational publisher, which acquired NCS and added the company to its portfolio of education businesses.

Today many of the components of NCS are based elsewhere, but three businesses of Pearson Education still call the Twin Cities home: Pearson Assessments, which has ties to NCS, is a premier provider of psychological assessments and scoring solutions; Pearson NCS, which also traces its roots to NCS, sells scanners and forms and provides data management services to commercial, government, and education customers; and Pearson VUE, a global leader in its sector, provides computer-based test delivery solutions for the professional licensure and certification market.

Pearson Assessments

NCS was started with the intent of finding a better way to score personality inventories. One of those instruments, the Minnesota Multiphasic Personality Inventory-2™ (MMPI-2™), is still marketed by Pearson Assessments and remains one of the most widely used assessment tools in the world.

Pearson Assessments also provides tools for use by professionals in clinical, medical, forensic, correctional, public safety, K–12, career, and counseling

settings. Other popular assessment tools offered by Pearson Assessments include the Millon™ Clinical Inventories, the Derogatis Checklist series, and the Beery™ VMI (Beery-Buktenica Development Test of Visual-Motor Integration).

Pearson Assessments is headquartered in Bloomington, Minnesota.

Pearson NCS

Nearly everyone is familiar with taking school tests and filling in the "bubbles" with a No. 2 pencil. If so, the test form was likely from Pearson NCS, or the exam itself was scored by one of Pearson's scanners. The company's proven solutions include optical-mark read and imaging scanners, scannable forms, software, and a full complement of services.

Pearson NCS has built its core expertise in data collection through testing and surveys. The company provides assessment solutions needed to facilitate student learning, improve instructional quality, and help meet schools' accountability requirements, as well as faculty evaluations and school-climate surveys. Pearson NCS also provides survey solutions that measure patient and customer satisfaction.

Pearson NCS is based in Eagan, Minnesota, and has facilities in Owatonna, Minnesota; Columbia, Pennsylvania; and Lawrence, Kansas.

Pearson VUE

Through a network of more than 350 company-owned and -operated sites in 20 countries and more than 3,700 authorized partner sites in 145 countries, Pearson VUE implements innovative testing solutions that enhance the performance, reliability, and security of professional licensing and certification programs.

This business was founded as Virtual University Enterprises in 1995 in Minneapolis and was acquired by NCS in 1997 to add computer-based testing capability to NCS's strong paper-based assessment businesses. Starting with creating certification exams for the likes of IBM, Cisco Systems, Microsoft, Novell, and others in the technology world, Pearson VUE has expanded to the growing professional licensure market.

Today, Pearson VUE provides testing materials for nurses, family physicians, and a host of other medical specialists, as well as for securities dealers. In addition, the business has expanded to offer driver's license exams in the United Kingdom (including Northern Ireland) and to provide the worldwide delivery of the Graduate Management Admission Test (GMAT).

These three businesses—Pearson Assessments, Pearson NCS, and Pearson VUE—are part of Pearson Education, which is headquartered in Upper Saddle River, New Jersey. As one of the largest education companies in the world, Pearson Education reaches 100 million people worldwide. This global leader in educational publishing provides quality content, assessment tools, and educational

services in all available media, spanning the learning curve from preschool to adulthood.

Pearson Education, in turn, is part of Pearson, which is based in London, England. Pearson owns the Financial Times Group, publisher of the *Financial Times* and other newspapers around the world, and the Penguin Group, the venerable book publisher.

Above: The Eagan facility of Pearson Education is headquarters for Pearson NCS, which provides data management and data collection solutions for education, government, and business.

Normandale Community College

This urban two-year college is known for excellence in instruction, preparing students for success by offering quality programs and courses that lead to associate's degrees, certificates, and transfers and providing adult classes for career and personal enrichment, with the motto 'This is your community . . . this is your college.'

Above: Normandale Community College, conveniently located near the Twin Cities in Bloomington, Minnesota, offers its diverse student body a welcoming environment that provides a wealth of educational opportunities. Right: Amid the college's lively campus activities is this traditional Japanese garden.

Since its founding in 1968, Normandale Community College has grown to become the largest community college in Minnesota. Providing educational opportunities for approximately 13,000 students each year, yet small enough for students and instructors to know one another, Normandale is located in Bloomington, just 10 minutes from Minneapolis and St. Paul. The college is a member of the Minnesota State Colleges and Universities system. It offers students a welcoming, accessible environment and is committed to opportunity, access, and lifelong education.

Normandale's general education courses lead to associate in arts degrees, associate in arts degrees with emphasis, the associate in fine arts degree, and professional certificates. Emphasis may be chosen in one of over 40 subjects in fields such as anthropology, languages, history, art, the natural sciences, mathematics, psychology, and education. Normandale has the only nationally accredited music program among two-year colleges in the state.

The college's career programs lead to associate of science and associate of applied science degrees and vocational certificates. The programs combine theory, training, and work experience to prepare students for employment in specific fields, including teacher education, computer technology, business, bioscience and engineering, nursing, radiologic technology, dietetics, dental hygiene, law enforcement, and hospitality management. Through the college's service-learning program, students can earn course credits and explore career options by working for local organizations. A program for study abroad is also available.

Many classroom courses are offered in the late afternoon or evening or on weekends to accommodate students' scheduling needs. Instruction also is available online via the Internet, and independent study programs can be arranged. Adult students may take continuing education or customized training programs, and prior work experience may qualify for course credit.

The Normandale campus is centered on a bustling quadrangle of educational facilities adjacent to a traditional Japanese garden. The Jodsaas Science Center, which was opened in 2003, houses state-of-the-art science laboratories, classrooms, and a greenhouse. The Fine Arts Building encompasses art, music, and theater arts. There is an auditorium for concerts and events and a theater for stage productions. The Kopp Student Center offers full wireless communications access, study and lounge areas where students can gather, and a full-service cafeteria; and the Activities Building supports athletics with gymnasiums and a fitness center. The campus also has a computer center and a large library. Throughout the year, there are extracurricular activities such as student

government, clubs, and organizations, and lectures, concerts, and cultural events.

Normandale offers an array of support programs for students, including tutoring in academics and communication skills, peer mentoring, assistance for students with disabilities, and financial aid and scholarships. The Nath Career and Academic Planning Center helps students plan their next step after Normandale.

Over the years, Normandale has enabled thousands of students to further their educations and achieve success. The college's faculty and staff continually strive to increase academic excellence, inspiring and challenging students to become knowledgeable, contributing members of their community.

University of Phoenix–Minneapolis

This pioneering university offers bachelor's, master's, and doctoral degree programs with a choice of instruction venues—in the classroom on campus, online via the Internet, or a combination of the two—making higher education flexible and convenient to serve working adults.

In 1976, the leading edge of the baby boom generation was just turning 30. That same year saw the prototype of the first mass-produced personal computer, signaling the birth of an economy in which intellectual capital would eventually replace industrial might as the dominant force.

These phenomena were noted by a Cambridge-educated economist and professor-turned-entrepreneur, John Sperling, Ph.D., who anticipated a demand for new job skills—and the return of working adults to formal higher education. In order to address these needs, in 1976 Sperling founded University of Phoenix.

At a time when colleges and universities were organized primarily to serve the educational needs of the 18- to 22-year-old undergraduate student, University of Phoenix was specifically designed to cater to the working adult—a revolutionary approach at the time. This focus attracted a tremendous response. During its first three decades, the university has experienced phenomenal growth. Its 2004 total enrollment was 227,760, including

students attending classes at its 158 campuses and learning centers, located in 33 states, Puerto Rico, and Canada, as well as 118,909 students taking courses via the Internet through University of Phoenix Online.

In 2004, University of Phoenix opened the doors of its Minneapolis campus, bringing its unique method of educating adults to the Twin Cities. Here, where the majority of adults has embraced technology, the university is focusing on its FlexNet learning option, which combines classroom lessons

with online course work. Students attend class on the first evening of each course and meet their instructor and classmates. They then complete the bulk of the course online before meeting one final time in class. This method provides valuable flexibility for students. It allows a busy working mother in St. Paul to spend time with her children before logging on to the computer to study late in the evening. It offers a businesswoman from Minnetonka the chance to complete course assignments while on the road. And it means that a father in St. Cloud can drive into

the Twin Cities for class just once a month, instead of once a week.

The University of Phoenix–Minneapolis campus serves working adults who live throughout Minnesota. As technology continues to evolve, the university evolves with it, remaining an education trendsetter for the region while staying true to the mission formulated by its founder.

Above and above left: University of Phoenix students enrolled in a campus program meet weekly between classes to work on projects as a "learning team"—a component of the university's education model. This innovative format of active participation is designed to replicate the way work is done in the business world and to facilitate studies.

Financial and Insurance Services

Profiles of Corporations and Organizations

U.S. Bancorp

Headquartered in Minneapolis and the sixth-largest financial holding company in the nation, U.S. Bancorp provides individuals, businesses, and institutions in 24 states with banking, brokerage, insurance, investment, mortgage, trust, and payment services.

With roots dating back to the birth of Minneapolis, U.S. Bancorp has grown from modest beginnings to become the sixth-largest financial holding company in the nation. U.S. Bancorp has always called Minneapolis home and is now the largest financial institution headquartered in the state.

Modest Beginnings

The First National Bank of Minneapolis received its charter in 1865 from the newly incorporated city of Minneapolis, while across the Mississippi River, First National Bank of St. Paul was establishing a foothold in Minneapolis's twin city. The two banks joined forces in 1929 to form First Bank Stock Corporation, one of the nation's first bank-holding companies. The company changed its name to First Bank System in 1968 and began the next phase in its expansion.

The 1990s saw an important transformation for the company as it shifted from a primarily commercial bank to a diverse financial services provider offering a wide range of banking, investment, mortgage, trust, brokerage, payment processing, and insurance services for individuals, businesses, government entities, and other financial institutions.

'A New U.S. Bancorp'

Through a number of mergers, the bank's name became U.S. Bancorp. Then in 2001, U.S. Bancorp merged with the Milwaukee-based Firstar Corporation, ushering in a new era of growth and prosperity.

Today, U.S. Bancorp serves more than 13.1 million customers and has nearly 2,400 U.S. Bank branch locations in 24 states and more than $195 billion in assets.

An Industry Leader

One of the nation's leading consumer banks, U.S. Bank serves individuals in cities large and small and nonurban communities across the country. The bank operates a broad network of traditional branch offices. In addition, it has more than 400 branch locations in stores, offering customers even more convenience and accessibility by providing extended hours and seven-days-a-week service. And its more than 4,600 ATMs use advanced technology to ensure that U.S. Bank is "open" for customers 24 hours a day.

Whether serving large corporations, midsize companies, or small businesses, U.S. Bank puts its full resources to work for its customers. It has a reputation for quality relationship management, flexibility, and the expertise to be a full financial partner.

U.S. Bancorp also is a leader in the payments industry. Its NOVA subsidiary is the third-largest provider of merchant processing services in the nation, and its corporate payment systems offer sophisticated management tools for corporate purchase programs and fleet programs. The bank also provides diverse wealth management, investment, advisory, trust, estate, and custody services for a wide range of clients.

U.S. Bank guarantees outstanding service to every customer. Its Five Star Service Guarantee is an integral part of its brand and sets the bank apart. Each employee is committed to providing the best service in the industry.

Dedicated to the Community

In 2004, the U.S. Bancorp Foundation made cash contributions of nearly $20 million to nonprofit organizations across the country. With financial support and countless employee volunteer efforts, U.S. Bancorp has demonstrated a strong commitment to strengthening Minnesota neighborhoods, education, and the overall quality of life in its communities.

In 2004, the company received a Corporate Citizenship Award from *The Business Journal (Minneapolis/ St. Paul)* in recognition of its six-year support of A Brush with Kindness, a program of Twin Cities Habitat for Humanity that focuses on revitalizing neighborhoods. Through the program, more than 1,500 of the bank's employees and their friends and family members volunteered to paint and repair a total of 60 homes in 2003 and 2004.

U.S. Bancorp also supports local education with the Financial Careers Institute and the Back 2 Schools program. The company formed a partnership with Metropolitan Community

and Technical College in 2003 to create the Financial Careers Institute, which encourages diversity in banking by providing specialized training and a two-year degree program. Through the Back 2 Schools program, Minnesota students are recognized for outstanding accomplishments in education, the arts, extracurricular activities, and athletics.

"U.S. Bancorp's Minnesota roots have helped us to become the successful and respected financial institution that we are today," says U.S. Bancorp chairman and chief executive officer, Jerry A. Grundhofer. "We are proud to support the city of Minneapolis, the community that we call home."

Opposite page: U.S. Bancorp Center, in the heart of downtown Minneapolis at 800 Nicollet Mall, is the seventh-largest building in the Twin Cities and headquarters for U.S. Bancorp. Above: U.S. Bank's Five Star Service Guarantee assures customers that their needs will be met with responsive, respectful, prompt service.

Minneapolis Regional Chamber of Commerce

Being 'the voice of business' is the business of the Minneapolis Regional Chamber of Commerce, which has advocated on behalf of its members, addressed pressing social and political matters, and contributed to the overall vibrancy of the region's economy for more than 120 years.

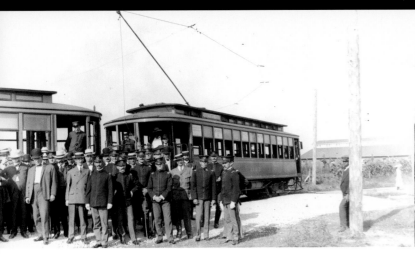

Above left: In 1895, local chamber of commerce members join soldiers at the opening of the Fort Snelling trolley line. Above center: In 1929, the Foshay Tower is the first of the downtown Minneapolis office towers. Above right: Nicollet Mall, as seen from 8th and Nicollet streets, is the center of activity in 1915.

A world-class chamber of commerce for the world-class Twin Cities, the Minneapolis Regional Chamber of Commerce (MRCC) has been serving the needs and best interests of its members for more than a century. Every day, the MRCC demonstrates its dedication and commitment to its mission—from advocating for long-standing business needs to creating innovative solutions for the new challenges posed by a global marketplace.

Founded in 1881, the first local chamber of commerce served the needs of mostly local businesses in the then-tiny city of Minneapolis. Today, 125 years later, the MRCC and its two affiliates, the Bloomington and the City of Lakes chambers, serve approximately 1,000 businesses in more than 68 communities across seven counties. And the MRCC is proud to offer programs tailored to the size and scope of all its member businesses, which range in size from one-person, in-home companies to multinational Fortune 500 corporations.

Thinking Locally, Acting Regionally and Nationally

The MRCC's main purpose is to "grow jobs in the regional economy."

To do this effectively, the chamber has found it necessary to "think locally and act regionally." Thus, the MRCC tackles issues not only on the local level but also on the regional, state, and sometimes even national levels.

This kind of broad focus means that the MRCC must often work in concert with other chambers and business organizations. So, over time, the MRCC has evolved into an organization that frequently joins forces with some or all of the 40 other chambers of commerce in the area in order to tackle tough regional issues, including transportation.

"This is one of the biggest issues we face," states Todd Klingel, MRCC president and CEO. "We're working to develop a comprehensive transit/transportation plan for the next 10 to 15 years, including the necessary funding to see it through." Another regional issue that appears on Klingel and the MRCC's agenda is working to attract "household-supporting-wage jobs," which would boost economic development in the entire area.

In public policy matters, the MRCC tackles legislative issues, ensuring that its member businesses have a strong say in policy matters that affect them, including health care. Says Klingel, "It's a huge issue for members in this era of rapidly rising insurance costs and fewer

businesses being able to offer adequate health care coverage to employees."

Being able to meet future workforce needs is also a major focus of the MRCC and its members. As the baby boomers begin to retire over the next several decades, with smaller numbers of younger workers available to replace them, "everyone in the country will be working to attract employees, not just companies," explains Klingel. "We also have to make our area increasingly attractive to workers as well as to businesses."

An issue of growing importance for the MRCC is the amount of total housing available, including affordable housing. With median new home prices

in the area skyrocketing, many lower-wage workers will not be able to afford a mortgage unless more affordable homes are constructed. Therefore, the MRCC has, over the years, created task forces and committees to look into making it more desirable to be a developer of affordable housing and to investigate the "red-tape issues" involved in constructing affordable housing.

Networks for Success
In its social and networking capacity, the MRCC provides events and services that are attractive to all its members, often in concert with other area chambers. The MRCC's programs—from networking groups to larger gatherings that host state and U.S. legislators—are designed to interest members of all levels.

For one example, the MRCC's Success Series brings in well-spoken, energetic community leaders to inspire MRCC members and to share tips to make their businesses more successful. Distinguished past and recent speakers include Mark Cuban, owner of the Dallas Mavericks; Norm Coleman, the U.S. senator from Minnesota; and Dr. Robert Bruininks, president of the University of Minnesota.

In addition, the MRCC offers two nationally honored programs—the Minnesota Keystone Program and the Voyager: Direction for Learning & Careers program. The Keystone program was created in 1976 to honor businesses that give back to

their communities and that serve as models for other businesses to follow. Each year, participants are celebrated at a gala luncheon. Voyager is a school-to-work curriculum developed by members of the MRCC to teach students the business skills that will ensure their success after college. Students begin the four-year program in their junior year in high school and are graduated from the program in their sophomore year in college. Voyager was implemented at Edison High School in Minneapolis and the curriculum has been published nationwide.

"The marketplace has changed drastically over the decades," states Klingel, "and the MRCC has stuck to its commitment to provide jobs and to evolve with the changing conditions. We take our responsibilities to our members and the region very seriously. If we want the region to celebrate its next 125 years, complacency is not an option."

Above left: Minneapolis's modern towers dwarf their forebears. Above center: After a 50-year hiatus, the Fort Snelling trolley returns in the form of light rail. Above right: As it has been for the past century, Nicollet Mall is the center of downtown activity.

ING

With roots in Minneapolis since 1885, this company offers 'fresh thinking in financial services,' including world-class banking, insurance, and asset management products for individuals, families, small and large businesses, and institutions as well as community support toward a thriving future.

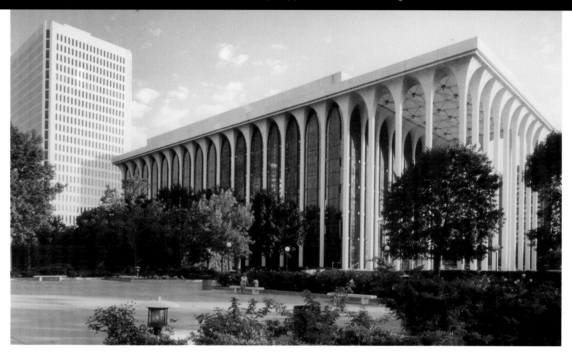

Right: The ING Minneapolis campus, located at the north end of Nicollet Mall, includes three architecturally significant buildings; the two shown here were designed by Minoru Yamasaki, who was also the architect of New York City's World Trade Center towers, and a third building was designed by BWBR Architects, of St. Paul.

A once-small insurance company with roots in Minneapolis is now part of a worldwide financial services organization. Northwestern National Life Insurance Company was founded in 1885 to serve the insurance needs of Minnesotans. The new home office it built in 1964, with serene design and stately pillars, became an instant Minneapolis landmark. The company was renamed ReliaStar Financial Corp. in 1995 to reflect its growth in financial services, and it became part of ING in 2000, maintaining its presence on the Minneapolis skyline.

ING affiliates work with individuals, employers, and institutions, providing financial solutions through the use of innovative products and services.

Customers of ING enjoy the benefits of working with a world-class provider of integrated financial products and services. ING's parent company, Amsterdam-based ING Group, is a global financial institution of Dutch origin with a diverse workforce of more than 125,000 employees worldwide. ING Group provides banking, insurance, and asset management to more than 60 million clients in over 50 countries.

In the United States, ING offers its clients a comprehensive array of financial services that includes retirement plans, mutual funds, managed accounts, direct banking, annuities, life insurance, financial planning, institutional investment management, employee benefits, and reinsurance. ING serves more than 14 million customers across the nation.

ING is committed to supporting diversity in the community and to enhancing the opportunity for all people to build a more secure financial future and to thrive. Its primary goal in community relations is to educate people in becoming financially independent by increasing their understanding of and comfort with financial services products. The company provides corporate sponsorships and grant programs targeted toward motivating individuals to be financially responsible. In addition, ING employees in Minneapolis volunteer thousands of hours every year to local charities.

AXA Advisors, LLC

With both a well-established local presence and the resources of a strong global organization, this Minneapolis firm provides individuals and businesses with custom-tailored strategies for achieving their financial goals.

A pillar of financial strength in the Minneapolis area for more than 100 years, AXA Advisors, LLC is an integral part of the local heritage. With thousands of clients in Minnesota, North Dakota, South Dakota, and western Wisconsin, the firm has helped generations of the community's residents and businesses seek their financial goals. Clients have come to rely on AXA Advisors for financial guidance in special focus areas ranging from wealth management and estate planning to executive benefits and business-succession planning.

A Tradition of Commitment

The firm has roots that extend back to the 1800s, when it was founded as part of The Equitable Life Assurance Society. It quickly developed a reputation as an industry innovator, pioneering new products to respond to the changing cycles of a dynamic marketplace. Then, in the 1990s, it became AXA Advisors, LLC. AXA Advisors, LLC (member, NASD/SIPC), headquartered in New York City, is a subsidiary of AXA Financial, Inc., which is part of the global

AXA Group. The move brought new synergy for the firm, allowing it to greatly expand its portfolio of products and services. As the local presence of a worldwide organization, the firm combines personal customer service with global financial strength.

At the core of AXA Advisors is a distinctive group of qualified professionals with a broad range of experience who are responsible for the firm's reputation as a financial services leader. Collaboration and teamwork are emphasized, upholding the tradition of a professional services firm. Financial professionals work together in partnership in order to provide clients with comprehensive guidance.

The firm's spirit of professionalism extends to its community. It has long-standing alliances with local attorneys, certified public accountants, and professional associations, which further enhance the level of service it can offer to clients. In addition, the firm is involved in neighborhood groups dedicated to art, music,

sports, and civic endeavors, supporting a rich cultural landscape and a thriving community.

AXA Advisors emphasizes the building of lifelong relationships with its clients. With this foundation, the

firm focuses on helping businesses to flourish, individuals to plan for their financial futures, and families to protect what is important to them. For additional information, visit the AXA Advisors, LLC Web site at www.axaonline.com.

Above: These professionals at AXA Advisors, LLC work together to expertly guide clients through the process of financial, estate, retirement, or business planning.

GE-31831 (4/05)

Winslow Capital Management, Inc.

Headquartered in Minneapolis, this investment management firm focuses solely on large-cap growth stocks, taking a disciplined approach to decision making that is based on direct research and formulated criteria for selecting and managing investments to achieve superior returns.

Founded in 1992, Winslow Capital Management, Inc. is a Minneapolis-based investment management firm that concentrates exclusively on investing in large-cap growth stocks and is approaching $1 billion in total assets under management. Clients include St. John's University, the Minnesota State Board of Investment, and the New York Life Insurance Company. The company's portfolio managers take a disciplined approach to analyzing, buying, and selling stocks. Working as a team, they conduct fundamental research and apply their collective analytical experience—gained at some of the nation's most prestigious investment management firms—to make decisions and build portfolios.

Winslow Capital Management's investment philosophy is that the best opportunities for achieving superior long-term returns are in buying stock in companies that have above-average earnings growth that is undervalued on Wall Street. The firm's technique for controlling risk involves a strong sell discipline that is maintained by using formulated criteria.

Stocks are selected by first choosing about 300 companies from the Russell 1000 Index. The companies represent nearly every industry and generally have a history of consistent growth, a market capitalization of more than $4 billion, and the potential for earnings to increase by at least 13 percent annually over the following three years.

The number of companies is then reduced from 300 to 100 by identifying those that have the best growth opportunities over the next two to three years. Criteria for these choices include above-average unit growth, leading market share, strong company management, sustainable competitive advantage, rising return on invested capital, and strong free-cash flow. Finally, after further analyzing each company's financial statements and competition, the investment team creates a portfolio of about 55 stocks.

"Our investment process is founded on the importance of fundamental research," says Clark J. Winslow, chairman, CEO, and founder. "We try to get our information directly from the company, not only from other analysts, to make the most informed decisions. If we can identify a strong business and determine why it should have greater growth than that predicted by Wall Street, then our stocks will outperform the market. This hands-on research leads to better judgments in constructing and managing a portfolio. The portfolio managers have substantial ownership in the firm," Winslow continues, "so their interests are completely aligned with success for clients, seeking quality longer-term growth."

A native of Minneapolis, Winslow graduated from Yale University and went on to earn an M.B.A. from Harvard Business School. He served as managing director at John W. Bristol & Co. in New York and as senior vice president at Alliance Capital Management in Minneapolis before starting Winslow Capital Management in 1992. Winslow works in collaboration with managing directors R. Bart Wear, CFA, and Justin H. Kelly, CFA. The combination of this team approach and the company's disciplined process has given Winslow Capital Management a competitive advantage in the growth stock investment field and has made it a business with strong growth potential of its own.

Allianz Life Insurance Company of North America

Focusing on wealth management, this Minneapolis-based insurer is one of the nation's largest providers of fixed and variable annuities and also offers universal life insurance, long-term care insurance, and more, making its products available through its extensive network of independent agents and registered representatives.

value-added products through independent agents and advisers, and we now have possibly the largest independent distribution system in the U.S. life insurance industry," says Mark A. Zesbaugh, Allianz Life CEO. "That is our long-term strategic direction, and it continues to produce outstanding results." A key ingredient in delivering these innovative products and services is recognizing the significance of changing demographics. Allianz Life recognized the impact of extended longevity as early as 1989 and proceeded to pioneer the development of products that place emphasis on the financial risks of living longer.

Allianz Life Insurance Company of North America, headquartered in Minneapolis, has parlayed a commitment to innovation, service, and performance into a position as one of the leading wealth management companies in the United States.

Founded in 1896, Allianz Life is an industry leader in the sale of fixed annuities through independent agents. Through its affiliate USAllianz Investor Services LLC, Allianz Life

has been one of the fastest growing providers of variable annuity products in North America. Through its Allianz Healthcare Risk Management division, Allianz Life serves HMOs, provider organizations, insurance companies, and employers that self-insure their employee benefit plans. Allianz Life also provides access to LifeTrac, a national network of leading organ and bone marrow transplant facilities and medical centers. USAllianz Securities Inc. is the

company's broker-dealer subsidiary, dedicated to serving the needs of independent registered representatives in the United States. Allianz Life is a primary company of the Munich, Germany–based Allianz Group, which offers integrated financial services in over 70 countries worldwide.

Allianz Life generated $9.7 billion in total production in 2003—a new record for the company. "We are committed to distributing innovative,

During its more than 100 years, Allianz Life has had a strong commitment to the communities where its employees live and work. The company supports health and social services, the arts and cultural diversity, and civic affairs. Its corporate-giving program is anchored by a philosophy of sharing financial resources, time, and expertise to build a stronger, more vibrant community that improves the quality of life for customers, employees, and the public.

Above left: Allianz Life Insurance Company of North America moved into its Minneapolis headquarters building in 2001. The company, which offers products that provide asset management, protection, and distribution, employs more than 2,000 people.

Marsh Inc.

Recognized and trusted internationally, Marsh Inc. is a provider of risk management, risk consulting, insurance brokering, financial solutions, and insurance program management services for businesses, public entities, associations, and private clients worldwide.

Minnesota played a significant role in the history of Marsh Inc., a modern-day leader in delivering risk and insurance services and solutions to clients in more than 100 countries.

Growth and Innovation

The origins of the company date back to 1904, when Duluth native Donald R. McLennan opened an insurance office in Chicago. He was considered one of the country's leading experts in railroad insurance because of his extensive knowledge of the St. Paul–based Northern Pacific and Great Northern railroads. In 1905, McLennan partnered with Henry W. Marsh to create the new firm of Marsh & McLennan.

These partners would go on to help transform America's insurance industry in the 20th century, and Minnesota would again provide a key connection in the growth of their firm. Marsh & McLennan was able to expand its foundation of fire insurance and core railroad clients to include marine insurance thanks to prominent Minnesota businessman James J. Hill,

founder of the Great Northern railroad. Hill turned to Marsh & McLennan for insurance coverage in 1905 after launching a new steamship line. In 1909, Marsh & McLennan opened its first Minnesota office.

Today Marsh & McLennan Companies is a global professional services firm with annual revenues exceeding $11 billion. It is the parent company of Marsh Inc., as well as Putnam Investments, one of the largest investment management companies in the United States, and Mercer Inc., a major global provider of consulting services.

Providing a Wealth of Global Services

Marsh Inc. provides global risk management, risk consulting, insurance brokering, financial solutions, and insurance program management services for businesses, public entities, associations, professional services organizations, and private clients. The company has more than 60 offices in

the United States, employs 38,000 professionals around the world, and serves clients in more than 100 countries. Since Marsh Inc. opened its first office in Minneapolis in 1909 with only two employees, its Minnesota staff has grown to more than 200 employees.

Marsh Inc.'s experience in the global insurance and reinsurance markets gives this company the ability to arrange and place the complex insurance coverages clients require. Marsh Inc. consultants and brokers provide increased access to the global insurance marketplace, more and better insurance products at competitive prices, and unsurpassed knowledge and professional risk management expertise.

As businesses continue to expand globally and risks grow more complex, Marsh Inc. will continue to help clients remain competitive through its unique ability to identify, analyze, mitigate, and/or transfer key business risks.

Right: Marsh Inc.'s stately building graces the skyline of Minneapolis. This national and international firm encompasses more than 60 offices across the United States, employs 38,000 professionals worldwide, and serves clients in more than 100 countries.

Wagnild & Associates, Inc.

This independent agency offers employers professional employee-benefit planning services, including employee-benefit counseling and assistance with plan selection, communicating with employees, and complying with government regulations.

As employers know, the process of providing employees with benefit packages that are comprehensive while also affordable can be challenging. Wagnild & Associates, Inc. of Mendota Heights, Minnesota, is committed to offering companies the expertise and guidance needed to find compatible employee-benefit plans.

Wagnild & Associates is an independent employee-benefit agency and consulting firm that leads companies through the numerous decisions of benefit planning. It represents more than 200 employer groups of varying sizes and specialties, providing benefit-plan counseling, assistance in complying with state and federal regulations, and event planning for wellness and benefits fairs.

Owner and president Jackie Wagnild founded the agency in 1991 to offer professional, custom-tailored benefit-planning services. After 25-plus years in the insurance industry, she wanted to give employers the chance to provide employee-benefit packages that reflected their business philosophy. Wagnild sees the

employer's role of benefit planning as a privilege as well as a responsibility. The agency assists employers in understanding the complexities of this role and communicating their choices to employees.

Wagnild & Associates has experienced staff members, most of whom have been with the company for more than 10 years. Employees appreciate

the family-friendly work environment and take pride in the satisfaction with the agency reported by its customers.

The agency provides customers with a quarterly newsletter that focuses on health and wellness matters. Customers also are invited to attend free informational seminars with lectures by industry experts. Seminars are designed to keep

customers informed about current industry issues and changing laws and regulations.

While Wagnild & Associates plans to expand its administrative capabilities in the future, it will continue to develop creative, practical solutions in providing services for its growing clientele, focusing on its motto, "Emphasis on Excellence."

Above: Vice President of Sales and Marketing Jim Stepka and President Jackie Wagnild of Wagnild & Associates, Inc. are proud of their team's commitment to professionalism and customer service. Together, they put Wagnild & Associates' corporate motto, "Emphasis on Excellence," into practice.

Exchange quickly established itself as a prominent business with a growing national reputation for ensuring fair trade in grain. The exchange was further vaulted into prominence through its connections to the industries and industrialists that were driving the growth of Minneapolis and the region. The railroads were expanding across the frontier by pushing their rail lines westward, and at the same time the milling industry in Minneapolis was expanding. All this activity created an increased demand for the high quality wheat that was grown west of the region, and at the center was the Minneapolis Grain Exchange, providing reliable markets for the commodities being traded.

At the heart of the operation is the trading floor, where daily trading sessions take place in a beehive of activity. The vast space is 32 feet high, with floor-to-ceiling windows and frescoes that depict the many ways wheat has been milled by different cultures. At the east end of the trading floor are the solid wooden trading tables, where merchants display the grains they have available for sale that day. Buyers wander the floor, carefully inspecting grain samples and negotiating purchases. At the opposite end of the floor is the octagonal trading pit, where spring wheat futures have been actively traded for nearly 125 years.

The Minneapolis Grain Exchange, a not-for-profit membership organization, was founded on October 19, 1881, and originally named the Chamber of Commerce of Minneapolis. Its name was changed to the Minneapolis Grain Exchange in 1947 to avoid confusion with the civic organization that is now the Minneapolis Regional Chamber of Commerce. Members of the Minneapolis Grain Exchange, including producers, millers, merchandisers, and investors, earn the privilege to conduct business as members and trade commodities at the exchange.

Through the actions of its visionary founders, the Minneapolis Grain

The Grain Exchange Building, located at Fourth Avenue and Fourth Street in Minneapolis, was built in 1902, and additions were constructed in 1909 and 1928 as the popularity of the business increased. The exchange still owns the property, which is on the National Register of Historic Places, and leases space to a variety of tenants.

During 2004, a record 1,416,282 contracts—representing seven billion bushels of grain—were traded at the Minneapolis Grain Exchange. December 16, 2004, marked the exchange's beginning of trading five agricultural index products exclusively on an electronic platform. It also marked the first time that the exchange offered hard red spring wheat via electronic overnight trading.

Real Estate Services

Profiles of Corporations and Organizations

Manley Companies

This family firm offers houses tailored to the client's taste and constructed with an array of fine interior and exterior materials and top brand-name product choices; realty, land, and commercial development; and real estate and financing assistance, all with a commitment to exceptional service.

Above: The Manley Companies is the creation of Kurt Manley, at right, and Kevin Manley, who have built a $100 million business that continues to grow.

Kevin and Kurt Manley are builders with a major presence in the Twin Cities, and their presence continues to grow. The two brothers build more than 120 custom-designed houses per year in the area, and they also have real estate companies. Their ventures now bring in more than $100 million annually. In fact, Manley Companies outgrew its offices and now has built new headquarters, a 36,000-square-foot office structure in Eagan, to accommodate the staff.

As children, the duo played at building, constructing little log cabins with Lincoln Logs. "I always wanted to build things, and I wanted to work in the building business," says Kurt. That was back in Ottumwa, Iowa, where they grew up. In high school, Kurt parlayed his work in shop class into part-time work on construction sites. At the University of Northern Iowa, where he majored in business management, he worked in construction on the side and read *Builder* magazine. After college, he moved to the Twin Cities and began working in real estate, but his focus shifted from selling properties to handling painting and repair jobs for properties listed by other agents.

Eventually, house painting became a business for him, and soon he persuaded his brother to leave a position as a grocery chain district manager and join him in his enterprise. The two built up a crew of 40 and put in long hours, and then as the painting business was taking shape they decided they could also build new houses.

Kurt took charge of the painting business, and Kevin started their construction company, building one house at a time. It took two years of perseverance until the new venture brought in enough money for them to work solely in construction. "We just kept at it," Kevin says. "It's easy to give up on things, and many times we might have, but we just stayed with it."

Today, Manley Brothers Construction custom-builds houses that are known for fine design and craftsmanship and distinctive style. More than 500 custom-designed houses have been completed, and the company has gained a reputation for performing quality work, being attuned to the tastes of its individual clients, and providing exceptional service.

The operations of Manley Companies also encompass Manley Realty, Inc., whose services can form a convenient "one-stop headquarters" for customers of the construction company;

Manley Land Development, which buys land in the Greater Minneapolis–St. Paul region; and Commercial Property Development Corporation, which manages the land for commercial businesses.

Manley Companies employs more than 100 people, including staff architects and design directors, and in 2005 it opened its first satellite office in Scottsdale, Arizona. Kevin manages the residential construction and real estate companies, while Kurt handles land development and commercial construction. They remain full partners.

"We are best friends," Kurt says. "I would do this work no matter what, because it is fun coming to the office and seeing my brother every day. And a lot of the people who work for us are friends or family members or people we have built houses for. Even as the company grows bigger, it is still a very enjoyable environment."

The brothers consider their finest professional achievement to be the growth of their company.

"Exceeding the $100 million mark in annual revenues was a huge milestone for us," Kurt says. "When we reached $10 million, we thought that was the limit. And when we went on to $50 million, we said, 'This is really the limit.'

And then we kept growing. By 2004 we needed more space, and now we have built our new corporate headquarters, a beautiful office building. And who knows, maybe we will reach the $200 million mark one of these days."

This page: The distinctive custom-designed houses by Manley Brothers Construction exemplify the firm's commitment to quality building materials, craftsmanship, and detailing. The contemporary craftsman model house shown above, located in Eden Prairie, features some of the many interior and exterior design styles, materials choices, and fine brand-name products available to the buyer. Clockwise from left: A comfortable living room, spacious kitchen with breakfast area, graceful foyer and formal dining room, and other living areas all maximize views to the scenery beyond.

The Opus Group

With more than 50 years in the industry, this $1.4 billion real estate development company, headquartered in the Twin Cities, brings a one-stop, comprehensive design-build approach to each client's project, resulting in positive experiences for those who work, live, or shop at a completed site.

Founded in 1953 as Rauenhorst Construction, today The Opus Group is an award-winning real estate development firm with extensive experience in bringing to life office, industrial, retail, institutional, and residential developments.

From inception through completion, Opus's streamlined design-build approach partners an Opus team of professionals with clients to bring together all elements of a development—land acquisition, architecture, engineering, and construction—to create a seamless, efficient process. Opus custom-designs projects based on client and community needs. Because of this process, Opus has acquired a solid reputation for building beyond expectations and delivering projects on time and on budget.

Headquartered in suburban Minneapolis, and with five regional companies, Opus has 1,400 employees in 28 offices in the United States and Canada. Opus has completed more than 2,200 projects, totaling more than 218 million square feet, and has 24 million square feet of space planned or under development.

Opus is ranked the 14th-largest privately held company in Minnesota and is the 10th most productive private company per employee, according to the *Business Journal–Minneapolis/St. Paul*. Nationally, Opus is also consistently rated as a top real estate developer. Accolades include being ranked first in "Top 25 Industrial Developers" by *National Real Estate Investor*, second in "Top 25 Office Developers" by *National Real Estate Investor*, and fourth in "Top Real Estate Developers" by *Commercial Property News*.

Marquis projects in the Twin Cities include The Shoppes at Arbor Lakes, in Maple Grove, Minnesota; the Minneapolis campus of the University of St. Thomas; Best Buy Co., Inc.'s world headquarters in Richfield, Minnesota; and the American Express Financial Advisors Inc. (AEFA) corporate headquarters in downtown Minneapolis.

Living Opus

Opus creates structures that meet the immediate needs of clients but that also stand the test of time. With more than 50 years of experience in office

and industrial design-build projects, Opus has entered into the residential sector with high-rise condominiums and master-planned housing communities.

As societal trends shift, so does the need for diversifying real estate development. In 2000, Opus took its core knowledge of office and industrial building and entered the residential market with Grant Park, a 327-unit luxury condominium in Minneapolis. The first high-rise condominium project in downtown Minneapolis in decades, Grant Park revitalized the downtown's

residential area and spurred an interest in urban dwelling for young professionals and empty nesters. Today, Opus has many residential projects across the Twin Cities metropolitan area, including The Carlyle, another luxury condominium in downtown Minneapolis, and The Bridges at Arbor Lakes, a 1,750-unit multifamily residence under development in Maple Grove.

Experiencing Opus

Locally and across the country, shoppers have experienced Opus. With 154 completed retail projects

totaling nearly 21 million square feet and 20 projects totaling more than 6.1 million square feet planned or under development in 2005, Opus continues to enhance its expertise in retail development.

Opus, in partnership with RED Development LLC, created Minnesota's first retail "lifestyle center," The Shoppes at Arbor Lakes, in Maple Grove. Designed with a Main Street setting, Arbor Lakes offers national retail stores, niche boutiques, and dining and entertainment

options in one central location. With Minnesotans embracing this shopping experience, Opus has next marked the grand opening of its second retail lifestyle center, Woodbury Lakes, in Woodbury, Minnesota.

Several other retail developments across the Twin Cities, including Nicollet Commons in Burnsville—a grocery store–anchored shopping area with a variety of other retailers —aim to create a convenient, central place for residents to gather and shop.

Being Community Stewards

Community stewardship has always been at the very core of Opus. The company contributes 10 percent of its pretax profits to community organizations. Nationally and locally, dozens of organizations have benefited from Opus's generosity, including Habitat for Humanity; the American Red Cross; Walter Reed Army Medical Center; and Progress Valley, Inc., a nonprofit organization founded and sponsored by Opus in Minneapolis and in Scottsdale, Arizona. Progress Valley provides comprehensive residential services to chemically dependent adults after they have completed primary treatment. More than 6,000 people have graduated from this program.

St. Joseph's Home for Children in Minneapolis is a shining example of Opus's giving spirit. The facility, which provides temporary shelter for children in crisis, had fallen into disrepair. During a three-month period, more than

200 Opus employees and family members volunteered more than 1,200 hours to refurbish sleeping rooms and common living areas. Now, children can feel the warmth of a homelike environment as they make their way through difficult times.

In 2004, the company launched the Opus Prize, an annual $1 million faith-based humanitarian award given to an individual or organization of any religion, anywhere in the world. The inaugural prize was presented to Helping Hands for the Poor, Inc. in honor of Monsignor Richard Albert, a New York–born clergyman who has spent nearly three decades helping the poor in shantytowns on the island of Jamaica.

With the company experiencing double-digit growth, Opus continues to see bright days ahead because of its ability to diversify, meet market demands, and give back to the community.

Left: The Shoppes at Arbor Lakes, in Maple Grove, Minnesota, is a shopping and entertainment destination where visitors can stroll along cobblestone sidewalks in a Main Street setting to shop at premier national retail stores and niche boutiques or dine at any of a variety of restaurants. Above right: Grant Park, located at 5th Avenue South and 10th Street South in downtown Minneapolis, has helped spur today's growth in condominium development by attracting young professionals and empty nesters who seek the culture and convenience of urban living. This 327-unit luxury residential project of condominium units, city homes, and town homes includes a fitness center, whirlpool spa, and glass-enclosed swimming pool; a business office for residents; guest rooms; and a club room for entertaining.

Gilbert Mechanical
Contractors, Inc.

Gilbert Mechanical Contractors, Inc. (established in Minnesota in 1978) and Gilbert Electrical Technologies
are turnkey providers of engineering, construction, building automation, and maintenance services.

For more than two decades, Gilbert Mechanical Contractors, Inc. has been trusted to deliver complete mechanical design and construction services for new buildings and existing-facility retrofits. Today, more than 80 percent of this company's $25 million in annual sales comes from the repeat business of loyal clients. Working in partnership with every client, Gilbert successfully applies in-house engineering services to five skilled construction trades: sheet metal, pipefitting, plumbing, electrical, and fire protection.

"We design and build most of our projects," states P. Dan Gilbert, P.E., the company's founder and president. "This is a proven delivery system that adds value for our customers through shorter construction times, greater project flexibility, and single-point responsibility. Repeat customers know they can count on our bid, our scope of work, and our project guarantees."

A solid team of professional engineers, experienced project managers, and trained craftsmen takes complete responsibility for a client's mechanical and electrical systems—from design through installation and service. Providing a quick response and dependable 24-hour service, Gilbert Mechanical's trained technicians ensure long equipment life and peak operating efficiency.

Gilbert Mechanical was founded in 1978 when P. Dan Gilbert purchased Temperature Control, Inc., a small heating, ventilation, and air-conditioning business located in St. Paul. As the company grew in size and capability, it was moved first to Minneapolis and finally to Edina, Minnesota. In 1998, the business was sold to Encompass Services Corporation and continued as a wholly owned subsidiary. In 2002, Gilbert, along with John T. Gorman, P.E., and Ed C. Dahlgren, P.E., bought back the assets from the publicly held consolidator.

Many of Gilbert's present 175 employees include loyal tradesmen and professionals originally hired back in the 1980s. "Excellent communication and teamwork within the trades and office staff account for much of our success," states Vice President Dahlgren.

"Our mission has always been to provide our customers with the best value and performance in the local mechanical and electrical construction industry," states Vice President Gorman. "We accomplish our goals through exceptional employees, who are strong on work ethic and who take personal responsibility. Safe work practices and honest dealings are employment musts. Our business philosophy also includes mutual respect for all individuals, the application of innovative methods, and a customer-oriented focus."

For additional information, call 952-835-3810; or visit the company's Web site at www.gilbertmech.com.

Right: Dedicated, experienced employees like Bill Riley (who has been with the company for more than 20 years) are integral to the success of Gilbert Mechanical Contractors, Inc. and Gilbert Electrical Technologies.

North American Properties

This innovative real estate company combines its experience and imagination to develop retail, apartment, office, and mixed-use projects designed to enhance the community and the lives of the people who live, work, and play there—now and in the future.

North American Properties is a privately held real estate company that develops, owns, and manages retail, apartment, mixed-use, and office properties across the United States. Since it was founded, in 1954 in Cincinnati, Ohio, the company has grown from a local owner and developer to a multifaceted, national industry leader with an annual development budget in excess of $100 million.

As one of the few real estate companies in the country with commercial and multifamily development capabilities under one roof, North American Properties manages a diverse and extensive portfolio of successful properties across the United States. Today, as it celebrates its 50th anniversary, the company continues to push the limits of traditional development by not only building buildings but also improving the lifestyles of the communities served.

The midwest office of North American Properties brings the company's award-winning brand of development to Minneapolis and its surrounding communities with upscale retail properties, luxury apartments, and premium office spaces in some of the fastest growing

areas. The company's passion for the city's future and respect for its past have created positive change time and time again.

North American Properties combines experience and imagination to take a visionary approach to development. Its innovative solution for the redevelopment of the Calhoun Square shopping and dining complex is designed to return this landmark to its premier status as the southwest gateway to Minneapolis.

Likewise, North American Properties creates vibrant communities, such as the ones found at The Watertower and SouthWest Metro Transit's SouthWest Station in Eden Prairie, which are designed to enhance the lives of the people who shop, dine,

live, work, and play there. By building these best-in-class types of communities, North American Properties creates a lasting, positive impression for present and future generations.

North American Properties remains steadfast in its commitment to the vitality of Minneapolis. Its belief in the

today, tomorrow, and future of the city, its citizens, and the community at large, reflect the company's legacy and its dedication to the future of Minneapolis.

For additional information, visit the North American Properties Web site at www.naproperties.com.

North American Properties redevelops properties into vibrant mixed-use complexes. Above: The project for Calhoun Square in Minneapolis is designed to revitalize the neighborhood. Above left: The Watertower, in Eden Prairie, blends apartment, office, and restaurant spaces.

American Express Financial Center, interior architecture by RSP Architects

RSP Architects

Established and respected as one of the top 100 architecture companies in the United States, RSP Architects provides the full complement of design services—from concept to implementation to space management—for its national clients from the private, corporate, and government sectors.

Until recently, people visiting RSP Architects' Web site were greeted with the following message: "What we imagine and build together is better than what any of us can create alone."

This phrase aptly expresses RSP's "total team" philosophy—one that has ensured the firm's strong, steady growth since it was founded in 1978. With more than 200 employees, RSP now ranks among the top 100 architecture companies in the United States. This leading Minneapolis-based firm has designed thousands of buildings and interiors for hundreds of clients throughout the Twin Cities and across the nation.

"Ideally, the architectural process should engage the expertise of all team members," states Dave Norback, AIA, president of RSP. "In practice, we actively encourage and integrate ideas from our clients, consultants, contractors, and other professionals from ideation through construction."

Award-Winning Creations

RSP's experience in renovating and designing the historic Grain Belt Brewhouse illustrates this firm's philosophy in action.

Located along the Mississippi Riverfront, northeast of downtown Minneapolis, the Brewhouse was closed in 1975 after more than eight decades of continuous operation. As the most monumental building on its historic site, the Brewhouse held great symbolic value for a neighborhood that was in transformation. City officials believed that renovating this landmark structure would catalyze other urban revitalization projects.

Once construction began, however, major unforeseen challenges arose. Mold and other environmental hazards were discovered. Portions of the building's structural system needed to be replaced or reinforced. The building was a maze of structures with sloped floors that did not align.

"This project clearly required the concerted, creative contributions of every team member, from

consultants to subcontractors to local manufacturers," states Norback.

To date, RSP's renovation of the Grain Belt Brewhouse has won nine awards and garnered positive media coverage at the local and national levels.

Client-Centric Designs

Successfully completing the Brewhouse renovation reinforced, for RSP, the importance that this company places on client-centric, business-based designs. Since the Brewhouse now serves as RSP's Minneapolis headquarters, RSP was both the client and the designer for the project.

"We have always known that the most innovative solutions flow from the mission, vision, and values of our clients," Norback states. "The Brewhouse renovation gave us a chance to relate design decisions to distinct aspects of our own corporate culture. For example, the tight spacing of interior columns made adapting the Brewhouse for offices especially difficult. We realized, however, that we could use the space left over between rows of

workstations to create teaming zones. This design decision has enhanced our daily operations while showing how important collaboration is for energizing the architectural process."

The portfolio section of RSP's Web site (www.rsparch.com) illustrates how this firm's designs reflect the broad diversity of its clients and their projects. "We don't have a signature style," states Norback. "For any design to be truly successful, it must capture and convey the client's vision with all of its unique characteristics and aspirations."

Top: In 1998, the Minneapolis-based RSP Architects opened an additional office in Phoenix, Arizona, to better serve its nationwide clientele. RSP's design for this Southwest location, Studio 5C (pictured here), has won awards from the architectural profession and the business community. Above: The renovated Grain Belt Brewhouse has been RSP's Minneapolis headquarters since early 2002.

Health Care, Medical Technology, and Bioscience

Profiles of Corporations and Organizations

Upsher-Smith Laboratories, Inc.

This rapidly growing company is a recognized leader in developing, manufacturing, and marketing cardiovascular and dermatological pharmaceuticals and is actively involved in licensing innovative compounds that are in clinical development.

Above: The state-of-the-art facilities of Upsher-Smith Laboratories, Inc. in Maple Grove, Minnesota are housed in a 200,000-square-foot building that includes corporate headquarters, offices, laboratories, and warehouse components.

Upsher-Smith Laboratories, Inc. is a pharmaceutical company with a long, distinguished history and an even more promising future. Founded in 1919 by pharmacist, chemist, and noted researcher F. A. Upsher-Smith, and purchased in 1969 by pharmacist and entrepreneur Ken Evenstad, the company has grown to become one of the world's top pharmaceutical companies and a leader in the development, manufacture, and marketing of an array of branded generic pharmaceuticals designed to advance human health.

Well known for Klor-Con®—the number one–dispensed potassium supplement in the United States—Upsher-Smith also is a leader in the

With state-of-the-art facilities in Maple Grove and Plymouth, Minnesota, as well as Denver, Colorado, family-owned Upsher-Smith is committed to providing reliable, affordable pharmaceutical products to meet the needs of its customers, who include pharmacists, physicians, managed-care organizations, and patients.

development of cardiology and dermatology products. Its Pacerone® Tablet, the leading brand of oral amiodarone for treating irregular heartbeats, is perhaps the company's best-known cardiovascular product. Jantoven®, a branded generic to a vital anticoagulation drug, which Upsher-Smith added to its product line in 2003, is another of the company's cardiovascular products.

In the area of dermatology, Upsher-Smith offers its AmLactin® family of moisturizing creams and lotions. This

line was expanded in 2004 with the launch of AmLactin® XL™ Moisturizing Lotion, a clinically superior, high potency, alpha-hydroxy lotion for moisturizing rough, dry skin. Another of the company's dermatology products, Clenia® Foaming Wash and Emollient Cream, introduced in 2003, further extends the company's product line in this field with an innovative skin care system. These products exemplify Upsher-Smith's commitment to providing comprehensive, high quality skin care that offers a low-cost alternative to other brands.

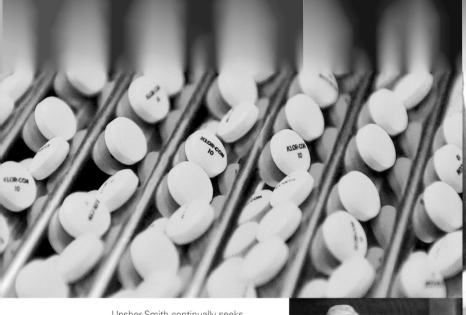

Upsher-Smith continually seeks new opportunities to fill unmet market needs. One result of this pursuit is its Folgard® OS Tablets, introduced in 2004. Folgard OS is a prescription-strength combination of calcium and folic acid and includes other vitamins and minerals. It is designed to help reduce the risk of developing osteoporosis and meet the increasing demand for supplementation with folic acid, which has been shown to provide a wide range of health benefits.

In addition to providing high quality products, Upsher-Smith serves the nation's physicians and pharmacists with continuing medical-education programs. Upsher-Smith's pharmacists provide drug information and offer technical training that covers pharmacology, physiology, and other medical information.

Upsher-Smith attributes the lion's share of its success to its highly skilled, committed, and innovative employees.

These include a pharmaceutical-research staff of scientists who analyze, probe, and contemplate the many aspects of a given medication or disease category; a manufacturing workforce dedicated to quality; a marketing team of creative individuals who strive to position the company's products to ensure maximum market penetration and growth; talented sales representatives who promote Upsher-Smith's brands across the nation; and a legal and regulatory affairs staff of scientists, lawyers, and regulatory experts who work to ensure that Upsher-Smith's products meet stringent

federal requirements. Ken Evenstad is the company's chairman and CEO, and his son Mark Evenstad is vice chairman and president.

Upsher-Smith considers that what counts is not merely what the company does but also how it does it. Its employees are continually devising new approaches to the firm's manufacturing and research efforts. These innovative efforts are based on a passion for maintaining state-of-the-art technologies and developing and producing the highest quality pharmaceuticals.

Upsher-Smith's contributions to the fields of pharmaceuticals and health care do not go unnoticed in the industry. Among the awards and recognition that have been bestowed

on the company are the Healthcare Distribution Management Association's DIANA Award for excellence in prescription-support systems, supplies, and service, and the National Wholesale Druggist Association's Best Overall Manufacturer Merit Award. In addition, both McKesson and Cardinal Health have named Upsher-Smith their Supplier of the Year for exemplary service and support.

Ever since its beginning, Upsher-Smith has consistently focused on excellence through innovation and growth through development, and today it is poised for continued success in developing, manufacturing, and marketing an array of products created to enhance human health.

Above: Company founder F. A. Upsher-Smith and his secretary are shown at their office in the downtown Minneapolis Sexton Building in the early 20th century.

Top left: Hundreds of millions of Klor-Con® 10 Tablets are produced in Upsher-Smith's advanced facilities and distributed to pharmacies nationwide.

Above left: Ken Evenstad, at left, is chairman and CEO of Upsher-Smith Laboratories, Inc., and his son Mark Evenstad is vice chairman and president.

American Medical Systems

Providing 'Solutions for Life,' American Medical Systems—established in Minnetonka, Minnesota, since 1972—develops, manufactures, and markets medical devices and creates therapies that assist physicians worldwide in restoring the pelvic health of their male and female patients of all ages.

American Medical Systems (AMS) is one of the world's leading independent companies dedicated to restoring male and female pelvic health by developing, manufacturing, and marketing innovative medical devices. AMS's implants and therapies address male and female incontinence, as well as erectile dysfunction, pelvic prolapse, benign prostatic hyperplasia (BPH), urethral strictures, menorrhagia, and other pelvic health conditions—all problems that diminish one's quality of life.

AMS collaborates with urologists and gynecologists to develop new technologies that can be delivered in the hospital or the doctor's office. The company's goal is to reduce the surgical risk to patients by offering devices that are minimally invasive, provide alternatives to long-term drug therapy, and simplify traditional surgical procedures.

At AMS's headquarters in Minnetonka, Minnesota, research and development engineers, clinical and regulatory specialists, and manufacturing and marketing personnel work together to develop novel and innovative therapies. Likewise, physicians work directly with product engineers in the operating room and in the AMS facility to come up with effective solutions. Because of such seamless, multifunctional collaborations, AMS is able to develop new products that are brought to market quickly and efficiently—allowing more people to benefit from AMS's advancements.

Since its founding in 1972 by Robert Buuck; Gerald Timm, Ph.D.; William Bradley, M.D.; and F. Brantley Scott, M.D., AMS has introduced many medical firsts, including the first urinary sphincter for incontinence and the first inflatable penile prosthesis for erectile dysfunction. The company's focus on women's health has led to a broad line of innovative and less invasive treatments for female incontinence and pelvic organ prolapse and an office-based treatment for excessive menstrual bleeding using a freezing technique called cryoablation.

In 2004 alone, more than 130,000 people throughout the world benefited from AMS solutions, and more than 2,800 physicians were trained to deliver AMS's innovative therapies. AMS has a rapidly growing business in terms of both revenue and profits. This growth allows AMS to channel its funds and energies into vitally important areas such as training, research and development, education, and outreach.

Today, AMS employs more than 700 people worldwide and has one of the industry's largest sales teams. The company's recent acquisitions include TherMatrx® for BPH and Her Option® for excessive menstrual bleeding. For the future, by listening to the needs of patients and their doctors, American Medical Systems will continue to help people of all ages enjoy a greater degree of physical health and a higher quality of life. For additional information, visit the AMS Web site at www.AmericanMedicalSystems.com.

Health Dimensions Group

An innovative, values-based leader, this Minneapolis-headquartered firm offers a complete array of integrated management and consulting services for the entire continuum of health care and senior services —a total solutions partner.

Health Dimensions Group is one of the nation's leading, fully integrated senior living and health care management and consulting firms. It works in partnership with providers of long-term care and senior-living facilities, as well as health systems and hospitals, to assist them in meeting the ever-changing needs in their markets and plan for the future while maintaining a healthy bottom line.

Headquartered in Minneapolis, Health Dimensions Group originated as a division of Health Dimensions, Inc., which was sold to the Benedictine Health System, a faith-based, nonprofit organization. Through the reorganization of the Benedictine Health System, an opportunity emerged for Health Dimensions Group to reform through private ownership. In 2000, Health Dimensions Group became a privately held entity, in order to expand its services and better meet the growing needs of its clients.

The firm draws on its staff's diverse knowledge and expertise to provide a comprehensive range of services that assist clients in addressing their specific needs. The Health Dimensions Group staff understand how each long term care, senior living, and post acute care component impacts the whole and tailor solutions to client's unique situations and specific challenges.

Health Dimensions Group's facility management services include

* startup management,
* interim management, and
* turnaround management.

The firm's consulting solutions address the areas of

* skilled nursing,
* senior living,
* hospitals and health systems,
* finance and reimbursement,
* PACE (Programs of All-inclusive Care for the Elderly) development, and
* rehabilitation.

The firm's turnaround management services offer the special resources needed to turn around difficult situations and have been particularly valuable for many of its clients. For example, when the Sisters of St. Francis of Marycrest in Denver, Colorado, decided to provide

residential care for low-income seniors and nonelderly persons with disabilities, it faced significant financial challenges. Health Dimensions Group worked closely with the Sisters to manage the operation, helping the organization to achieve profitability within 18 months and enabling the Sisters to continue their mission.

Health Dimensions Group's clients also include mortgage companies, investment bankers, independent investor groups, religious and other faith-based organizations, municipalities, and civic organizations.

In all endeavors, the firm provides tailored solutions to meet today's challenges, along with industry leadership that envisions tomorrow's opportunities.

Above: Health Dimensions Group works in partnership with providers of senior health care to assist them in meeting the challenges of tomorrow.

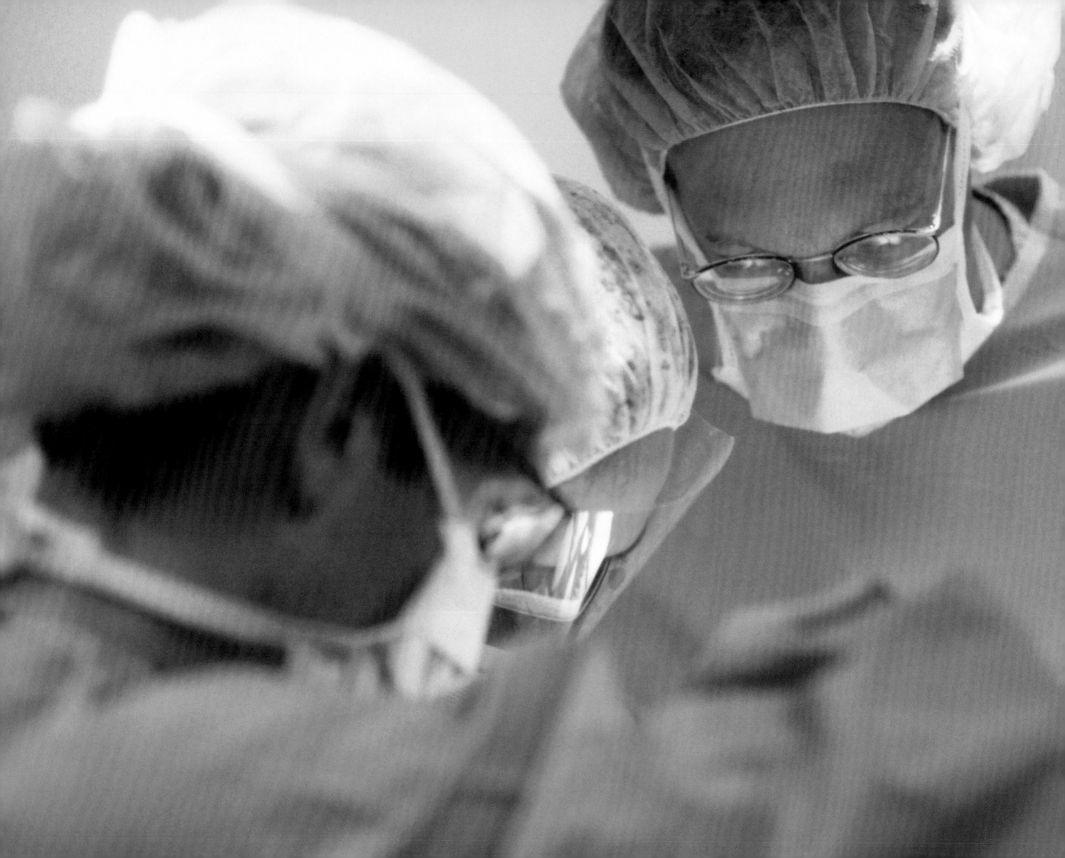

Boston Scientific

Delivering on the promise of medical innovation, this industry-leading and award-winning company improves the quality of patient care and the productivity of health care through its minimally invasive cardiovascular technologies and products.

Boston Scientific's continued pursuit of innovation has led to tremendous growth and investments in Minnesota. Since 1997, Boston Scientific has hired more than 1,200 employees in Minnesota, bringing its statewide total number of employees to 3,500. The company, headquartered in Natick, Massachusetts, has 16 plants and 17,000 employees worldwide. In 2004, the company grew 62 percent and earned $5.6 billion in net sales.

With locations in the northwest Minneapolis suburbs of Maple Grove and Plymouth, Boston Scientific develops less-invasive medical technologies and devices that are used by interventional cardiologists, vascular surgeons, and radiologists. These technologies and products are used to diagnose and treat cardiovascular and peripheral vascular diseases, as well as other cardiovascular disorders.

Overall, Boston Scientific's growth is a result of both acquisitions—more than 45 since 1995—and internal research and development. This company's research and development teams in Minnesota are responsible for the creation of the TAXUS® drug-eluting stent system, a revolutionary technology that helps prevent the regrowth of plaque in arteries. These teams continue to lead the industry in developing innovative technologies, devices, and materials. They have a strong pipeline of product advancements and next-generation solutions.

Boston Scientific's Minnesota teams have been recognized for their outstanding efforts. Collectively, they received the Cadence Management Corporation's 2004 award for Customer Excellence in Project Management. The Maple Grove Operations team was awarded the 2005 Shingo Prize (known as the Nobel Prize of manufacturing) for Excellence in Manufacturing. In 2004, the Maple Grove facility was selected by *IndustryWeek* magazine as one of the Top Ten Best Plants.

Boston Scientific's growth in Minnesota is also evidenced by the construction of a new 150,000-square-foot research and development facility. Opened in 2005, this expansion brings Boston Scientific's total area of operations in Minnesota to 600,000 square feet. The new building contains state-of-the-art laboratory space and work areas, plus a 300-seat conference center.

Through the efforts of local employee teams and a strong leadership vision, Boston Scientific is improving the quality of patient care and the productivity of health care through its innovative cardiovascular solutions. For more information, visit www.bostonscientific.com.

Above left: Boston Scientific's Maple Grove, Minnesota, campus encompasses state-of-the-art laboratories, work areas, and conference centers.
Above center: This company's exceptional research and development teams are renowned for their ground-breaking work, including the creation of the TAXUS® drug-eluting stent system.
Above right: In 2005, Boston Scientific broke ground for its new research and development facility in Minnesota.

Information Technology and Telecommunications

Profiles of Corporations and Organizations

McCaa, Webster & Associates, Inc.

Unique in its corporate culture and services, McCaa, Webster & Associates, Inc.—a leading information technology consulting firm—provides 'the right talent, the right solutions, and the right experience' for its diverse clients.

Private and public corporations, including many Fortune 1000 companies, and government organizations have relied on McCaa, Webster & Associates, Inc. for cost-effective solutions since this company was established in 1994. McCaa, Webster & Associates' powerful combination of information technology (IT) experts and the in-house use of advanced human-capital management technologies, such as intelliMATCH, distinguishes this forward-thinking firm.

Based in Minneapolis, Minnesota, McCaa, Webster & Associates was organized to provide the full range of IT solutions and staff-augmentation services. Systems analysis, design, and development; custom-application and database design and development; project management; and job placement are among McCaa, Webster & Associates' areas of expertise that are personalized for every client. Recognizing that object-oriented and Internet technologies represent the future of application and system development, McCaa, Webster & Associates specializes in the uses of these technologies to deliver its solutions.

Such innovation is part of McCaa, Webster & Associates' "Different Approach" corporate philosophy and culture, which encompasses its inspired employment practices. This "Different Approach" emphasizes serving the mutual interests of clients and employees. Through its family-friendly hours, prosperity sharing, opportunities to work on projects of great significance, and many other options and benefits, McCaa, Webster & Associates is able to recruit and retain top personnel. These motivated, talented consultants function as critical extensions of clients' internal teams. By actively listening to clients and assigning the right personnel with the right skill sets, McCaa, Webster & Associates ensures the right results.

For the consistent success of its efforts, its culture of collaboration and innovation, and its standard-setting employment practices, McCaa, Webster & Associates was named to *The Business Journal*'s 2004 "Top 25" list of minority-owned businesses in the Minneapolis–St. Paul metropolitan area. "We are very pleased to have made this list, because it shows that the hard work and dedication of our employees is making an impact in the marketplace," states Sam McCaa, the company's CEO and president.

With new solutions for the new millennium, McCaa, Webster & Associates provides the clear, competitive IT advantages that evolve with the business needs and strategies of its clients.

Right: Since 1994, McCaa, Webster & Associates has been providing mission critical IT solutions to Fortune 1000 North American companies. Shown here, from left, are McCaa, Webster & Associates staff members Robert Haley, director of sales and marketing; Sam McCaa, CEO and president; Cynthia Castelline, director of human resources; and Matthew Prestegaard, director of operations.

Thomson West

Publishing more than 66 million books and 500 CD-ROM libraries each year, and offering integrated software and online services, this company—one of the largest employers in Minnesota—provides the legal industry with a broad range of valuable tools for accessing and managing legal information.

Since the company's founding in St. Paul in 1872, Thomson West has played a key role in supporting the American justice system and helping legal professionals better serve their clients. While the company's roots are in legal publishing, Thomson West also offers a broad range of services and software applications designed to support the practice of law. Today, Thomson West is a leader in providing integrated information solutions to legal and regulatory professionals, thanks to its keen focus on customer needs, its unrelenting drive to innovate, and the talent and expertise of its 8,000 colleagues worldwide.

Thomson West, which is headquartered in Eagan, Minnesota, became a business of The Thomson Corporation (NYSE: TOC; TSX: TOC) in June 1996. Thomson West is home to its industry's most highly respected brands, including Westlaw, its leading online legal research service; KeyCite, its award-winning citation-checking service; and West km, its knowledge-management system, which enables law firms to index and research in-house documents using Thomson West search technologies. Additionally, Thomson West publishes more than 66 million books and 500 CD-ROM libraries annually.

With more than 6,000 employees based on its Eagan campus, Thomson West is one of Minnesota's largest employers. Thomson West recognizes that its employees are critical to the organization's success and continually demonstrates its commitment to fostering a knowledge-rich work culture and promoting career and personal development among its employees.

The awards Thomson West has received are as diverse as its people and represent the breadth of services the company offers to help employees manage their life and work priorities. Thomson West is repeatedly ranked among the nation's "100 Best Companies for Working Mothers" by *Working Mother* magazine. For four consecutive years, Thomson West has been honored as a leading information technology employer on the *Computerworld* list of the "Top 100 Best Places to Work in IT." In addition, Thomson West was named "one of the 10 best companies for promoting employee work/life initiatives" in a study cosponsored by Bright Horizons Family Solutions and William M. Mercer, Inc.

Thomson West has a long tradition of supporting the communities in which it does business. Its Community Partnership Program, established in 1998, supports a wide variety of community organizations and programs and also encourages employee civic involvement. Each year, Thomson West employees have the opportunity to donate to their favorite charitable organizations through employee-giving campaigns. Thomson West also has a policy that allows employees to receive up to 16 hours of paid time off to participate in corporate-sponsored volunteer activities. In addition, the company partners with the community through grants, through matching contributions to enhance the gifts of individual employees, and through corporate fund drives and volunteer efforts. Involvement in the community is at the heart of Thomson West's corporate values.

By providing products and services that are among the best in the industry and by building a strong reputation as a world-class employer, Thomson West has become a hallmark of quality and service excellence for the legal profession.

Left: The Thomson West headquarters campus in Eagan, Minnesota, houses 6,000 of the company's employees. Thomson West is one of the largest employers in the state.

Kaltec of Minnesota, Inc.

This technologically advanced company provides experienced design engineering, rapid manufacturing, and software solutions to help customers in a wide range of industries develop innovative concepts and bring new products quickly and cost-effectively to market.

As a provider of product development services, Kaltec of Minnesota, Inc. has been delivering innovative solutions to its customers for nearly 20 years. Founder Bruce Kallevig, P.E., originated the venture in 1986 as KFA Engineering, which provided design-engineering services. In 1988, it became apparent that many customers could be further served by having a finished product delivered—ready to be tested, displayed, and sold. The company became Kaltec of Minnesota, initiated to complete the cycle by incorporating manufacturing with design engineering.

Evolving from its traditional approach, Kaltec began maximizing the use of advanced technologies in its services. By 1990, it had delivered one of the first-known models in Minnesota created via stereolithography (SLA), rapidly building a prototype directly from a product design.

Over the years, the Kaltec mechanical design team has worked with companies in numerous diverse industries and created successful designs for products such as

- automotive components
- computer equipment
- consumer products
- cosmetics packaging
- earth-moving equipment
- electronic devices (handling, testing)
- food packaging
- lawn care equipment
- medical equipment
- power tools
- railroad maintenance equipment
- shipping containers
- sporting goods

With key projects for companies such as Select Comfort and

Kaltec of Minnesota Clientele

Among the companies for which Kaltec has provided product development are:

Select Comfort	Aveda
Avecor Cardiovascular	TriMark
Medtronic	Lockheed Martin
Carl Zeiss	Reliance Telephone Systems
General Motors	Loram Maintenance of Way
Ford Motor Company	SciMed Life Systems
Sawhorse Designers and Builders	SPX Fluid Power

Avecor Cardiovascular, Kaltec has been able to play a role in the development of products that had their inception in Minnesota and now are distributed around the globe.

In the early 1990s, Kaltec branched into developing software, and in 1996 it teamed with Microsoft as a provider of software solutions. Kaltec now delivers software based on Microsoft technology for use in a variety of industries, from telephone systems to home remodeling. Kaltec is a prominent supplier of correctional facility software that includes inmate-management systems and integrates with Minnesota's CriMNet initiative. The CriMNet system, with operations at the Minnesota Bureau of Criminal Apprehension (BCA), is the first

system in the nation to enable inmate data collected at the county level to be linked to a state BCA.

Kaltec has undergone 14 marked expansions since it began. In 2002, it relocated to a facility in Monticello, Minnesota, that provides 33,000 square feet of manufacturing space and enables sophisticated data-transfer capabilities for its engineering and administrative staffs.

Kaltec of Minnesota, Inc. continues to expand its services to meet its customers' needs. By carefully blending advanced technologies with old-fashioned innovation, the company continues to exceed expectations in the products and services it delivers.

Eschelon Telecom, Inc.

This rapidly growing telecommunications company provides voice, data, and Internet services and business telephone systems, offering flexible product sets, scalable systems, a secure, reliable network, and enhanced customer service.

In the challenging telecommunications industry, Eschelon Telecom, Inc. has emerged as one of the leading telecommunications providers in the United States. Founded in 1996 in Minneapolis as Advanced Telecommunications, the company steadily expanded and in 2000 changed its name to Eschelon Telecom, Inc. Today it serves more than 60,000 business customers in eight midwestern and western states, offering integrated communications systems that include voice, data, and Internet services and business telephone systems and equipment.

Eschelon focuses on small to midsize businesses and strives to set itself apart with product and service advantages, described as "Service at the Next Level." Its Precision Integrated T-1 combines voice and data lines into a single circuit. Businesses that select this option can have up to 16 telephone lines and high-speed Internet access. For smaller businesses, Eschelon's Simple Solutions bundles local, long-distance, and Internet services into one package at one low monthly rate. Eschelon offers flexible product sets and systems that are designed to

accommodate changing needs and future growth.

Eschelon focuses on maintaining long-term relationships with clients by providing the highest level of service and support. The specifications of new orders are custom-tailored to precise client requirements, and each new system is vetted in a "five-point quality control" review. Once service is implemented, quality is tracked via customer surveys. Network quality is maintained through continual monitoring, an advanced troubleshooting system, and state-of-the-art security. The quality of equipment and service from outside suppliers is monitored through service report cards. Calls to customer service are answered in 20 seconds or less. Eschelon's efforts to continuously improve service levels have helped this company achieve customer retention rates that over a more-than-five-year average are among the highest in the industry.

Eschelon also makes its products and services available through members of its Elite Partners Agent Program such as telephone systems vendors, telecommunications consultants,

and other professionals who assist clients with telecommunications.

Strong leadership is a key component of Eschelon's success. Founder and chairman of the board Clifford M. Williams was an Ernst & Young Entrepreneur of the Year. President and CEO Richard Smith, with 32 years in the industry, serves on the executive committees of several industry trade associations. Eschelon employs 1,200 talented telecommunications and Internet professionals.

Eschelon has been named among the 50 fastest growing Minnesota-based companies by *The Business Journal–Minneapolis/St. Paul.* Throughout its history, Eschelon Telecom, Inc. has proved to have the right vision and the right product mix to serve a growing customer segment successfully.

Above, from top: Eschelon Telecom is guided by Clifford M. Williams, founder and chairman of the board, and Richard Smith, president and CEO.

www.eschelon.com

Media and Communications

Profiles of Corporations and Organizations

Gage

Gage sets itself apart as a forerunner in the new breed of marketing agencies by combining creativity, technology, and a focus on achieving measurable results for its clients, using complementary marketing services to produce dynamic possibilities.

Above: Some of the world's largest companies and most prestigious brands turn to Gage for its combination of creativity, technology, and strategic acumen. Above right: CEO Edwin "Skip" Gage founded Gage in 1992. While the company has evolved over the years, its focus on driving sales results for its clients has never changed. In 1999 Skip Gage won "Entrepreneur of the Year" honors from Ernst & Young for Gage and other start-up companies and investments.

Once upon a time, all a company really needed in order to promote a product was a really great TV commercial or a super-slick ad or direct-mail piece.

Advertising agencies set themselves and their clients apart by aiming raw creative talent at any given marketing problem. For decades, agencies produced advertisements that shocked, titillated, or seduced buyers. They were funny, or tugged at your heartstrings, appealing to either the intellect or selfish impulses.

Ushering Out the Old Method of Marketing and Selling

Cable TV and the proliferation of media—a magazine or channel for every interest and every demographic—wounded the old model of marketing and selling. The rise of one-to-one marketing, the invention of TiVo, and, finally, the rise of the Internet eventually killed it.

Now consumers get information and make buying decisions in a highly complex manner. The old model—running a clever ad during the Super Bowl, for instance—no longer works. What is called for is a whole new kind of agency. Gage is that kind of agency.

Expertly Combining the Five Most Important Disciplines in Marketing

Consumers—and, increasingly, the distribution channel—gain information about brands from a spectrum of sources. Gage calls them brand "touch points." Controlling that spectrum ultimately drives buying decisions to go a certain way.

Gage experts focus on the five segments of that spectrum that work most effectively to achieve the results that clients demand. These segments are:

- Branding and Strategic Communication
- Interactive and Traditional Direct Marketing
- Customer Relationship Marketing (CRM)
- Incentive Programs
- Sales Promotion

Gage has focused on these specifics because they are highly measurable as well as highly effective. Most important, in the right hands they can be directly interwoven to create complete, robust solutions to marketing challenges.

Set Apart by the Method of Combining the Five Core Disciplines

Most marketing agencies have a legacy of being founded as "above-the-line" ad agencies. They are often predisposed toward coming up with an advertising solution. Gage was founded by Edwin "Skip" Gage in 1992 as a below-the-line company focused on less glitzy, more high-impact solutions.

Over the years, the company has incorporated proprietary technology, perfected its processes, and built a senior staff that is uniquely equipped to build large-scale marketing solutions that gain attention, drive sales, and create brand preference at all levels.

Other agencies offer adjacent areas of expertise that can be mixed and matched. Gage focuses on five Core Disciplines and fuses them using a combination of branding and technology.

The highly synergistic solution that results creates significantly more impact. A Web site created by Gage, for instance, goes far beyond "brochure-ware." Instead, it is a highly interactive online environment that may include:

- A sweepstakes or an online game (from Gage's Sales Promotion Core Discipline)
- Outbound e-mail (from Gage's Interactive Direct Marketing Core Discipline)
- Database-driven offers and communications (from Gage's CRM Core Discipline)

And Gage's attention to brand and its robust technology make the entire offering seamless.

Short-Term Results, Long-Term Successes

Gage has a history of typically beginning with a client in one or possibly two Core Discipline areas in order to achieve a specific result, such as a spike in sales for the duration of a sales promotion.

Gage automatically and efficiently builds in connections to its other disciplines so that at the appropriate time an even better, deeper, more comprehensive solution can be quickly deployed.

A Web site, for instance, becomes the cornerstone for a complete e-based Customer Relationship Marketing effort that in turn can incorporate sales promotion tactics to drive sales or gain customer information.

Creating Intelligent Solutions for Some of the World's Smartest Companies

Gage is deploying solutions for companies as diverse as Sony Corporation, Microsoft, Best Buy, Nestlé, Wells Fargo, and many others. Most started as a single project that rolled out into a complete program, generating ever-greater sales. Looking ahead, as media and target audiences fracture into ever-smaller pieces, Gage anticipates a growing need for its unique ability to combine marketing disciplines into huge successes.

Gage

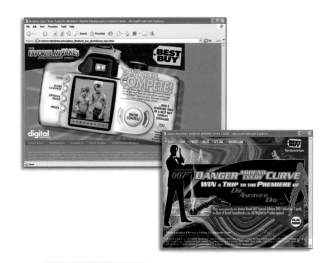

Above left: Gage's roots in sales promotion plus its technical expertise have moved the company heavily into online marketing strategies, providing interactive sweepstakes, games, and contests for brand-name retailers such as Best Buy. Left: Lawry's tapped into Gage's creativity and promotional expertise for its "Grilling" effort, which fired up sales of the company's marinades and seasonings during the summer months. Consumer promotions drove demand, while trade promotions ensured that retailers would be all stocked up to meet it.

Star Tribune

This respected Minnesota company brings quality journalism to more than a million readers, believing that its newspaper and Web site should be at the heart of the community by providing comprehensive news coverage, extensive consumer information, and independent editorial commentary.

The Star Tribune is a thriving media company that produces one of the top 20 largest newspapers in the nation, as well as startribune.com, the most frequently used local news and information Web site in the Twin Cities.

The Star Tribune is owned by The McClatchy Company (NYSE: MNI), which is headquartered in Sacramento, California. The McClatchy Company dates back to the California Gold Rush era, when the company's first newspaper, *The Sacramento Bee*, was founded in 1857 by James McClatchy. The McClatchy Company acquired the Star Tribune company from Cowles Media in 1998 and made a commitment to continue the newspaper's local autonomy in news coverage and editorial commentary.

The Star Tribune company history begins in 1867 with three newspapers— the *Minneapolis Tribune*, the *Star*, and the *Minneapolis Journal*. In 1935, the Cowles family of Des Moines, Iowa, purchased the *Star*, and over the next few years it purchased the *Tribune* and the *Journal*, as well. From these acquisitions and through a series of consolidations, the evening *Minneapolis Star* and the morning *Minneapolis Tribune* emerged.

In 1982, the *Star* and the *Tribune* combined to make one daily morning newspaper—the *Minneapolis Star and Tribune*. In 1987, the name changed to the *Star Tribune*, *Newspaper of the Twin Cities*, to reflect the newspaper's growing presence across the entire metropolitan area, especially in St. Paul.

In 1996, the Star Tribune launched the Web site www.startribune.com, an electronic news and information service that also provides a vibrant online marketplace.

Beginning in 2003, the *Star Tribune* launched a series of suburban sections focused on community news in specific geographic regions. The company also produces a variety of direct-marketing products, as well as publications custom-designed to reach target audiences.

"We are proud of our rich history of involvement in the life of the Twin Cities area and of our commitment to deliver quality journalism to millions of people every day," says J. Keith Moyer, publisher and president of the *Star Tribune*. "As we continue to grow, we will honor our tradition as Minnesota's preferred source of information and as one of the best and most respected media organizations in the country."

Padilla Speer Beardsley

Named Midsize Agency of the Year in 2005 by the prestigious *Holmes Report,* Padilla Speer Beardsley serves a diverse list of clients throughout the United States from its Minneapolis headquarters and New York office, and serves clients around the globe through its Worldcom Public Relations Group.

The institutions that make Minneapolis a great city in which to work, live, and play have trusted Padilla Speer Beardsley to help build their reputations with the people who are important to their success.

Don Padilla and David Speer created this public relations firm in 1961. Speer was a dreamer who captured the imaginations of his clients and the loyalty of their customers. Padilla was the corner-office guy. He knew that big ideas mattered only if they moved a business forward. The integration of Speer's captivating ideas and Padilla's business savvy has driven the success of Padilla Speer Beardsley for four decades and through three leadership transitions.

Today, Padilla Speer Beardsley's 90 employee-owners serve clients throughout the United States from the firm's Minneapolis headquarters and New York office. The client list is diverse by design, from pre-IPO emerging growth companies to many of the largest, most recognized corporations, including General Mills, Rockwell Automation, BASF, Ernst & Young, and MetLife.

Common threads do exist, however. According to this firm's market research, clients choose Padilla Speer Beardsley for its experienced, cohesive teams (some members have worked together for more than 20 years); its commitment to above-and-beyond service; and its

creative approaches to helping organizations compete in crowded markets. Padilla Speer Beardsley's independent, all-employee-owned status has also been a drawing card for many clients since it formed an ESOP (employee stock ownership plan) in 1992.

To serve clients outside the United States, Padilla Speer Beardsley also cofounded a worldwide network—the Worldcom Public Relations Group. Today, this international group is the world's largest network of independently owned

public relations firms, with more than 100 offices in 35 countries.

At the heart of Padilla Speer Beardsley's mission is the knowledge that organizations thrive only when they build and maintain good relationships with all important constituents. That's why this firm's practices are focused on customer, investor, voter, and employee relations. Specialized services that are available to all clients include media relations, Internet communications, opinion research, and crisis communications.

Above left: Proudly founded and still headquartered in Minneapolis, Padilla Speer Beardsley was honored as Midsize Agency of the Year for its award-winning work and successes by the *Holmes Report,* published by The Holmes Group—one of only two organizations that rate public relations firms in the United States and Europe. Above: Some of Padilla Speer Beardsley's experienced, cohesive teams have worked together for more than 20 years.

Manufacturing

Profiles of Corporations and Organizations

Alliance Steel Service Co.

From an industry pioneer to a modern-day standard setter, Alliance Steel Service Co. has defined the business of scrap-metal recycling and brokering on a national and international scale—and in a safe and environmentally conscious manner—for nearly half a century.

Right: For nearly five decades, Alliance Steel Service Co. has succeeded as a family business and an industry leader. In 2005, former owner Harold Goldfine (pictured at left) handed the reins of the company to his son-in-law Mike Zweigbaum, who now shapes the future of this dynamic company.

When Alliance Steel Service Co. was created in 1957, the company was a pioneer in the scrap-metal recycling industry. Nearly 50 years later, this northeast Minneapolis–based firm remains at the forefront of an evolving industry. Partners Henry Davis and Fred Schwartz launched what, at the time, was a fairly new concept. Both had worked for other scrap-metal processing companies, and they realized that the time was right to create a niche operation that catered to industrial accounts.

Davis and Schwartz took advantage of the opportunity to engage in brokering scrap from other dealers on Alliance Steel's orders. As the industrial scrap business increased, Alliance Steel teamed up with a local rubbish hauler to provide scrap containers at their clients' manufacturing facilities. Business flourished as more and more customers were attracted to the concept of the "lugger" truck system to handle their scrap.

National and International Scope

Today, Alliance Steel services more than 200 industrial accounts and provides needed scrap to more than 25 corporate customers. The company works exclusively with industrial scrap materials. The brokerage business started by the founders remains an important part of Alliance Steel, and the firm now has national and international brokerage abilities. Alliance Steel purchases, sorts, packages, and transports recyclable materials including steel, aluminum, copper, stainless steel, and brass. The customer base for these materials encompasses industrial manufacturing companies, custom fabrication and machine shops, commercial printers, other scrap brokers, and additional related businesses.

In 1976, Davis's son-in-law Harold Goldfine and Schwartz's son Charles joined the company. As business increased, Alliance Steel outgrew its existing Minneapolis facility, and the firm constructed a larger building at 31st Avenue North. The facility featured a much larger yard operation and enabled Alliance Steel to increase its capacity. This state-of-the-art facility, which today provides clients with a variety of services, is directly connected to a rail spur line for mill-direct shipping within a 24-hour period. Moreover, the firm's modern equipment ensures prompt, safe material handling. A knowledgeable on-site staff is available to address questions related to the processing, storing, and transportation of the materials.

Environmental Stewardship

To its credit, Alliance Steel recognizes that taking care of the environment is also an important aspect of doing business. This company has a proactive environmental attitude toward its recycling practices. Alliance Steel's full-time environmental staff is committed to following compliance issues such as storm-water permit requirements, storm-water pollution-prevention plans, and the collection and disposal of stockpile runoff. In addition, the company maintains an on-call environmental

consulting firm that is ready to step in and assist with issues when needed.

One hundred percent of Alliance Steel scrap is recycled using only licensed, reputable contractors. The company scrutinizes incoming materials, rejects hazardous materials, and has a select client base that allows detailed tracking of both incoming and outgoing materials. In addition, Alliance Steel has expanded its Environmental Compliance Program, which includes the operation of a newly constructed environmental containment system.

Dynamic Growth

Charles Schwartz and Harold Goldfine purchased the company in 1984, and Goldfine later bought out his partner when Schwartz decided to retire in 1995. Over these years, acquisitions played an important role in the company's dynamic growth. Between 1984 and 1998, Alliance Steel purchased the assets of Opatz Metals; H. Winnick Co.; E & S Iron and Metal; and KWA Metals, Inc. Those acquisitions have been key to the firm's growth over the past two decades. The flow of ferrous scrap has increased from 14,000 tons per year in the early 1970s to its current level of more than 150,000 tons per year.

Alliance Steel has continued its pattern of natural progression in acquiring companies whose operations mesh with its own operations, and who are already doing business with Alliance Steel. In 2002, Alliance Steel acquired Silverberg Metals, the scrap branch operation of Quality Metals. In keeping with that natural progression, Mike Zweigbaum, son-in-law of then-owner Harold Goldfine, purchased the company in 2005 and is leading Alliance Steel Service Co. successfully into the 21st century.

Far left and left: Also valued as part of the "family" of this family-run business, the expert yard personnel and office staff contribute greatly to the success of Alliance Steel Service Co. Currently, Alliance Steel and its employees provide recycled scrap materials and comprehensive services to more than 200 industrial accounts and more than 25 corporate customers.

Entegris, Inc.

This leading materials integrity management company provides quality products and services to purify, protect, and transport critical materials and components before and during manufacture, serving the semiconductor industry and technology-based sectors such as data storage, life sciences, and fuel cells.

Above: Entegris, Inc. creates products and processes to manage the integrity of critical materials, which is essential for efficiently and economically manufacturing computer chips and other electronic devices. Shown here, from left, are wafers used in the semiconductor industry, reticles used in the semiconductor industry, and advanced analytical capabilities using FTIR (Fourier Transform Infrared) spectroscopy.

Most materials that go into the manufacturing of today's technologies need special care while being processed or stored within a manufacturing facility or transported to an outside location. As a leader in managing materials integrity, Entegris, Inc. provides products, systems, and services to purify, protect, and transport critical materials, from development through delivery.

Entegris is known worldwide for its core competencies in filtration, purification, polymer material science, sensing and control, comprehensive design and manufacturing, and microelectronics process applications knowledge. Applying these strengths in materials integrity management has made the company a valuable supplier to the semiconductor, data storage, life sciences, and fuel cell industries.

Entegris products are used to protect and reliably transport more than half of the world's silicon wafers, upon which computer chips are built. For the semiconductor industry, Entegris makes products for handling and purifying wafers, devices, and fluids, along with measurement and control components. For the data storage industry, the company supplies products such as disk carriers and shippers and read/write head trays that are used to protect and transport more than half of the world's disks.

In the life sciences area, Entegris makes clean-in-place (CIP) equipment for biopharmaceutical and medical device technology companies. It also makes fluoropolymer components for metal-sensitive applications.

Entegris serves the fuel cell industry from concept to commercialization, supplying components and services designed to reduce fuel cell size, weight, and cost. Among its products are bipolar plates, plate shipping containers, and balance-of-plant components. The company's product advances improve reliability and maximize productivity and, in turn, help to increase fuel cell use. Worldwide, more than half of the vehicles that operate on fuel cells use products by Entegris.

As a result of technical innovations in materials science achieved through its research and development operations, Entegris has significant patents as well as trade secrets that it applies to serve its customers.

Around the globe, at regional service centers strategically located near customers' facilities, Entegris also offers services to maximize productivity, enhance predictability, and reduce costs. Entegris provides logistics, precision-cleaning, maintenance, replacement, and environmental services at the customer's facility or off-site. These programs, integrated with Entegris's well-engineered products, form total materials integrity management solutions.

In 2005 Entegris merged with Mykrolis Corporation of Billerica,

Entegris Products and Services

Entegris provides products and services for these industries:

Semiconductor
- wafer growing
- wafer handling
- wafer processing
- component handling
- chip and component assembly and packaging
- finished wafer handling
- chemical and fluid handling and filtration
- chemical and fluid controlling and measuring

Data Storage
- disk manufacturing
- disk handling
- disk processing
- component handling
- component assembly and packaging

Life Sciences
- biopharmaceutical components
- biopharmaceutical equipment
- medical technologies
- engineering design

Fuel Cell
- cell stack components
- balance-of-plant components and subsystems

Services
- cleaning equipment
- on-site services
- off-site services
- environmental services
- polymer services

Massachusetts, creating the new Entegris. The company has had 39 years of annual profitability. Publicly owned, Entegris (Nasdaq: ENTG) is headquartered in Chaska, Minnesota, and its global infrastructure allows it to serve clients anywhere in the world. In the United States, it operates manufacturing facilities in Chaska, Minneapolis, and Gaylord, Minnesota; South Beloit, Illinois; Gilroy and San Diego, California; Allen, Texas; Billerica and Franklin, Massachusetts; and Colorado Springs, Colorado. Its manufacturing and service facilities abroad are located in Japan, Malaysia, Singapore, South Korea, Taiwan, China, Germany, and France.

Customer support is provided world-wide, directly and through distributors.

"When you consider our market focus and financial strength, Entegris is positioned for growth opportunities in both our current and expanded markets," says John D. Villas, chief financial officer.

"Along with providing great products and services, at Entegris we develop great leaders," says Gideon Argov, president and CEO. "We are a values-based organization. As our people train and work, they are empowered to do what they need to do to achieve our goals and best serve our customers."

Above left: Entegris is headquartered in Chaska, Minnesota, and operates manufacturing facilities across the United States and in Asia and Europe. It can provide service for customers anywhere in the world.

The Foley Companies

Since 1926, this family-owned Minneapolis company has been making machines that sharpen cutting tools —from early handsaws to the blades that groom today's finest golf courses—and its product lines have expanded to include diverse items such as cutting boards, home training courses, and CD/DVD replication.

Formerly the Foley Manufacturing Company, The Foley Companies, also known as Foley-Belsaw Company, was started in northeast Minneapolis in 1926 by Walter M. Ringer Sr. Then, its sole product was a grinder to sharpen butchers' meat saws. Today, the company still manufactures grinders, which now sharpen reel-mower blades for golf course mowers.

The business's evolution in sharpening applications has been matched by its diversification into a variety of proprietary product lines. The products included the Foley Food Mill, cookware and bakeware, mess kits for the U.S. Army during World War II, lawn mowers, woodworking equipment, and woodenware, as well as winter clothing and vocational home study courses.

The founder's son, Walter M. Ringer Jr., drove the diversification of The Foley Companies to the business it is today. He began working at the company in 1936 and was company president for over four decades. Now, as chairman of the board of directors, he presides over the mix of divisions and subsidiaries that make up The Foley Companies. His sons John Ringer and Walter M. "Joe" Ringer III, along with a team of seasoned professionals headed up by Richard Hentges, president, are actively involved in the management of the businesses.

Today, The Foley Companies manufactures and distributes its reel-mower grinders through its Foley-United division, located in River Falls, Wisconsin.

The Foley Companies also markets and distributes wooden and plastic cutting surfaces under the trade names Foley-Martens and Grande Epicure from facilities located in Arab, Alabama. In addition, the company sells home study courses in vocational skills such as home inspection and locksmithing, which are fulfilled from the Foley-Belsaw Institute, with facilities in Kansas City, Missouri, and Chaska, Minnesota. And in 2001, the Duplication Factory, which replicates CDs and DVDs and duplicates videotapes, became a member of the Foley group through a joint venture. The Duplication Factory is located in Chaska, Minnesota.

Proud of his family's five-generation history in the company, Walter Ringer Jr. is most positive about the futures of the company's businesses and the people active in the businesses, past and present associates, and future associations. One of his favorite expressions, "changing with the times," expresses a belief that is ever in practice at The Foley Companies.

Left: Headquartered in Minneapolis, The Foley Companies has operations in several states. Shown here is the Duplication Factory in Chaska, Minnesota. Far left: The founder's son, Walter M. Ringer Jr., formerly president of The Foley Companies and now chairman of the board of directors, presides over all company divisions and subsidiaries.

Food Processing

Profiles of Corporations and Organizations

General Mills

Trusted worldwide brands, product excellence and innovation, respected business practices, and leading philanthropy have forged this 'Company of Champions'—a multibillion-dollar consumer foods corporation with a global reach, local headquarters, and a rich heritage nurtured in Minneapolis for more than 100 years.

Above: General Mills has been based in Golden Valley, Minnesota, since moving its headquarters from downtown Minneapolis in 1958.

General Mills' commitment to its values has always been part of its story—a rich heritage that began well before its incorporation in 1928. The history of General Mills reaches back to the 1860s, to a pair of Minneapolis flour mills on opposite banks of the Mississippi River. These two mills would grow to build a city, anchor a region, and change the milling industry forever.

Since its beginnings, General Mills has remained grounded in its values: championship brands, people, innovation, and performance. The company leads by example to make a positive difference in the lives of its consumers, employees, retail partners, shareholders, and communities.

Company of Champions

The quality of General Mills' consumer food products is second to none—hardworking, dedicated employees make sure of that. From teams at a dough plant in Inofita, Greece, to dieticians at the company's Bell Institute of Health and Nutrition in Minneapolis, General Mills innovates and produces consumer foods found in more than 100 countries on six continents.

General Mills' largest business division—U.S. Retail—earns yearly net sales of more than $7 billion. Three additional business divisions—Bakeries & Foodservice, International, and Joint Ventures—earn yearly net sales of more than $1 billion each.

The U.S. Retail business includes General Mills' Big G cereals, meal and baking products, yogurts, snacks, and organic products. Among the company's 100 leading U.S. brands are well-known favorites such as Wheaties, Cheerios, Betty Crocker, Pillsbury, Yoplait, Hamburger Helper, Gold Medal, and Bisquick.

The Bakeries & Foodservice business markets mixes and dough products to retail, supermarket, and wholesale bakeries. It also markets a variety of products to restaurants, cafeterias, convenience stores, and food-service distributors.

Around the globe, General Mills' International division markets products in more than 100 countries. Notable brands include Old El Paso, Green Giant, Pillsbury, and Häagen-Dazs, as well as local leaders such as Wanchai Ferry in China and Latina fresh pasta in Australia. These international markets are supported by offices and manufacturing facilities in more than 30 countries.

General Mills is involved in successful joint ventures, the largest of which is Cereal Partners Worldwide, an international joint venture with Nestlé. The company also markets 8th Continent soy milk through its joint venture with DuPont.

Community Champion

As a leader in philanthropy, General Mills is a champion for stronger communities. This company awards monetary grants through the General Mills Foundation to nonprofit organizations that are focused on education, youth nutrition and fitness, social services, and arts and culture. Founded in 1954, the General Mills Foundation has since contributed more than $330 million to such community efforts.

Beyond financial contributions, General Mills directly partners with inner-city neighborhoods in Minneapolis and nationwide; encourages and

supports employee volunteerism such as mentoring in school-based programs and building Habitat for Humanity homes; and is one of the largest contributors to America's Second Harvest food bank network.

General Mills also builds environmental stewardship into its business strategies. Areas of environmental focus include methods to continually evaluate the use of raw materials, fuels, and utilities in production systems; improve energy efficiency; reduce or eliminate negative environmental impacts; minimize waste and use of hazardous materials; and maximize the use of renewable resources.

Recognizing the results of these corporate practices, *Fortune* magazine named General Mills as one of the Most Admired Companies for four years running. This honor is one in a long list of honors that have been awarded to General Mills over the years, including the following 2005 recognitions:

- "100 Best Companies to Work For," *Fortune*;
- "Most Admired Companies," *Fortune*;
- "100 Best Corporate Citizens," *Business Ethics* magazine;
- "Top 50 Companies for Diversity," *DiversityInc* magazine.

Today, General Mills continues to build and maintain trust by focusing on champions—its brands, people, innovation, and performance. General Mills' steadfast dedication to consumers and its commitment to providing innovative new products have not only advanced the company's consistent growth but continue to direct its future—as one of the most trusted and respected food manufacturers in the world.

Above: From its first flour mill in Minneapolis to the most recent headquarters expansion, General Mills has a long history of launching products and brands that today span the globe.

Philanthropy and Culture

Profiles of Corporations and Organizations

The Minneapolis Foundation

Through The Minneapolis Foundation—one of the first community foundations created in the United States—Minnesotans support cultural and educational institutions as well as thousands of organizations that improve people's lives locally, nationally, and around the world.

This page: The Minneapolis Foundation has always supported organizations that provide children with an enriched experience of the world around them. The Wells Memorial House, an early foundation grantee, provided a safe space for neighborhood children to gather. Opposite page, left: Sponsored by The Minneapolis Foundation, Minnesota Meeting is the state's oldest and most prominent public affairs forum for exploring new ideas, educating leaders, and fostering civic discourse on critical issues. Opposite page, center: A student achievement and scholarship program, Destination 2010 is a Minneapolis Foundation multiyear initiative. The program is designed to improve student achievement, increase high school graduation rates, and advance educational reform. Opposite page, right: The Minneapolis Foundation helps raise community awareness through public education about issues such as racism and immigration.

The Twin Cities businessmen who created The Minneapolis Foundation in 1915 could not have foreseen the emergence of AIDS, the Internet, or urban sprawl. They did, however, recognize that community needs would change over time, and they established a way for Minnesotans to meet those changing needs through philanthropy.

Ninety Years of Minnesotans Making a Difference

The Minneapolis Foundation provides a convenient way for individuals, families, and businesses to create charitable funds and, through their contributions, to support nonprofit organizations in Minnesota, across the country, and around the world. Donors create funds at The Minneapolis Foundation for specific purposes—like scholarships or a favorite charity—or for the general benefit of the community.

Many Minnesotans also leave planned gifts and bequests through The Minneapolis Foundation. Whether they appoint their children and grandchildren or entrust The Minneapolis Foundation to carry on their philanthropy, hundreds of Minnesotans continue to make a lasting and positive difference in the community every day.

Creating a Philanthropic Model and Tradition

Prior to the creation of The Minneapolis Foundation, no local institution existed to manage, invest, and distribute charitable gifts to meet changing community needs and honor donors' wishes in perpetuity. Despite profound social needs at the turn of the century, the principal means of relief were religious charities (which were usually open only to members of the denomination), political patronage, or through direct appeal to wealthy individuals.

A community foundation represented a new model, since it was open to everyone. The Minneapolis Foundation was among the earliest community foundations in the country, and it offered all Twin Cities residents—of both vast and limited means—the opportunity to participate in building a common endowment to benefit the community forever.

Minnesotans have long been known for being generous, so it is not surprising that they embraced the community foundation concept from the start. Among The Minneapolis Foundation's early grant recipients were the Boy Scouts of America, The Salvation Army, settlement houses, Little Sisters of the Poor, and other agencies that provided direct services to the city's most disadvantaged residents.

Over time, as more government aid became available for social services, The Minneapolis Foundation's trustees began awarding grants for capital expenses and for "character-building institutions" such as museums and theaters, the Fort Snelling Park Association, and, later, the "new" public television channel—now Twin Cities Public Television.

Today, The Minneapolis Foundation sees the results of generations of giving—results that are evident throughout the community and the entire region. The Dunwoody Institute, the Washburn Child Guidance Center, Pillsbury Neighborhood Services, and many other respected community institutions exist today due in part or entirely to the gifts contributed by Minnesotans 10, 20, 50, and even 90 years ago.

Building a Community for Future Generations

The Minneapolis Foundation is also a catalyst for meeting ongoing and emerging community needs. The foundation's grant-making work, public awareness programs, community events, and special initiatives help bring Minnesotans together to identify, explore, and address some of the region's

greatest challenges and most pressing issues.

The Minneapolis Foundation supports efforts to tackle the root causes of poverty and injustice in order to serve the greatest number of people and make the broadest impact. Foundation donors complement that support with grants to direct-service programs, which provide food, shelter, and other assistance to individuals in need.

Through its public awareness campaigns and forums, The Minneapolis Foundation invites Minnesotans to participate in community-wide discussions about issues such as homelessness, immigration, and racism, as well as disparities in education and achievement. Minnesota Meeting, The Minneapolis Foundation's public affairs forum, draws together business leaders, community members, policy makers, and students to discuss issues and share ideas.

Minnesotans Will Continue to Make a Difference

Through their funds at The Minneapolis Foundation, people make a tangible difference in the lives of the state's residents—both during their lifetimes and through their legacies. A recent grant from the Emma B. Howe Memorial Foundation, established upon her death in 1984, will be used to create Teen Central, a space designed just for teenagers, in the new Minneapolis Central Library. Other donors include families, corporations, and individuals who contribute to thousands of nonprofits and cultural organizations each year.

It is hard to imagine what life in Minnesota will be like 100 years from now. Whatever may come, however, Minnesotans will continue to make a difference in this community and far beyond through their charitable giving.

Maybe you're just not sure what to make of all these new Minnesotans bringing in all these strange new cultures and customs.

But hey, have you ever really thought about lutefisk?

Surveys show that Americans have always believed earlier waves of immigrants were useful citizens, but that the newly arrived are somehow less desirable. The same holds true in Minnesota. Many people just a generation or two "off the boat" from Europe can't seem to find it in their hearts to welcome newcomers from Asia, Africa and elsewhere. They say they're too different. Different language, different color, different customs, different religion. Funny, we always thought being tolerant of other people's differences was one of those things that made Minnesota a great state to live in. Learn more about these new immigrants. Call us at 612-672-3869 and we'll send you our free booklet *Immigration in Minnesota*.

THE MINNEAPOLIS FOUNDATION

Professional and Business Services

Profiles of Corporations and Organizations

Lindquist & Vennum PLLP

Founded on the belief that practicing law and performing public service should go hand in hand, the law firm of Lindquist & Vennum PLLP has grown to become a dynamic force in both the metropolitan community and national legal circles.

Above: Leonard E. Lindquist, with partner Earl R. Larson, founded in 1946 the Minneapolis law firm that became Lindquist & Vennum PLLP. Above right: Minnesota governor Orville Freeman shares the stage with soon-to-be-president John F. Kennedy in Minneapolis in 1960. In the foreground are, from left, Minnesota U.S. senator and former mayor of Minneapolis Hubert H. Humphrey and Minnesota U.S. senator Eugene McCarthy.

The people associated with the law firm of Lindquist & Vennum PLLP have been a part of the fabric of Minneapolis life and business since the mid 1940s. Today, the firm is a thriving business-oriented general practice law firm with offices in Minneapolis and in Denver.

Growing Up with the City

Lindquist & Vennum was the creation of two Minneapolis attorneys who shared a philosophy about the practice of law: "Work hard for your clients and give back to the community in which you live." The firm has grown from a handful of attorneys to nearly 200 today. It has built strong regional business practices in the Upper Midwest and Rocky Mountain regions, and some of its practice areas, notably corporate finance, agribusiness, banking, and life sciences, have extensive national practices.

Lindquist & Vennum attorneys have achieved success for regional and national clients in noteworthy court cases and in important business enterprises and transactions. Through seasoned legal skill and diverse business experience, Lindquist & Vennum lawyers are personally engaged in helping their clients succeed.

The list of the firm's alumni reads like a who's who of notable leaders in Minneapolis and the nation: the longest serving mayor in the history of Minneapolis; a three-term governor of Minnesota and U.S. secretary of agriculture; a chief justice and several associate justices of the Minnesota Supreme Court, including the first African-American to serve on this court; one of the first women to make partner in a larger Minneapolis law firm; the first woman to hold a federal judgeship in Minnesota; the president of the American Civil Liberties Union (ACLU); and many others.

As well as being a force in public service, Lindquist & Vennum also has been uniquely active in community service and pro bono work in the Twin Cities throughout the firm's history. Service to the community involves numerous projects and ongoing volunteer opportunities, with a substantial part of that commitment focusing on providing uncompensated legal services to less fortunate members of society.

Lindquist & Vennum and Minneapolis have grown up together, maturing through the ups and downs of 50 years, well prepared for the challenges that this new century will bring.

Pro Bono and Community Service

With giving back to the community as one of the founding philosophies of the firm, Lindquist & Vennum is involved in charitable causes that cover a wide range of activities:

Law Firm Pro Bono Challenge

Lindquist & Vennum attorneys have participated in the Law Firm Pro Bono Challenge (formerly the ABA Law Firm Pro Bono Challenge) since 1995. In this effort, the nation's larger firms are challenged to contribute a percentage of their attorneys' billable hours to pro bono work and community service. Lindquist & Vennum attorneys have raised the bar and developed their own policy, which establishes an expectation that each partner, associate, and paralegal will participate in this challenge. Since 1997, Lindquist & Vennum has met and exceeded its goals and is one of only a few firms in the nation with 100 percent participation.

Pro Bono

Lindquist & Vennum lawyers provide pro bono services at outreach clinics throughout the Twin Cities, such as the

Division of Indian Works and the Ubah Somali East African Education Center, among many others. The firm's lawyers also participate in a wide variety of individual pro bono cases and major pro bono projects through organizations such as the Volunteer Lawyers Network.

Community Service

The firm supports the community in many ways, ranging from performing volunteer work to serving in leadership positions on the boards of nonprofit organizations to making financial contributions. Examples of the groups in which Lindquist & Vennum attorneys hold leadership positions are the Fund for Legal Aid Society, the Girl Scout Council of Greater Minneapolis, and Jewish Family and Children's Service of Minneapolis. The firm is also committed to the arts and has long been a supporter of the Tony Award®–winning Children's Theatre Company, the Minnesota Orchestra, and the Minneapolis Institute of Arts.

Winter Closet Foundation

Lindquist & Vennum's Winter Closet Foundation annually provides new

coats, hats, mittens, and boots to disadvantaged children in local schools and day care centers. Each year, Lindquist & Vennum raises

thousands of dollars in donations and distributes hundreds of coats, hats, and pairs of boots and mittens to locations that assist children.

Left: Angel Flight America (AFA) is the largest charitable air transportation organization in the world, representing more than 90 percent of all charitable flights in America. In 2004, AFA pilots flew 16,240 missions. AFA is a not-for-profit grassroots network of six regional, autonomous Angel Flight organizations plus Mercy Medical Airlift, covering North America, with a corps of more than 5,000 volunteer pilots who fly under the AFA banner. Lindquist & Vennum is a proud sponsor of AFA, providing free legal assistance and financial support for this vital service.

The Firm, Its People, and Its Character

The Minneapolis firms Lindquist, Magnuson & Glennon and Vennum, Newhall, Ackman & Goetz joined together in 1968 to form Lindquist & Vennum PLLP. Lindquist & Vennum has gained a well-deserved reputation for the quality of its attorneys, who work hard for their clients, go on to lives of public service, and willingly give of their time for pro bono work and community service.

The quality of people associated with the firm over its history exemplifies the philosophies of the firm and its founders: "Work hard for your clients and for your community." Here are just some of the people who contributed to the character of one of the state's stellar law firms:

Leonard E. Lindquist was a man of both compassion and a hard-nosed passion for the law. Early in his career, he worked for the Minnesota Railroad and Warehouse Commission, where he was charged with putting an end to the corrupt activities of local gangsters. He eventually drove the mobsters out of town, but not before he and his family had suffered threats and harassment. Lindquist returned to his own law practice in 1952 and successfully represented groups that wanted to organize unions, such as the Minnesota Nurses Association, the Honeywell Teamsters, and the National Football League Players Association. He also won a seat in the state legislature in 1954. Until his death in 2004, Lindquist remained involved in the charitable organizations he cared deeply about, such as Life's Missing Link, which operates Lindquist Apartments, providing housing and supportive services for youth at risk; and the Winter Closet Foundation.

Thomas Vennum was an adventurous spirit, heading off to China after graduating from Yale in 1923. He had gone with fellow Yale classmates to teach German, but was also caught up in the political turmoil of the day. A young Mao Zedong was beginning his own history-changing career as a revolutionary during this period. On Vennum's return to the United States, he pursued his law degree and began practicing in Minneapolis. He cared a great deal about his community and became the first president of the Minneapolis Junior Association of Commerce (J.A.C.), the precursor to the Minneapolis Junior Chamber of Commerce. In 1968, Vennum and Leonard Lindquist joined forces, resulting in the firm of Lindquist & Vennum.

Louise Herou Saunders was a groundbreaker for women in Minnesota in many ways. As a student, she was the only female on the University of Minnesota Law School's *Minnesota Law Review*; she was the first woman to clerk for a Minnesota Supreme Court justice; and after she joined the Lindquist firm in 1951 she became one of the first female partners in a larger Minneapolis law firm. In 1961, she left Lindquist & Vennum to care for her ailing husband, Charles Saunders, who owned the landmark Minneapolis restaurant Charlie's Café Exceptionale. She took over management of the restaurant after her husband's death and ran the well-known eatery for many years. She also was the first, and until 2004 the only, woman to have served as president of the Minneapolis Downtown Council.

Orville Freeman was one of Minnesota's most respected political figures. Freeman joined the Lindquist firm right out of law school in 1946 and remained with the firm until 1954, when he was elected governor of Minnesota, a post he held for three consecutive terms. Governor Freeman had the distinction of nominating John F. Kennedy for president at the 1960 Democratic National Convention.

When Kennedy was elected later that year, Freeman was appointed U.S. secretary of agriculture and continued in the post for eight years. Freeman dedicated his legal and political careers to global economic growth, often lecturing on the importance of agriculture in a world of ever-changing needs.

Judge Earl R. Larson was Lindquist's partner in the law firm they created in 1946. The two had attended the University of Minnesota Law School together and wanted to create a law firm rooted in the

beliefs that their law school mentor, Dean Everett Fraser, had instilled in them: tie together the practice of law with the interests of the community

and public service. Larson worked in private practice until 1961, when he was appointed to the position of U.S. District Court judge for the District of Minnesota. He remained in this post until he retired in 1977 with senior status. During his judicial tenure, Larson made a number of rulings in landmark cases. He was also the first president of the Minnesota branch of the ACLU, which was formed in 1952, and he served as chair of the Minnesota Human Rights Commission. Larson established the Earl R. Larson Chair in Civil Rights and Civil Liberties Law at the University of Minnesota Law School in 1993. The honor recognizes excellent teaching in these areas.

Left: Orville Freeman was a three-term governor of Minnesota and served as U.S. secretary of agriculture for eight years. He dedicated his legal and political careers to global economic growth and the importance of agriculture. Below left: Judge Earl R. Larson became a distinguished U.S. District Court judge for the District of Minnesota. He was also noted as a leader in civil rights affairs, for which he established a chair at the University of Minnesota Law School. Far left: Lindquist & Vennum attorney Louise Herou Saunders was the only female on the *Minnesota Law Review* and the first woman to clerk for a Minnesota Supreme Court justice. At Lindquist & Vennum, she became one of the first female partners in a large Minneapolis law firm.

Lindquist & Vennum PLLP

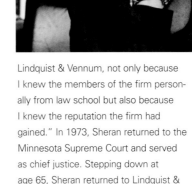

Above: Robert Sheran served in the state legislature and as Minnesota Supreme Court chief justice. Top right: Diana Murphy began her legal career with the firm and now serves on the U.S. Court of Appeals for the Eighth Circuit. Right: Alan Page is a Minnesota Supreme Court justice. He is the first African-American to serve on the Minnesota Supreme Court. Far right: Nadine Strossen is a professor of law at New York Law School and president of the American Civil Liberties Union (ACLU).

Robert F. Kennedy. In 1963, Loevinger became commissioner of the Federal Communications Commission, where he developed the idea of the 911 universal emergency telephone system.

Larry Ackman and Norman Newhall were also early partners of the firm. Both earned reputations as consummate business attorneys. Ackman served as president of the Minneapolis Club and was active on the boards of directors of many organizations, including the Minneapolis Institute of Arts and the Citizens League. Among Newhall's accomplishments was his work with the Minneapolis Area Chapter of the American Red Cross in creating (during World War II) one of the area's first blood banks. That effort would eventually lead to the formation of Memorial Blood Centers, which now collects more than 100,000 units of blood per year and serves 36 hospitals in the region.

Dean Fraser's son Donald M. Fraser joined the firm in 1946 before launching a career in public service that would culminate in a tenure as the longest serving mayor of Minneapolis. That same year, Lee Loevinger became a partner in the firm, practicing until 1960, when he was appointed to the Minnesota Supreme Court. Within a year, Loevinger was called to Washington to head the antitrust division of the U.S. Department of Justice under Attorney General

Robert Sheran joined Lindquist & Vennum in 1970. Previously, he served two terms in the state legislature (1947 and 1949) and was appointed by Governor Elmer L. Anderson to the Minnesota Supreme Court in 1963 and elected to a six-year term in 1964. At the end of his term, Sheran decided to return to private practice. "The only firm I thought of applying to was

Lindquist & Vennum, not only because I knew the members of the firm personally from law school but also because I knew the reputation the firm had gained." In 1973, Sheran returned to the Minnesota Supreme Court and served as chief justice. Stepping down at age 65, Sheran returned to Lindquist & Vennum until his retirement in 1991.

Gerald Magnuson, who was responsible for bringing noted trial attorney Ed Glennon into the firm, worked with law school classmate and friend Melvin Orenstein to merge the firms of Lindquist, Magnuson & Glennon and Vennum, Newhall, Ackman & Goetz in 1968. Magnuson exemplified the spirit of Lindquist & Vennum, serving as director of the Fund for the Legal Aid Society. He has been honored for his years of community leadership, including assisting in the establishment of a program to help support legal services for vulnerable Minnesota citizens.

Diana Murphy joined Lindquist & Vennum immediately after law school

in 1974. She spent two years with the firm before being appointed by Minnesota governor Wendell Anderson to the municipal bench. Murphy was appointed to the U.S. District Court for the District of Minnesota by President Carter in 1980 and now serves on the U.S. Court of Appeals for the Eighth Circuit. Murphy is the first woman to hold a federal judgeship in Minnesota.

Alan Page played professional football for the Minnesota Vikings at the same time that he attended the University of Minnesota Law School, graduating in 1978. He joined Lindquist & Vennum in 1979 and remained with the firm until 1984, when he assumed a series of positions with the state of Minnesota. He was special assistant attorney general and assistant attorney general and ultimately won election to the Minnesota Supreme Court. Page is the first African-American to serve on this court.

Nadine Strossen started her legal career at the firm before heading to New York to practice and teach law.

She joined the ACLU's national board of directors in 1983 and later became the organization's first female national president.

The Lindquist & Vennum Practice Today

From the earliest days of Lindquist & Vennum, business law has been the bedrock of the firm, and it remains so today. For example, the firm is consistently among the top law firms in the Upper Midwest selected to represent publicly held companies. The nature of the firm's practices is constantly evolving to keep pace with the changing needs of the business community.

Corporate and Business

Lindquist & Vennum attorneys are experienced in representing a wide array of businesses and are best known for their work on complex acquisition and financing transactions. Clients include many of the region's leading publicly held manufacturing, technology, medical device, and communications enterprises. The firm also represents a large number of closely held companies and has extensive knowledge and experience in assisting emerging companies with their special needs, particularly financing methods and sources.

Financial Institutions

From 2000 through 2005, the financial institutions attorneys of Lindquist & Vennum have represented more institutions in the firm's Federal Reserve District in mergers and acquisitions than any other law firm, placing Lindquist & Vennum among the leading firms in this practice nationally. This group provides a full range of services to the financial institutions industry, serving clients representative of the largest and smallest members of the industry.

Agribusiness and Cooperatives

Lindquist & Vennum has represented agricultural producers since 1946, when Orville Freeman began his practice with the firm. Today, the firm is recognized nationally as a leader in representing agribusinesses and cooperatives. It assists traditional agribusiness clients while also helping to develop and shape the value-added movement in agriculture created by producers who seek to gain new markets for their commodities through ownership of processing and distribution facilities.

Life Sciences

Life sciences attorneys provide experienced legal services to clients in the health care, pharmaceutical, biotechnology, and medical device industries. Clients range from start-up ventures to

mature, publicly traded companies. The group works with clients in the areas of private capital, venture finance, and public offerings; distribution and licensing; intellectual property protection; noncompetition; confidentiality and employment matters; health plans and benefits; regulatory matters; and litigation.

Litigation

Lindquist & Vennum litigators represent clients of all sizes in trials, arbitrations, and appeals in disputes ranging from multimillion-dollar commercial conflicts to personal legal matters. Working in specialized areas, attorneys provide litigation services in securities, antitrust and trade regulation, white collar crime, employment and labor law, intellectual property, environmental law, commercial matters, insurance coverage, and shareholder disputes.

Individuals

The firm provides an extensive array of services to individuals, including trusts and estate planning and financially complex family matters involving all types of assets, business and partnership interests, tax concerns, and complicated compensation and income structures.

Values

The history of Lindquist & Vennum is tightly intertwined with the history of Minneapolis. The firm has grown and prospered for more than 50 years, as has the city, but it has never lost sight of the values that, its members believe, characterize life in Minneapolis: hard work, honesty, generosity, and a sense of commitment to community, values that make living and working in Minneapolis a true gift.

Above: The thriving city of Minneapolis has been home to the law firm of Lindquist & Vennum since the mid 1940s.

Ellerbe Becket, Inc.

Iconic in its stature and creations, this top-ranked leader in architecture, engineering, and construction is world recognized for its expertise in designing nearly every major building type—from health-science and sports facilities and campuses to general buildings and mixed-use complexes—in all 50 states and more than 20 countries.

Right: An Ellerbe Becket client since 1914, the Mayo Clinic in Rochester, Minnesota, has continually evolved to meet the challenges of growth and ever-changing health care delivery and patient needs. The clinic's Gonda Building, designed by Ellerbe Becket in collaboration with Cesar Pelli & Associates, is a highly flexible structure that allows for expansion, redesign, and accommodation of evolving technology advances and biomedical discoveries, making the facilities ready to support the next 100 years of medical advances.

For Ellerbe Becket, "Success without limits" is more than a marketing catchphrase—it is the foundation upon which the firm's vision and decades-strong legacy of significant projects are based. Founded in 1909 and head-quartered in Minneapolis, Minnesota, Ellerbe Becket is an integrated firm that provides expertise in architecture; interior design; mechanical, electrical, and structural engineering; and construction to clients worldwide.

For nearly a century, Ellerbe Becket employees have worked for their clients' success in an environment that demands specialty knowledge, collaboration, and innovation. These values drive the firm to deliver high quality buildings that incorporate ingenious solutions to clients' challenges. Each project is approached with a spirit of collaboration, resulting in inspired design that accommodates growth and change while positively impacting clients' business outcomes.

World Leader in Health Facilities

A pioneer in design for health care projects, Ellerbe Becket has led the planning, design, and construction of countless facilities that support healing.

One such project is the Leslie & Susan Gonda Building, the centerpiece of Mayo Clinic's Rochester, Minnesota, campus. The building provides a welcoming entrance to the storied institution while also ushering in a new level of patient care. The proximity of diagnostic and treatment facilities enables teams of specialists to collaborate in centers of care—which translates into greater convenience and a more streamlined patient experience. This integration of facilities is one of the most sophisticated of its kind. A new standard of health care efficiency and flexibility is set with the Gonda Building—placing the facility in the forefront of current thinking in health care design.

Halfway around the world, Yonsei University Medical Center's New Severance Hospital celebrated its grand opening in spring 2005, becoming the most significant new health care facility in Seoul, South Korea. The 1,006-bed hospital weaves the best of the West's health care design expertise into an appropriate Korean cultural context.

Innovative Designs for Sports

Ellerbe Becket is well-known as a world leader in multipurpose arena and

stadium design. Its sports portfolio encompasses professional and collegiate facilities, both domestic and international, including Lambeau Field in Green Bay, Wisconsin; Centennial Olympic Stadium in Atlanta, Georgia; Guangdong Olympic Stadium in Guangzhou, China; Bank One Ballpark in Phoenix, Arizona; and Autzen Stadium at the University of Oregon, in Eugene, Oregon.

Notably, the Seattle Seahawks' Qwest Field—an icon for the city—incorporates many green-design features. Qwest Field was built on the site of the former Seattle Kingdome, and its design incorporates 90 percent reused

or recycled materials from the imploded facility. The reuse/recycling efforts saved the city of Seattle millions of dollars in transporting material off-site, which subsequently saved countless gallons of fuel, reduced vehicle emissions, and avoided landfill costs. More importantly, these efforts helped to maintain the natural environment of Washington state.

Designs Support Client Success

Ellerbe Becket has also earned accolades for its design of advanced learning environments. The firm's impressive roster of clients includes the University of Minnesota; Georgetown University; Yale University; and the

University of California, Berkeley. In 2006, the Ellerbe Becket–designed Rady School of Management at the University of California, San Diego will be opened. Situated in a globally recognized hotbed of innovation, the business school is uniquely poised to offer access to both cutting-edge research and a fully engaged San Diego business community.

Target Corporation is among the many organizations that have sought Ellerbe Becket's expertise in the design of workplace environments. A primary function of the design for this company's headquarters, which is located in Minneapolis, is to promote communication and a sense of community while reinforcing the Target brand. At the same time, the facility provides an efficient, functional, and flexible environment that is designed to support Target's business objectives well into the future.

The design for Energy Management Center, a new, state-of-the-art control center for City Public Service (CPS), San Antonio, Texas's natural gas and

electricity provider, responds to unique client goals: to be highly secure, reliable, efficient, and adaptable. In a crisis situation, the CPS staff could be required to remain on duty for 24 or more consecutive hours, so it is also important that the space be comfortable for employees and provide them with the facilities necessary to perform their jobs. The complex includes an adjacent training center that is available for use by both CPS employees and the community.

Building upon CPS's legacy of harnessing alternative energy resources, Ellerbe Becket designed a sophisticated system for collecting rainwater and water from cooling towers for use in landscape irrigation. A photovoltaic system enables the training center to be lighted using solar power. In a display at the training center, alternative energy performance is tracked, showing the amount of water collected and used, how much solar power is generated, and describing other sustainable aspects of the building, such as environmentally friendly surface finishes and individual temperature controls.

Left: The National Football League Seattle Seahawks' home in the city's historic Pioneer Square district provides fans with dramatic views of the downtown skyline, Puget Sound, and snow-capped mountains, creating a unique Seattle experience. In a city famous for rain, 70 percent of fans are protected from the elements by the stadium's distinctive 1.4 million-pound roof, which spans 720 feet and features the largest post-tensioned arches in the United States.
Far left: Over its 96-year history, Ellerbe Becket has made significant contributions to the Minneapolis built environment. Shown here on the city's famed Nicollet Mall is a four-building, three-block development (designed by Ellerbe Becket and developed and constructed by Ryan Companies US, Inc.) featuring, from left, Target Corporation headquarters; 900 Nicollet, a mixed-use building; and US Bancorp Center. The development has transformed the south end of the mall and brought a new vitality to Minneapolis.

Allen Interactions Inc.

This custom e-learning development group, one of the world's most influential, creates fascinating e-learning experiences—engaging, challenging, and fun experiences—that people use every day to improve the way they work.

Its client list would impress even the biggest technology companies. Its corporate headquarters in the Minneapolis–St. Paul suburb of Mendota Heights brings together three award-winning studios. And Fortune 1000 clients keep lining up. No wonder the people at Allen Interactions Inc. remain excited about their future in e-learning.

"We understand changing behavior through interactive events," says Allen Interactions founder, chairman, and CEO Michael W. Allen, Ph.D. "We understand multimedia, learning, and behavior. By putting this understanding to work, we have seen what quality e-learning applications can do for people and their organizations. Our e-learning training motivates. It inspires. It helps build meaningful business results."

Live Local, Think Global

Allen Interactions came into being because another Minnesota company, Control Data Corporation, made Allen an offer he could not refuse—to leave his research and development post at The Ohio State University and take a corporate job to identify how computer technology can help people learn faster and more easily.

Control Data had invested millions of dollars in a system that used computers to teach, and it wanted someone like Allen, with a doctorate in educational psychology and demonstrated results working with computers in education, to move this concept from the laboratory to the business world. Upon arriving in Minnesota, Allen was charged with turning complex mainframe code into software that enabled the computer to serve as a teacher.

One result of Allen's work was Authorware®, a powerful software program that simplifies the development of instructional interactions. When Control Data ran into difficulties and narrowed its business focus, Allen worked to separate the program from its parent, and in 1987 he formed Minneapolis-based Authorware, Inc. He invested personally in refining the technology and raised venture capital to take the product to market.

In 1992, Authorware merged with the San Francisco animation software and 3-D imagery company Macromind-ParaComp to form Macromedia, Inc., which soon became a public company, making many people, including Allen, financially independent. Rather than move to San Francisco, Allen decided to stay in his adopted Minnesota home and retire. He was 46 years old.

Aim for 'A-Ha' Experiences

The retirement was short-lived. In 1993, Allen became disappointed with the quality of instruction being developed with the technology he had pioneered. Gathering a few of the people who had helped him build Macromedia, he started Allen Interactions Inc. This company would develop training experiences—complete with interactive stories and lively simulations that would help people improve the way they work—with a focus on doing, not just knowing. These e-learning experiences would meet Allen's three criteria for effective instruction: they would be memorable, meaningful, and motivational. "All three criteria are critical, or you should not even bother," says Allen. "If you really want your security personnel to perform, for example, they need to actively participate in a realistic hands-on simulation."

When Allen Interactions was hired by automaker DaimlerChrysler to teach statistical process control to its engineers, it did away with boredom by creating an animated machine designed to stamp out plastic fish of uniform size. Sometimes the manufactured fish varied in size, and learners had to figure out why and correct the problem. By temporarily removing automotive personnel from their familiar world, the Allen Interactions program helped them quickly understand quality-control principles and apply them.

"A lot of vendors told us what they could achieve with multimedia, but they could not show us applications that matched their descriptions," says Mike Groszko, manager of the DaimlerChrysler Quality Institute. "The simulations that Allen Interactions used were more sophisticated and a lot closer to the real problem-solving that people would be doing on the job. Learners were able to internalize complex concepts as opposed to having a superficial understanding or a memorized definition. By

the time they were done, they had had an 'A-ha' experience."

Experience. The Difference.

More than a decade after its founding, Allen Interactions continues to provide interactive multimedia consulting and custom-developed e-learning to meet business needs, as well as specialized training for organizations that want to improve internal performance. The landmark *Michael Allen's Guide to e-Learning* reigns as a best-selling e-learning book on Amazon.com and continually receives industry awards and client accolades.

Allen Interactions has won several Excellence in Learning awards from e-learning authority Brandon-Hall.com, and it received another in 2004. The award, which recognizes outstanding examples of innovative learning, cited an Allen Interactions application developed for a St. Paul–based Fortune 500 client to replace some of the client's traditional classroom training programs and augment others. While reducing overall training costs, the action-oriented program moved executive leaders to think more productively about business

solutions and their potential impact on the corporate culture.

"We were excited and honored to receive this prestigious award again," says R. John Welsh, vice president of sales and marketing for Allen Interactions. "This project is a powerful example of how e-learning can deliver incremental benefits to the bottom line. It was a fun project, a challenging project, and a project our studios delivered with great creativity."

Clients of Allen Interactions value its strong e-learning products. One customer, Ecolab Inc., used an Allen Interactions training tool to increase sales. After a yearlong study, the program proved to be a success, with an impressive 119 percent increase in new business by Ecolab sales professionals who had taken part in the training over those who had not.

Allen Interactions is regarded by many as the premier e-learning

company in the nation. Sales in 2004 increased by more than 50 percent over the previous year, and the company projects continued growth on this scale. "We did some soul searching about whether to be a small company or move up," Allen says, "and we decided to grow. We want to spread our influence as widely as possible to save every learner we can from all the boring e-learning programs that, instead, could be high-impact, success-generating events."

Top left: An "Allen Interaction" results in a 119 percent sales increase. Top right: Sales professionals and designers share a creative space at the Allen Interactions Minnesota facility. Above left: Allen Interactions operates a local office in Mendota Heights. Above right: Security training is guided with hands-on simulations—a focus on *doing*, not just knowing. Center: The "No Boring e-learning" symbol represents Allen Interactions' belief that e-learning can and should be both fun and effective.

G&K Services

With a rich 100-plus-year history of service to Minneapolis, G&K Services continues to meet the needs of the community, offering innovative, custom-branded, high quality apparel and merchandise that enhance image and safety in the workplace.

Above: Richard M. Fink serves as chairman of the board for G&K Services. Right: Founded in 1903 by Alexander and Allen Morris Gross in the Twin Cities, Gross Brothers Minneapolis Dye House introduced door-to-door laundry pick-up and delivery service via horse and buggy in 1910. The company later became part of G&K Services, which currently has more than 9,000 employees and processes more than 18 million garments each week from over 140 locations.

Located in the Minneapolis metropolitan area, G&K Services is a North American market leader in branded identity apparel programs and facility services. Known for enhancing image and safety in the workplace through innovation, the company attributes its reputation to its founding principles.

Hard work and a commitment to customer satisfaction formed the foundation for Gross & Kronick Dyers and Cleaners (formerly named Twin City Steam Dye Works). The company was established in 1902 in the Twin Cities by two sets of brothers— Alexander and Allen Morris Gross, and Charles and Maurice Kronick. The following year, the partners divided along family lines, forming separate businesses in the Twin Cities: Kronicks French Dry Cleaners and Dyers; and Gross Brothers Minneapolis Dye House.

The friendly competitors courted the region's elite families, such as the Pillsburys, the Daytons, and the

Washburns. They expertly cared for the era's extravagant fashions, particularly women's dresses made of tulle, chiffon, silk, and satin with brocade trims and ornamented with pearls, beads, lace, and crochet.

In 1910, Gross Brothers took customer service to a higher level by introducing door-to-door laundry pick-up and delivery service. The company's route sales representatives traveled via horse and buggy to the area's most distinguished families and businesses, catering to customers' laundering needs.

By 1935, the Kronicks' company had suffered from the Great Depression. That year, the family sold its business to the Gross brothers, who had already recruited additional family members I. D. Fink (Alexander's son-in-law) and Leo Gross (Allen Morris's son). Throughout the years, more family members would join the business.

In 1943, the company changed its name to G&K. During World War II, the company serviced uniforms for all branches of the armed forces. G&K also instituted a diaper service in 1948.

G&K greeted the midcentury by initiating a pick-up and delivery laundry service for Minnesota's college students, charging 99 cents for eight pounds of clean clothes and linens. G&K's "Blue Bundle" deliveries, named for blue packaging, became a familiar sight in college dormitories.

During the 1950s, G&K produced one of television's first infomercials by sponsoring a show called *Masterpiece Theatre*. During commercial breaks, G&K then-president I. D. Fink educated viewers about laundering and dry-cleaning techniques used by his company. The result was a boom in business—and local celebrity for Fink. Also during the 1950s, G&K entered the uniform rental market.

Success marked the 1960s as well, when G&K opened a chain of drive-in cleaners. In 1969, G&K became a public company (NASDAQ: GKSRA).

The following decade, as home washing and drying machines became commonplace, the company shifted its focus more to uniform sales and rentals. The change invited opportunities for nationwide expansion, which continues to be a company strategy today.

During the 1990s, G&K increased its business reach by acquiring Work Wear of Canada, a major uniform-rental company in eastern Canada. The move allowed G&K to add 20 locations in that country. Further expansion occurred in 1997, when the company acquired 29 National Linen Service processing facilities and related branches.

In 2002, G&K Services celebrated its 100-year anniversary, continuing to

focus on its commitment to quality, service, and innovation. The company now serves more than 160,000 customers—in a broad range of market segments—throughout the United States and Canada. Each day, more than one million workers wear uniforms supplied by the company.

With President and CEO Richard Marcantonio at the helm, G&K is committed to growth by using the best technology in garment care and hygiene solutions and by constantly adapting to the changing workforce in North America.

The company's market-leading services include:

G&K Apparel Rental Services, which provides branded identity apparel including uniforms, executive apparel, and corporate casual wear. All items can be customized to clients' image, safety, and security needs;

G&K TeamWear®, which provides companies with the ability to purchase and/or custom design apparel to boost customers' brand image and identity;

G&K First Step® Facility Services, which enhances customers' image, safety, and hygiene in the workplace with its selection of branded floor coverings, restroom solutions, and dust-control products;

G&K Cleanroom, which offers state-of-the-art technology for cleanroom garments and process-control services for high-tech industry needs;

And G&K ProSura™ Food Safety Solutions, which offers a full line of garments, personal protective equipment,

and facility products and services. ProSura features G&K's unique patent-pending Sanitation Standard Operating Procedures (SSOPs), designed to minimize the risk of cross-contamination in food processing and handling.

The company's quality services, coupled with more than 9,000 committed employees (with approximately 1,000 employees in Minnesota) and a savvy and committed leadership team, ensure G&K's future success—in the next year, the next decade, and the next 100 years.

Left: Richard Marcantonio serves as president and CEO of G&K Services. Above: For more than 100 years, G&K has helped companies throughout North America enhance their image and safety in the workplace through innovation.

Personnel Decisions International

This global management and human resources consulting firm uses a systematic approach to help each client organization achieve a genuine leadership advantage with the confidence that its current and future leaders are distinctively strong in its field, resulting in sustained superior organizational performance.

In 1967, Lowell Hellervik, then a doctoral candidate in organizational and counseling psychology at the University of Minnesota, a top-ranked psychology institution, joined Marvin Dunnette, Ph.D., at a fledgling consulting company. From a tiny office in the Foshay Tower in Minneapolis, the two set out to determine whether they could improve the performance of organizations by drawing a link between their training in behavioral science and the needs of businesses.

Hellervik quickly completed his Ph.D. and became the driving force behind their firm, Personnel Decisions, Inc., now Personnel Decisions International (PDI). In the ensuing decades PDI has touched the lives of hundreds of thousands of leaders and positively impacted the performance of hundreds of well-known organizations. Today the company has operations on five continents, and Hellervik, chairman and CEO, has endowed two and one-half chairs at his alma mater. PDI has fulfilled Hellervik's prediction that "PDI will become what its people become." This is its story.

The Firm

PDI began by helping local businesses make better decisions about people. Today, as a global human resources consulting firm, PDI has distinctive expertise in building leadership talent that provides real competitive advantage. Hundreds of PDI team members serve clients who represent the majority of the world's top firms, and in the process they have reshaped an industry. PDI's success and its focus on where to make a difference are the products of decades of measurement, learning, and innovation. At the heart of the company's success is the passion and energy of PDI consulting experts who continue to pursue the founders' original quest to link the art and science of human behavior with business needs to help individuals and organizations meet their goals and achieve enduring success.

The PDI Advantage

PDI offers its clients the benefits of:

- a large, proprietary database of information on global leaders, covering a full spectrum of leadership roles, challenges, and measures;
- nine specialty practice areas that consistently define industry standards in linking leadership talent to business objectives;
- 27 full-service offices in 15 countries;
- 250 consultants who extend thought leadership on leadership talent topics;
- 600-plus dedicated team members who provide a local resource in supporting the work of PDI and its clients.

The Work

The rigors of scientific inquiry, research, and measurement serve as a foundation for PDI consultants, helping them to advance their expertise and lift their recommendations to the highest level of predictive validity in the industry. Their approaches have produced some of the world's most detailed understanding of leadership—its roles, challenges, and transitions—and have created the metrics and means to identify, develop, and deploy successful leaders.

PDI's work has evolved from the impact of individual leader decisions to the impact of whole pools of organizational talent. Along the way, PDI has added new capabilities to improve human resources effectiveness, develop human resources strategy, better execute business strategy, and affect top-line growth.

The secret of PDI's success, however, lies not only in the data obtained or the tools used, but in the innovative ways that PDI team members connect with their clients. They convert understanding into insight and then into new, practical constructs that can be applied by leaders of organizations. As one client says, "PDI rolls up its sleeves and gets the job done." This hands-on approach has produced a framework for isolating, measuring, and blending critical factors such as an individual's performance in a current job, readiness for a substantially new role, long-term potential, and ability to fit and thrive within an existing culture and set of expectations. Today, PDI consultants use these constructs not only to define, measure, and develop individual leaders, but also to select and develop entire leadership pools—in essence, to build the talent management DNA that organizations require for sustained success.

The Team

Clients are at the root of PDI's reputation for gaining insight, creating innovation, and making an impact. Ever curious and passionate about what they do, PDI team members value growth, and they grow personally and professionally by doing work that makes a difference for clients and contributes to clients' success. PDI consultants work in partnership with their clients to build effective leadership and talent development processes and enable them to consistently make more effective decisions about leaders and about leaders' development. Whether PDI consultants are studying the context of a client's business, exploring options, applying PDI data and methods, determining how to best meet a client's business needs, or sharing expertise, they are expert partners in helping to identify, develop, and deploy the kind of superior leaders that clients need in order to gain a genuine business advantage.

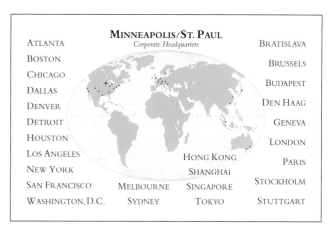

MINNEAPOLIS/St. PAUL *Corporate Headquarters*		
ATLANTA		BRATISLAVA
BOSTON		BRUSSELS
CHICAGO		BUDAPEST
DALLAS		DEN HAAG
DENVER		GENEVA
DETROIT		LONDON
HOUSTON	HONG KONG	PARIS
LOS ANGELES	SHANGHAI	
NEW YORK		STOCKHOLM
SAN FRANCISCO	MELBOURNE SINGAPORE	STUTTGART
WASHINGTON, D.C.	SYDNEY TOKYO	

PDI Leadership

In the decades since its inception, PDI has achieved many firsts as it has expanded and built its core capabilities. PDI was the first to

—develop a framework that an organization can use to create a competitive advantage through its choice of leaders; namely, a method of using performance predictions to improve decision making in choosing leaders in order to sustain improved organizational performance;

—build a complete set of assessment processes for all primary leadership transitions and roles to ensure a pipeline of leaders;

—provide a simulation-based, public assessment center for leader selection;

—develop a center where leadership development can be custom designed;

—use executive coaching as part of its leadership development process;

—create a comprehensive framework and practical tools to help human resources personnel become partners in strategic thinking;

—design a 360-degree feedback tool that includes embedded suggestion for leadership development;

—publish a book of development suggestions for executives called the *Successful Executive's Handbook*; and

—publish a book of development suggestions for managers called the *Successful Manager's Handbook,* now with more than one million copies in print.

PDI Clientele

PDI's client organizations are among the world's top firms, including:

80 percent of the *Fortune* 100 (U.S.);

75 percent of the *Forbes* Global 100;

70 percent of the *BusinessWeek* Top 100 Brands (Global);

25 percent of the *Forbes* Global 2000.

Parker Durrant International

Parker Durrant International, headquartered in Minneapolis, is the worldwide division of Durrant and is engaged in the design and construction of numerous master plans and international high-rise and mixed-use projects, offering clients local access and global reach.

When it is completed, the Lotte World II mixed-use tower in Busan, South Korea, will be among the tallest buildings in the world, climbing to over a quarter of a mile. It will be a 107-story facility housing offices, hotels, and entertainment and retail establishments and is projected for completion in 2010. Across the globe in Minneapolis, Stephan Huh, FAIA, Gary Mahaffey, FAIA, Keun Heung Lee, KIA, and the project team see to the designs, plans, and budgets for the tower. Huh is the chairman of Parker Durrant International (PDI), the firm behind the building's design and engineering.

PDI, a division of Durrant in Minneapolis, provides architecture, engineering, planning, interior design, and project-delivery services for an international clientele. Its financial arm, Durrant Capital Resources (DCR), works with clients in procuring the funding for new facilities.

With a mission to be involved in the design and construction of an increasing number of global projects, PDI works with clients in South Korea, Japan, Taiwan, Vietnam, China, Russia, the Philippines, and other countries. Among its many completed projects in South Korea are major convention centers in Daegu and Busan and a luxury housing complex in Seoul. In China, a three-million-square-foot retail, hotel, housing, and entertainment complex in Dalian was opened recently to much local acclaim.

The firm is sensitive to the need for combining its own skills with those of the international community. PDI takes care in determining a client's needs and in maintaining an awareness of the local cultural and political values throughout a project. The PDI staff includes employees from many countries, including South Korea, Malaysia, China, Russia, Armenia, and Tunisia, as well as the United States.

PDI has won numerous international design competitions and has received more than 100 design awards. Its projects have been recognized not only for their aesthetics but also for program execution, function, innovative use of materials, energy conservation, and accessibility. Among its accolades are awards from the Asian Habitat Society for excellence in the design of housing projects in Choon Chun and Seoul, South Korea.

Today, PDI continues to expand its presence in South Korea, Japan, China, Russia, Taiwan, and Vietnam, leveraging its high-rise and mixed-use facilities design expertise in the corporate and government sectors.

Far right: Among the large-scale multiuse projects designed by Parker Durrant International (PDI) is Lotte World II tower in the city of Busan, South Korea. The landmark building will reach skyward to 107 stories upon completion, scheduled for 2010. Near right: For the United States Embassy in Santiago, Chile, PDI created a structure of high quality that fulfills the needs of a challenging site, advanced security technologies, and cost-effective design. Stately interiors welcome world visitors.

Durrant

This longtime Minneapolis firm, born out of The Leonard Parker Associates, offers comprehensive architectural, interior design, engineering, and project-delivery expertise, serving clients in the Twin Cities and all of Minnesota, throughout the United States, and, through its international division, around the globe.

"Seeking Excellence in Everything We Do" expresses the level of commitment and quality that Durrant delivers to its clients.

Durrant is a multidisciplinary firm that offers architectural, engineering, planning, project-delivery, financing, and interior design services for clients in the private and public sectors. The firm operates through its Minneapolis headquarters, its network of 12 other Durrant offices nationwide, and its international division, providing clients across the country and around the globe with local access to Durrant services. The firm was founded in 1957 in Minneapolis by Leonard S. Parker as The Leonard Parker Associates.

In 1999 The Leonard Parker Associates merged with The Durrant Group, which provides architectural, interior design, project-delivery, engineering, and financing services. The merger enabled both entities to expand their reach. Durrant today has over 330 professionals assisting clients through its 12 offices across the Midwest and the West, in

Minnesota, Illinois, Wisconsin, Missouri, Iowa, Colorado, Arizona, and Hawaii.

A primary focus of Durrant is the role of architecture in the public sector. It has successfully completed more than 35 major civic projects, including libraries, justice buildings, and cultural facilities, bringing an individual approach to each design that incorporates the uniqueness and vitality of its surroundings. Over its history, the firm has made an impact on the quality and character of the Twin Cities through its work in both new construction and renovation. It is noted for producing buildings that are at once aesthetically distinguished

as well as highly functional and environmentally responsive.

Numerous awards have been received by Durrant, including a recent Historic Preservation Honorable Mention from the American Society of Interior Designers, for Temple Israel in Minneapolis; an Honor Award from the American Institute of Architects–Minnesota, for development of the Inver Glen Library in Inver Grove Heights, Minnesota; and an International Illumination Design Award from the Illuminating Engineering Society of North America, for design expertise for the auditorium of the

Minneapolis Convention Center. In 2004, the firm was included on *Engineering News-Record*'s list of the nation's top 500 engineering design firms.

Working through the Durrant Foundation, a not-for-profit organization, Durrant provides scholarships and internships for students in the fields of architecture, engineering, interior design, and construction management.

Durrant strives "to create architecture of enduring value in which we, our clients, and the community can take great pride."

Above left: For the Minnesota Judicial Building, prominently located adjacent to the Minnesota state capitol in downtown Saint Paul, Durrant provided a renovation and addition that preserves the historic existing building. Far left: For the Minnesota Department of Public Safety in Saint Paul, Durrant created a state-of-the-art forensic laboratory and office space.

Above: Designed by Elness Swenson Graham Architects Inc., the Excelsior & Grand community is a unique representation of a new mixed-use, downtown-environment concept that is transit related, pedestrian friendly, and vertically integrated.

"Creating environments that endure" is the hallmark of Elness Swenson Graham Architects Inc. (ESG), founded in Minneapolis and headquartered there since 1973. The firm's principals—Mark Swenson, David Graham, Dennis Sutliff, Paul Mittendorff, and Art Weeks, all members of the American Institute of Architects—lead a team of more than 80 professionals with wide-ranging skills and market-specific insights. This creative team consistently delivers design solutions that are innovative, cost-effective, and tailored to meet and exceed each client's requirements.

With strong roots seeded and nurtured in Minneapolis, ESG has a deep commitment to the city it calls home. From panoramic urban-design projects to the creation of impressive commercial buildings, ESG believes in the continuous revitalization of Minneapolis and its surrounding metropolitan area.

An impressive example of ESG's commitment and dedication to its own backyard is the role the company has played and will continue to play in the redevelopment of the bustling Minneapolis riverfront. ESG has planned and designed structures along the riverfront that will turn heads for years to come, including the four-story Depot Office Center and its neighbor, the historic Milwaukee Road Depot Hotels and Water Park.

ESG excels in providing clients with exceptional design quality and service across all markets and industries. By constantly keeping a finger on the industry's pulse, ESG is able to understand and recognize trends that are shaping the future of architectural design. For example, ESG designed a highly successful and unique mixed-use urban development in St. Louis Park, the Excelsior & Grand community. This project brings the convenience and energy of business and entertainment to the front doors of residents of the contemporary apartment units that are the core of the project.

On the residential side, the modern design of the luxury mid-rise 301 Kenwood Parkway, which overlooks the Walker Art Center and the Guthrie Theater in Minneapolis, showcases ESG's creative capabilities. The combination of glass and steel with simple, rectilinear lines, a flat roof, a stone base, and carefully detailed entryways fits elegantly into the prestigious Lowry Hill neighborhood that surrounds this building.

Beyond the city it calls home, ESG's work enhances the skylines and cityscapes in more than 25 states. Whether the design expression is traditional or contemporary, inspirational or mood setting, ESG's projects display timeless quality and style.

Firm Specialties

Elness Swenson Graham Architects' expertise is seen in a variety of markets and projects, including:

- Residential
- Hotels
- Urban Design
- Mixed-Use
- Senior Living
- Student Housing
- Corporate Office

"At Elness Swenson Graham Architects, we continually strive to go above and beyond what clients expect in all aspects of design and service," states President Mark Swenson. "Our firm's philosophy of teamwork extends beyond our walls, in that our architects embrace the values and expertise of our clients and the consultants and contractors with which we work."

Overall, ESG has earned more than 70 local and national awards, which attests to the company's commitment to excellence, the talent of its respected staff, and the company-wide emphasis on collaboration between the firm, its clients, and its contractors. These are the key elements of style and success for Elness Swenson Graham Architects Inc., a leading Minneapolis enterprise.

Best & Flanagan LLP

Diversified in its areas of legal expertise and unified in its commitment to ethical practice, this top-ranked law firm provides a full range of services for its clientele, which includes individuals, publicly traded corporations, state and local governments, and labor unions.

Best & Flanagan LLP has remained committed to providing clients with practical results and individual attention for nearly 80 years. This highly regarded Minneapolis law firm was founded in 1926 by Jim Best and Bob Flanagan. Initially, the two focused on providing estate planning, trust services, and probate administration to individuals and closely held companies. As Best & Flanagan grew over the years, it extended that commitment and expertise to the practice of real estate, business, public finance, government, and Native American law, as well as litigation.

Today, this firm of over 50 attorneys serves a highly diversified clientele and represents clients in all areas of civil practice. Individuals, publicly traded corporations, state and local government, and labor unions have benefited from Best & Flanagan's legal expertise. With respect to state and local government finance, the firm has broad experience with all aspects of tax-exempt financing in the state of Minnesota and the greater Midwest. Best & Flanagan lawyers also have represented investment banking firms and nonprofit charitable

organizations in connection with traditional governmental infrastructure projects. The firm's work also has included hospital financings, senior-housing projects, low- and moderate-income multifamily housing facilities, manufacturing plants, higher education institutions, charter schools, urban renewal and tax increment projects, and student loan bonds. Uniquely, the Native American Law Practice Group at Best & Flanagan provides the full range of legal services that Native American tribal clients need to achieve their social, educational, and economic goals.

Throughout the years of growth and change, the one constant for the firm has been serving clients well with an emphasis on delivering practical results. Best & Flanagan has cultivated a client-centered practice, and it continually adjusts its procedures in order to apply the best means available in solving clients' problems. For example, attorneys share knowledge and expertise with each other and also direct clients' work to those attorneys who have the particular experience and qualifications needed to deliver the most practical results cost-effectively. Accordingly,

each Best & Flanagan attorney is free to develop a specialized expertise—upon which all the other attorneys can draw —and the collective experience and resources of the firm provide comprehensive, yet personalized, services to clients.

"From the very beginning, Best & Flanagan has been dedicated to building strong relationships with our clients," explains Managing Partner James C. Diracles. "Our philosophy is

simple. We serve our clients best when we provide legal advice and legal services that will produce immediate and effective results."

Above: The Minneapolis-based law firm of Best & Flanagan LLP serves clients throughout Minnesota and the greater Midwest.

Best & Flanagan LLP Practice Areas

Public Finance
- 501(c)(3) financing
- general obligation bonds
- private activity revenue bonds
- essential function bonds
- securities and blue-sky law
- continuing disclosure
- tax increment financing
- debt restructuring
- workouts

Government and Land Use
- administrative proceedings
- eminent domain
- land use and zoning
- municipal law
- housing and redevelopment
- state legislative lobbying

Business Law
- business and succession planning
- bankruptcy/debtor-creditor
- employee benefits and compensation
- intellectual property/technology
- Native American law
- securities/mergers and acquisitions
- taxation/nonprofit and tax exempt

Litigation
- commercial litigation
- employment and civil rights
- family law
- personal injury
- real estate litigation
- probate litigation

Real Estate
- commercial real estate lending
- title registration, title examination, and foreclosures
- Section 1031
- mixed-use development
- condominium and town house development

Estate Planning and Trusts
- wills
- trusts
- probate
- trust administration
- gift tax planning

Patterson, Thuente, Skaar & Christensen, P.A.

Practicing law with a passion for maximizing potential for every client—from established to newly formed companies, individual inventors to multinational corporations—is the hallmark of this intellectual property law firm with a local, national, and international reach.

Protecting Intellectual Property

Patterson, Thuente, Skaar & Christensen, P.A. provides services for its clients that enable them to protect one of their most important assets—their intellectual property. The firm's areas of legal practice include:

- patents
- copyright, trademark, trade secrets
- entertainment and the arts
- intellectual property litigation
- licensing
- international law
- technology and telecommunications

Trusted by its diverse clientele and esteemed by its peers, Patterson, Thuente, Skaar & Christensen, P.A. provides intellectual property services that open, protect, and expand the windows of opportunity for clients. From idea to prototype to the realization of a viable, thriving enterprise, this firm provides strategic, efficient, and cost-effective counsel at every stage of the creative and production process.

Areas of legal practice include patents; copyright, trademark, and trade secrets; entertainment and the arts; intellectual property litigation; licensing; international law; and technology and telecommunications.

The firm was founded in 1991 in Minneapolis and now has an additional office in Atlanta. It maintains its mission of providing full service to clients. Says cofounder James H. Patterson, "We work with clients and their intellectual properties with the goal of having a very positive, very real effect on the bottom line of their business." This corporate philosophy and daily goal has contributed to the success of the firm, as it has to the success of its clients. Today Patterson, Thuente, Skaar & Christensen comprises 32 top attorneys, most of whom have advanced degrees and work experience in technical fields, from mechanical engineering to life sciences, which gives them a unique understanding of their clients' needs.

This impressive legal team assists clients in building complete patent portfolios that build market share, at home and abroad, and will withstand potential future litigation. In the area of litigation, 12 experienced attorneys focus entirely on protecting clients' intellectual property rights at the local, national, and international levels.

The firm is experiencing dynamic growth in international law as many of its clients move to global markets. It maintains close relationships with associate firms in Europe, the United Kingdom, and the Pacific Rim, where it also counsels foreign companies about U.S. patent law. In fact, Patterson, Thuente, Skaar & Christensen has participated as a U.S. patent law expert in European courts of law.

By diligently and consistently providing innovative, lasting solutions to complex intellectual property matters, Patterson, Thuente, Skaar & Christensen has distinguished itself and earned the trust of its clients.

Washburn-McReavy
Funeral Chapels

Based in Minneapolis since 1857, this oldest and largest independent funeral establishment in Minnesota operates chapels throughout the city and surrounding suburbs, as well as a cemetery and crematories, offering its customers a complete range of quality facilities and professional, caring service.

Washburn-McReavy Funeral Chapels is the oldest independent, family-owned funeral establishment in the state of Minnesota. The business began in 1857, a year before Minnesota was declared a state. Today the company has 150 employees and operates funeral facilities throughout Minneapolis and the surrounding suburbs. Its management consists of William L. McReavy ("Bill Sr."); his wife, Kathleen ("Kay"); and two of their four children, William Washburn McReavy ("Bill Jr.") and Cyndi McReavy-Seitz.

William P. Washburn was originally a partner with William Glessner in a furniture and undertaking company— an enterprise combination that was common at the time. The furniture portion was sold in 1917, and Washburn kept the funeral portion as the Washburn Undertaking Company. William P. Washburn invited his nephew Donald R. McReavy, now married to Lillian Ponsonby, to join the business. Donald R. McReavy became a successful manager and subsequent partner.

The company was renamed Washburn-McReavy, and after Washburn's death in 1932, Donald McReavy guided it through many challenging years. Upon his own death in 1949, his wife took over operations with the help of their son William, now known as Bill Sr., who went on to earn a degree in mortuary science. Under Bill Sr.'s leadership, the firm has strategically expanded. In 1954, Bill Sr. married Kathleen "Kay" Boyd Hammer. Their son Bill Jr. and daughter Cyndi represent the fourth generation to join the business.

Together, the McReavys operate the business in the tradition that began nearly 150 years ago. All aspects of service are available, including pre-arrangements; handling documents; transportation; professional care, caskets, and visitation rooms; memorial services; funeral vehicles; cremation; and cemetery arrangements. The company's funeral facilities encompass 12 Washburn-McReavy chapels. Six are in Minneapolis, including the first Washburn-McReavy chapel, the Southeast Chapel. This chapel was also Minnesota's first funeral chapel. It is located near the banks of the Mississippi River, where the city began, and across from downtown Minneapolis. The additional Minneapolis chapels are the Northeast Chapel; Swanson Chapel; Nokomis Chapel; Welander Quist Davies Chapel, where the Washburn-McReavy flower shop is located; and Hillside Chapel.

The other six chapels, located in surrounding suburbs, are the DuSchane Chapel in Robbinsdale; Edina Chapel in Edina, which offers an area for luncheon receptions; Strobeck Johnson Chapel in Hopkins; Columbia Heights Chapel in Columbia Heights; Seman Chapel in Coon Rapids; and Eden Prairie Chapel in Eden Prairie, Minnesota's only funeral chapel that offers a columbarium, with glass-encased recesses for cremation urns. Washburn-McReavy also owns and operates Hillside Cemetery in Minneapolis, which provides comfortable, well-equipped facilities for receptions and includes a cremation viewing room, one of the first in the area.

Overall, Washburn-McReavy Funeral Chapels still follows the core philosophy of delivering quality service, facilities, equipment, and personnel and of giving customers the very best value for the dollars spent on traditional funeral and cremation services.

Above: Family-owned and -operated for 148 years, Washburn-McReavy Funeral Chapels is today guided by William L. McReavy; his wife, Kathleen; and two of their four children, William Washburn McReavy and Cyndi McReavy-Seitz.

Right: The law firm of Briggs and Morgan, P.A.—with offices in Minneapolis in the IDS Center, shown here, and in St. Paul—employs more than 160 attorneys.

For more than a century, the law firm of Briggs and Morgan, P.A., has represented businesses that have played central roles in the economic development of Minnesota and the upper Midwest. Today, Briggs maintains its position as a leading full-service regional business and trial law firm by attracting talented lawyers and support staff members dedicated to delivering unparalleled client service, a core value of the firm. The firm's clients include emerging growth companies and other businesses ranging from sole proprietorships to Fortune 500 companies, government agencies, and individuals.

Overall, Briggs is recognized nationally for its expertise in complex litigation, class-action defense, and practice in the areas of real estate development, energy, public finance, and commercial banking and finance. The firm has offices in both Minneapolis and St. Paul and employs more than 160 attorneys.

A tradition of responsiveness, common sense, straight talk, and honest answers has earned Briggs several distinctions, including being selected as one of the top law firms in the Twin Cities by *Corporate Board Member* magazine and being chosen as a "Go-To Law Firm" by *Corporate Counsel* magazine.

Internationally, Briggs is a founding member firm of Lex Mundi, "The World's Leading Association of Independent Law Firms." Lex Mundi is a mark of excellence for legal services globally. With more than 15,000 lawyers in 560 offices, Lex Mundi member firms are present in more than 160 countries, states, and provinces. Membership in Lex Mundi gives Briggs global reach and access to legal resources that enhance its ability to serve the needs of its clients worldwide.

At its core, Briggs is dedicated to exceeding the expectations of its clients, embracing diversity, and serving its community. The firm looks to the future with an optimistic eye, balancing its responsibility to evolve as its clients' businesses require with its responsibility to the community. While Briggs and Morgan, P.A., may have traditional beginnings, its future is being written by skillful lawyers who blend experience with progressive, innovative solutions.

culture while addressing concerns for quality, cost, and service.

Founded in 1978, the practice has grown from a sole proprietorship to a 75-person partnership. Today, the name BKV Group represents a firm that offers architecture and interior design; structural, mechanical, and electrical engineering services; and construction administration. Its innovative designs have garnered numerous awards, including multiple national and local American Institute of Architects (AIA) design awards.

BKV Group is a practice with multidisciplinary and team-focused expertise. The diverse collective knowledge of the staff allows design teams to apply their distinct capabilities and provide a service-oriented approach to a project from its inception. The firm believes that good design is the result of clear communication among the entire team. Staff members blend, build on, and cross-reference one another's experience to provide the most comprehensive services possible.

BKV Group develops designs and services to satisfy the needs, schedule, and budget of each client's building

program. BKV Group design teams take on challenges with client and community objectives firmly in mind. Clients rely on the team to approach each project with a proactive, problem-solving mind-set. This approach is carried throughout the firm's core project types of corporate, government, and mixed-use developments. Its portfolio includes diverse residential, retail, corporate, financial, educational, and governmental projects.

At BKV Group, a client-architect relationship might begin with a single project, such as a city hall, an office tower, a bank, or a residential building, and evolve into an ongoing collaboration to envision and plan a community's future. With each project, the firm continues to grow in breadth and depth, responsiveness and flexibility.

BKV Group's work creatively defies stylistic categorization, although the community-based project types on which the firm was built remain at its core. With a dynamic group of skilled specialists who are confident in their ability to build on their collective knowledge, BKV Group is positioned as a leader in community architecture and planning, in the region and across the nation.

A full-service architectural, interior design, engineering, and construction administration firm, BKV Group (Boarman Kroos Vogel Group) of Minneapolis works closely with corporate, financial, governmental, mixed-use development, and residential clients to develop solutions that fit their organizational needs and

Left: Among BKV Group's distinctive projects in Minneapolis are the mixed-use Heritage Landing apartments and townhomes. A dedication to the client-architect relationship and to innovative community-based projects has earned this leading firm numerous prestigious American Institute of Architects design awards.

Gray Plant Mooty

GRAY PLANT MOOTY

Recognized as the longest continuing law practice in Minneapolis, Gray Plant Mooty—established in 1866—is an award-winning full-service firm with a distinguished tradition of excellence in providing creative thinking and innovative legal strategies to its clients.

Above and above right: Members of Gray Plant Mooty gather at the firm's Minneapolis offices in the IDS Center for monthly meetings led by Bruce Mooty, managing officer. "Gray Plant Mooty is the firm of choice for clients who want a progressive law firm and smart, approachable lawyers," states Mooty.

The history of Gray Plant Mooty is the history of Minneapolis business. The law firm opened its doors shortly after Minnesota officially became a state. In the center of the city, with its unpaved streets and wooden sidewalks, the firm was founded in 1866 by the first justice of the peace of Minneapolis, Charles Woods.

As the oldest continuing law practice in Minneapolis, the firm has expanded and evolved over the years, but its founding principles and commitment to exceptional client service have not wavered. In 2002, Gray Plant Mooty combined with Hall & Byers of St. Cloud to better serve clients throughout the Midwest.

Today, more than 150 lawyers serve an impressive roster of regional, national, and international clients from the firm's Minneapolis and St. Cloud locations. This award-winning firm offers individual and business services and has built a reputation for its legal expertise in numerous areas, including business law and litigation, mergers and acquisitions, franchise, health and nonprofit organizations, employment, intellectual property, employee benefits, real estate, estate planning, entrepreneurial services, bankruptcy, corporate finance, and more.

Gray Plant Mooty considers its people to be its most valuable resource. "Throughout the halls, impressive resumes abound, yet egos do not," says Managing Officer Bruce Mooty. By working together and sharing ideas, members of the firm foster a culture of integrity, fairness, and respect for each other and for the firm's clients. In fact, Gray Plant Mooty has received the "Great Places to Work" award multiple times from *The Business Journal Minneapolis–St. Paul*.

Everyone at Gray Plant Mooty is focused on the same goal: rolling up their sleeves and doing the best possible job for clients. This philosophy also applies to the firm's commitment to community involvement, which is marked by generous time investment and action. Lawyers, paralegals, and staff members make a positive difference in their local and national communities through involvement in a variety of charitable organizations and pro bono activities.

Gray Plant Mooty (Web site: www.gpmlaw.com; phone: 612-632-3000) has proudly served Minnesota for nearly one and a half centuries and continues its tradition of providing business-oriented legal counsel with consistently effective results for clients.

AAA Minneapolis

One of the first auto clubs, this motoring and travel organization provides members with emergency road service and traffic safety programs, as it did a century ago, plus many other benefits—including airline, cruise, and rail tickets; tours; hotel and car rental reservations; auto, home, life, and health insurance; and the AAA Travel Store.

At the turn of the 20th century, Americans began experiencing a bold, new type of independence—one of increased mobility. When automobile pioneers such as Henry Ford and Ransom Eli Olds opened the world to motorized carriages, it was just the start of the journey. AAA Minneapolis has remained a reliable partner on that trek for more than 100 years.

Founded in 1902 by automobile enthusiasts as the Automobile Club of Minneapolis, AAA Minneapolis today helps the community experience adventures, fulfill dreams, and enhance life. And it still is guided by the principles of its founding "automobilists"—fairness, reliability, and honesty. AAA Minneapolis offers support for its nearly 180,000 members in Hennepin County in all areas of their lives—on the road, at home, in the office, and around the world—by telephone and online via the Internet. AAA Minneapolis members rely on its trusted core benefits of emergency roadside assistance and travel services. In 2004 alone, the club responded to more than 100,000 local calls for vehicle assistance.

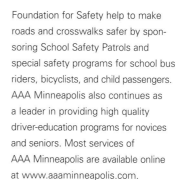

From humble beginnings as one of the first motoring clubs, AAA Minneapolis has grown to become one of the largest full-service travel agencies in the Twin Cities. Club members and nonmembers can purchase airline, cruise, and rail tickets and charter and escorted tours, reserve hotel rooms and rental cars, and obtain travel documents and accident insurance for trips throughout North America and beyond.

AAA Minneapolis members also benefit from AAA, the independent insurance agency that represents leading companies offering exclusive rates

on automobile, home, life, and health insurance. In addition, members can visit the AAA Travel Store, an expanding source for good values in top-brand luggage, travel books, specialty maps, travel security goods, convenience items, automotive accessories, and more. AAA's popular member discount program—Show Your Card & Save—represents well-known national and local retailers, services, lodging, and tourist attractions.

Working as responsible corporate citizens, AAA Minneapolis and its member-funded Minneapolis Auto Club

Foundation for Safety help to make roads and crosswalks safer by sponsoring School Safety Patrols and special safety programs for school bus riders, bicyclists, and child passengers. AAA Minneapolis also continues as a leader in providing high quality driver-education programs for novices and seniors. Most services of AAA Minneapolis are available online at www.aaaminneapolis.com.

AAA Minneapolis—celebrating more than a century of service to its members and community—looks forward to its journey into the 21st century.

Above left and inset: AAA Minneapolis's emergency road service has been relied upon for more than 100 years. Above and inset: School Safety Patrols are sponsored by AAA Minneapolis and its Minneapolis Auto Club Foundation for Safety.

Goodin Company

This 'Source of Supply' equips contractors, manufacturers, utilities, governmental agencies, and industrial end users throughout the Twin Cities, nationwide, and outside the continental United States with a wide range of plumbing, HVAC, pipe, valves and fittings, water well, and industrial supplies.

Above: Centrally located, just minutes from downtown Minneapolis, the Goodin Company's main facility includes the corporate headquarters and 100,000 square feet of warehouse space.

An outstanding product selection, sleek showrooms (with a full complement of kitchen and bath fixtures and accessories), innovative computerized systems, and extraordinary customer service distinguish the Goodin Company. This industry wholesaler has dedicated itself to "total customer satisfaction" since it was established in Minneapolis in 1937. Its products are marketed to contractors, manufacturers, utilities, governmental agencies, and industrial end users throughout Minnesota, western Wisconsin, North Dakota, and South Dakota. Upon request, the company also makes shipments nationwide and outside the continental United States.

Across the Twin Cities alone, the skylines are graced by gorgeous monuments and buildings whose mechanical contractors turned first to Goodin to purchase the highest quality products for their projects. Goodin was involved in the outfitting of the Mall of America, the Federal Reserve Bank, Target Center, and the Minneapolis–St. Paul International Airport, to name just a few.

From its present headquarters and its modern 100,000-square-foot central warehouse located minutes from downtown Minneapolis, Goodin oversees the operations of eight additional locations—in St. Paul, Duluth, Detroit Lakes, St. Cloud, Brainerd, and Rochester, Minnesota; in Fargo, North Dakota; and in Eau Claire, Wisconsin. All of these Goodin branches, regardless of size, are "full line," and each is conveniently located for customers to obtain materials and to consult with trained customer service representatives. In addition to the 300 employees in these locations, Goodin sales representatives are on hand in towns stretching from Wisconsin to the Dakotas and in all of Minnesota.

While excelling at the state of its business, Goodin also excels in its state-of-the-art capabilities. The company efficiently manages more than 18,000 stock items from 700 manufacturers through fully computerized sales-transaction and inventory systems. At all times, staff members at each location have instant, shared computer access to all inventory and all ordering and reordering information. Current pricing, available stock, and product specifications are available online, 24 hours a day. In addition, customers can peruse catalogs online, access their own accounts and inventories, and enter orders at any time.

The legacy of Goodin's founders— Al Goodin, Les Reisberg, Irv Larson, and Howard Nelson—continues to guide the company. Their vision and philosophy-in-action—"Building trust over decades, trust in knowledgeable people who can be depended upon to deliver the right products on time"— have ensured the company's success. Using its more than 68 years of experience as its benchmark and customer goodwill as its daily goal, the Goodin Company and its employees will set industry standards well into the future.

Wilkerson, Guthmann + Johnson, Ltd.

Serving as client advisers since 1923, this CPA and consulting firm's team of professionals has been impacting the success of businesses and individuals by providing expertise in a wide range of financial and technical areas.

When Lyle Hines established this firm more than 80 years ago, a tradition of exceptional client service was established. Upon Hines' retirement, Hartwell Wilkerson, Howard Guthmann, and Wallace Johnson lent their names to the firm and carried on the tradition of caring client service to individual clients, not-for-profit groups, and for-profit businesses of all sizes.

In a competitive, ever-changing business world, the professionals at Wilkerson, Guthmann + Johnson listen carefully to understand their clients' needs and objectives. Then, by providing trustworthy advice in the areas of general tax, financial reporting, financial consulting, organizational consulting, resource planning, and business software, the advisers become catalysts for action to affect the futures of businesses and the lives of individuals. From the firm's offices in Minneapolis, St. Paul, and Scandia, Minnesota, they bring their creative energies to diverse clients locally, nationally, and internationally.

The professional teams at Wilkerson, Guthmann + Johnson integrate their multiple disciplines, which include not only tax, financial reporting, consulting, and resource planning but also technology. A team of contract accountants assists businesses with special software to keep financial information up to date and available for evaluation, to improve efficiencies, production, and profitability.

While resource planning is a service that the firm has provided for many years, today the financial planners also can objectively help clients take advantage of investment strategies to manage their resources more effectively and ultimately reach their retirement lifestyle goals. The advisers do not sell investment products of any kind.

Many of the firm's leaders also are leaders in the community, including past presidents of the Minnesota Society of Certified Public Accountants. Howard Guthmann, at Wilkerson, Guthmann + Johnson since 1943, has been affiliated with the Boy Scouts of America for more than 70 years. Roger Katzenmaier, CEO, hired in 1965, has been a board member of the Twin Cities Habitat for Humanity since 1999. President Randall Kroll, who joined the firm in 1980, served as a board member of the Minneapolis Regional Chamber of Commerce for eight years.

The firm's leaders and employees alike strive to make their clients' lives better with their professional services and advice, and they continue to contribute countless hours to their communities.

Left: At Wilkerson, Guthmann + Johnson, Ltd., from left, staff members Amy Slachta and Andrew Muntifering confer with Howard M. Guthmann.

"Our company was acquired by a multinational company, and we continue to operate as a subsidiary. During the acquisition, Messerli & Kramer P.A. provided us with expert legal counsel. This was a complex, multifaceted transaction, and the special attention and expertise provided to us was outstanding. A successful outcome achieved in a cooperative environment is a testament to the representation we received from Messerli & Kramer P.A."
—*Dennis Holbert, Founder and President, Foam Enterprises, Inc.*

"For many years, Messerli & Kramer P.A. employees have supported Volunteers of America Minnesota, by both volunteering and contributing financially. They participate in several of our annual special events. The staff is fabulous to work with, not only because of their enthusiasm, reliability, and sincere desire to help but also because they eagerly reach out to the less-typical or hard-to-fulfill situations. We very much appreciate the staff at Messerli & Kramer P.A."
—*Pam Hoepner, Director of Corporate Partnerships, Volunteers of America Minnesota*

"Messerli & Kramer P.A. staff members consistently meet and exceed our expectations. They provide us with great representation and possess exceptional skills in advancing our interests in the legislature. Credibility is key for a lobbying firm and Messerli & Kramer P.A. is at the top of its profession."
—*David Minkkinen, Managing Director, BearingPoint, Inc.*

Above: "At Messerli & Kramer P.A., we value the relationships we have with our clients. We measure our success by their success," states William M. Habicht, president of this legal firm that has garnered numerous awards and accolades.

Messerli & Kramer P.A. understands the importance of relationships—in particular, the relationships between the firm's legal professionals and its clients. That is why this professional association has created an environment where relationships and results go hand in hand.

When clients choose Messerli & Kramer, they are not just hiring a lawyer, they are hiring a legal team. This firm provides personal attention and uses its expert resources to make sure each client's needs are met.

Messerli & Kramer's diverse areas of expertise include business litigation, corporate finance and securities, credit and collections, elder law, employment and labor, estate planning, family law, general business and banking, government relations, and real estate.

Since its founding in 1965, Messerli & Kramer has been in the forefront of the legal profession. With offices in Minneapolis, Plymouth, and St. Paul, the firm has demonstrated its ability to quickly respond to an ever-changing economy and business environment.

It was one of the first law firms in Minnesota to take its credit and collections practice online, and its Web site (www.messerlikramer.com) has been voted one of the top 20 in the state by *Minnesota Law & Politics*.

Messerli & Kramer's lawyers are hired to produce results. The firm's work has received accolades from peers in business and law. For example, its real estate department is well known throughout Minnesota for its expertise in representing developers, property owners, and real estate lenders. Also, the firm's credit and collections department received

national honors for superior net-liquidation performance by Midland Credit Management, Inc.; Chrysler Financial; Ford Credit; Discover Card; and Target. Members of the firm's government relations group operate one of the largest such practices in Minnesota and have been consistently recognized as one of the best lobbying organizations in the state.

As Messerli & Kramer P.A. celebrates its 40th anniversary in 2005, the firm looks forward to building upon its relationships with existing clients and to creating future relationships with new clients.

Norman G. Jensen, Inc.

This Minneapolis-based customs brokerage firm—one of the nation's largest—provides importers and exporters worldwide with high-level service, expertise, and streamlined electronic data transactions, guiding the shipment of goods across borders and providing freight-forwarding services for international cargo transport.

In 1937, a young man named Norman G. Jensen recognized that Canadian businesses had a need for guidance in shipping their goods into the United States and for the services of a customs broker. Jensen created Norman G. Jensen, Inc. (NGJ) and, with his brother Gordon W. Jensen, began opening brokerage offices along the U.S.-Canada border to provide these services for the southbound flow of goods. First based in Portal, North Dakota, NGJ has been headquartered in Minneapolis, Minnesota, since the mid 1940s.

Customs Brokerage

Today, NGJ processes nearly 1.5 million shipments per year. It is one of the nation's largest customs brokers and is still family owned, operated by a second generation of Jensens. NGJ employs a staff of nearly 500 people and has an office at every major U.S.-Canadian highway and rail crossing as well as coastal and inland offices in Seattle, Spokane, Los Angeles, Salt Lake City, Houston, Laredo, Minneapolis, Chicago, Detroit, Miami, and New York City. A worldwide network of agents in more than 70 countries assists in handling

shipments to and from the United States. In addition, in 2002 NGJ began an operation based in Canada, which provides customs brokerage services to companies shipping goods into Canada from the United States and other countries.

Freight Forwarding

NGJ also is a freight forwarder, assisting both importers and exporters by facilitating the movement of their cargo. Freight forwarders make arrangements to transport shipments by air, ocean, or ground to and from all the major cities of the world. Services can include packing, insurance, documentation, shipping, tracking, warehousing, and distribution.

The processing of shipment data today is conducted in a nearly paperless environment, with most forms and information received, processed, transmitted, and released electronically. NGJ maintains a Web site (www.ngjensen.com) to keep its clients advised of import-export regulation changes, which are frequent. Looking to the future, NGJ provides a link to the global marketplace for Midwest businesses.

Left: Shown here in the 1940s are, from left, Norman G. Jensen and Gordon W. Jensen. The two brothers built Norman G. Jensen, Inc., which today has offices in Minneapolis and other major import-export locations across the United States, as well as agents in 70 other countries around the globe.

Professional Sports

Profiles of Corporations and Organizations

Minnesota Vikings

Boasting a tradition of athletic and personal excellence and a fiercely loyal fan base, the Minnesota Vikings—consistent contenders for the most coveted title in professional sports—provide community strength on and off the field, through donations of time, money, and resources.

victory over the Chicago Bears. And the rest, as they say, is history.

In the years since then, star players and winning coaches have come and gone, but the Vikings' tradition of excellence has remained the same. General manager Bert Rose and head coach Norm Van Brocklin were replaced by Jim Finks and Bud Grant. Metropolitan Stadium was abandoned as the team's venue, and the Hubert H. Humphrey Metrodome took its place as the Vikings' home field. Today the team is under a new ownership group led by Zygi Wilf and his family, who have pledged that the Vikings "will be in the Minneapolis area forever," and is coached by Mike Tice, the team's first head coach to have been a former Vikings player.

Champions On and Off the Field

The Vikings football franchise, named for the widespread Scandinavian heritage found throughout the region, enjoys an extremely loyal fan base that receives as much as it gives. The team's commitment to making life better for Twin Cities residents takes the form of community outreach programs and

donations of time, money, and resources that help citizens of all ages.

The Viking Children's Fund, with a total grant history of over $7 million since 1978, is one way for team members to give back to the community. The fund awards more than half of all proceeds to the University of Minnesota Department of Pediatrics to support research of major childhood diseases and disorders. It awards the remaining funds to nonprofit organizations that focus on education and family services that help children. These include organizations that offer treatment and rehabilitation for drug and alcohol abuse, education regarding child abuse, programs that mentor at-risk youths, shelters for homeless families, and child protection services.

Special events such as the Mike Tice/United Way Youth Football Day also encourage young people to envision a brighter future and make positive choices. Vikings players and coaches teach children the importance of hard work by putting them through football drills and giving them pointers about the game. Other Vikings programs

From the beginning, the Minnesota Vikings have been at the top of their game. Since 1960, when five of the state's businessmen were awarded an NFL franchise, the Vikings have played in four Super Bowls; made 24 playoff appearances; and won 15 division championships, three NFC titles, and

one NFL championship. Even their very first game was a stunning example of the athletic talent and team spirit that would characterize the Vikings in the decades to come. On September 17, 1961, rookie quarterback Fran Tarkenton threw four touchdown passes and ran for a fifth to lead the team to a 37–13

include Fine Money for Fine Causes, which donates money from the Players' Fine Fund to local charities, and the free Youth Football Coaches Academy, designed to help high school and youth football coaches improve their skills and learn from the pros.

Vikings players, coaches, and staff eagerly donate time and money. They make numerous appearances including visits to hospitals and schools on Community Tuesdays, a league-wide initiative pioneered by the Vikings.

Whether they are winning on the football field or winning in the community, the Minnesota Vikings prove that being a champion means working hard and making good choices. The organization's philosophy that a strong community derives strength from its families is demonstrated in all of its endeavors. As the entire Vikings family becomes personally involved in the betterment of the community, it becomes stronger as a team and sets a winning example for all of its present and future fans.

Carl Eller (1964–78) A quick and agile defensive end with a knack for sacking the quarterback, Eller won the George Halas Award as the NFL's leading defensive player in 1971 and helped the Vikings' defensive line earn the nickname "the Purple People Eaters."

Jim Finks (1964–73) An executive who elevated the struggling Vikings to championship status, Finks was not afraid to make controversial decisions that proved successful in the long run.

Bud Grant (1967–83 and 1985) One of the NFL's all-time greatest coaches, Grant led the Vikings on a path of championship seasons that included winning 10 division titles in 11 seasons.

Paul Krause (1968–79) The leading pass interceptor of all time (81 steals), safety Krause achieved more interceptions (12) than any other NFL player during a first season.

Alan Page (1967–78) A defensive tackle who was named the NFL's Most Valuable Player in 1971, Page was a master at recovering fumbles and blocking kicks. After retiring from pro football, he became a lawyer and was elected to the Minnesota Supreme Court.

Fran Tarkenton (1961–66 and 1972–78) During Tarkenton's second tour of duty with the Vikings, he led the team to win six NFC Central Division titles and three Super Bowl appearances. When he retired, Tarkenton held the record for pass completions, passing yards, and touchdowns.

Ron Yary (1968–81) A lean, mean football machine, six-foot five-inch Yary was an outstanding tackle who played with the Vikings for 14 years. He was named All-Pro six times and was instrumental in the team's championships throughout the seventies.

Far left: Vikings' legend Fran Tarkenton played at Metropolitan Stadium, which served as the team's home from 1961 through 1981. Left: Daunte Culpepper, like Tarkenton in the early years, ranks as one of the top field generals in the NFL.

The Hubert H. Humphrey Metrodome

An important gathering point for people from across Minnesota and beyond, the domed stadium in Minneapolis hosts not only sports but also big-name concerts and major expositions, cultural celebrations, and other community events of all kinds.

Right: The Hubert H. Humphrey Metrodome brings great vitality to the downtown east section of Minneapolis. The Metrodome, which was opened in 1982, is the regular season home of Major League Baseball's Minnesota Twins, the National Football League Minnesota Vikings, and the Big Ten University of Minnesota Golden Gophers football team.

The nation's most versatile stadium also is an essential connecting point for the community.

It is the only stadium in the world to have hosted the National Football League (NFL) Super Bowl (1992), Major League Baseball's World Series (1987, 1991) and All-Star Game (1985), and the Final Four of the National Collegiate Athletic Association (NCAA) Division I Men's Basketball Championship (1992, 2001).

It is the regular season home of the American League Minnesota Twins, the NFL Minnesota Vikings, and the Big Ten University of Minnesota Golden Gophers football team.

It was created by a legislative charter that ensures that it remain a community facility, not the sole province of professional athletes. And it also is the only public stadium in the nation that does not rely on a continuous tax subsidy to keep it operating.

It is the Hubert H. Humphrey Metrodome—a remarkable example of both civic cooperation and public stewardship.

'Minnesota's Rec Room'
The Metrodome was opened in 1982, and since then more than 60 million people have witnessed or participated in Metrodome events, both large and small. In fact, of more than 300 event days per year at the stadium, fewer than 100 feature professional sports or major college sports. The rest of the event days are used by high schools and colleges or for community and cultural events.

"We pride ourselves on being an important gathering point for people throughout Minnesota and beyond," says Roy Terwilliger, chair since 2003 of the Metropolitan Sports Facilities Commission, which owns and operates

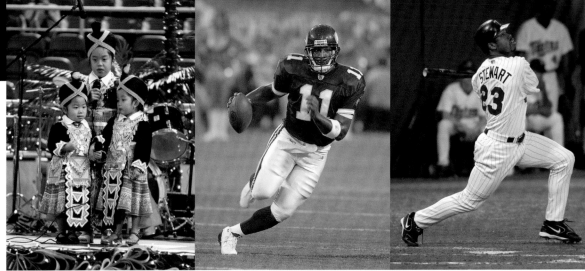

the Metrodome. "We call ourselves 'Minnesota's Rec Room' because what goes on in the Metrodome is so varied and brings together so many diverse people—fans of professional sports, music lovers, high school athletes, joggers, in-line skaters. This stadium is important, and it means something different to everyone."

Memorable Moments

The stadium has certainly had its share of memorable moments. Two of the most exciting World Series (1987 and 1991) were played in the Metrodome. In both cases, the Twins returned to the Metrodome for Game 6 facing elimination. And in each case, the Twins won the game to force a Game 7, and then won that game to take the series. The 1991 World Series will long be remembered for the gutty performance of Twins' pitcher (and St. Paul native) Jack Morris, who pitched all 10 innings of the team's extra-inning victory.

As exciting as that victory was, something happened in the Metrodome just days later that revealed even more about the Metrodome's importance to the community. Unrelenting record snowfalls

threatened to wipe out the remainder of Minnesota's high school football season. Over several days, 73 high school football games were moved into the Metrodome, salvaging the season and paving the way for the Prep Bowl, Minnesota's six-class high school football championship, a Metrodome staple since 1982.

The Prep Bowl is just one thread in the varied fabric of the Metrodome. For example:

- more than 500,000 people attended Metrodome concerts by such performers as Paul McCartney, the Rolling Stones, Bob Dylan, Tom Petty, the Grateful Dead, Pink Floyd, Guns N' Roses, Metallica, and George Strait;
- the Minnesota Timberwolves set a National Basketball Association (NBA) single-season attendance record of 1,072,572 in 1989–90 when they played their inaugural season in the Metrodome;
- the Reverend Billy Graham once preached to 349,000 people over a five-day period in the Metrodome.

In addition, the stadium has hosted such diverse events as motor sports;

the International Special Olympics; the Scandinavia Today exposition; the AIDS Memorial Quilt exhibit; the U.S. Olympic Festival; amateur baseball and volleyball games and soccer matches; surprise birthday parties; model airplane fly-offs; weddings; police canine training programs; and firefighter recruitment tests. And skating, running, and walking events have been enjoyed by up to 60,000 people each year.

According to an editorial in the *Star Tribune* of Minneapolis–St. Paul, "the Dome has been a remarkable success and an incredible bargain. . . . The $124 million it took to finance the building has generated $2.75 billion from fans. That's a return 22 times the original investment."

Metrodome Remains Vital

In 2004, more than six million people entered the Metrodome to witness or participate in a wide range of events, including watching the Twins roll to their third consecutive American League West title. Those six million guests and patrons were greeted by major improvements to the stadium, designed to make the games better, accessibility greater, and the fan experience richer.

Constantly improving and updating the stadium is a central part of the mission to protect the public's investment in the Metrodome. Another is making sure that tremendous statewide events such as the Prep Bowl are never left out in the cold.

Above right: The Minnesota Twins have won two World Series championships in the Metrodome. Shown here is left fielder Shannon Stewart.
Above center: The Minnesota Vikings are among the most intense in the National Football League. The player is quarterback Daunte Culpepper.
Above left: The Metrodome is also a cultural center, hosting a wide variety of events, such as an annual Hmong New Year celebration.

Transportation

Profiles of Corporations and Organizations

Murphy Warehouse Company

A proud partner in the history and progress of the Twin Cities for more than 100 years, the Murphy Warehouse Company—with locations throughout the Twin Cities—succeeds as one of the Upper Midwest's largest logistics companies and offers the services of its sister company, Murphy Rigging and Erecting, Inc.

Above: The prosperous Murphy Transfer & Storage Co., Inc., circa 1919 (left), evolved into today's dynamic Murphy Warehouse Company, with a modern truck fleet (right), state-of-the-art warehousing facilities, and a full range of logistics services for local, regional, and national customers in all business sectors.

In 1904, a St. Paul Irishman named Edward L. Murphy Sr. bought a team of horses and a wagon. In creating his small business, he also laid the foundation for a family business and a legacy that would endure for more than a century.

Edward Murphy's founding business evolved into the Minneapolis-based Murphy Warehouse Company, one of the Upper Midwest's largest asset-based logistics companies, and into

Murphy Rigging and Erecting, Inc., a premier rigging and millwright organization in the region. Today, these multimillion-dollar operations employ approximately 225 people in nine locations throughout the Twin Cities, and they serve more than 200 customers— from start-up to Fortune 500 companies—across the nation and the globe.

President and CEO Richard T. Murphy Jr. is the fourth generation of the Murphy family to guide the

enterprise. "As a family, we have come to recognize that our history is in many ways one of our most precious assets," states Murphy, who continues to build on his family's legacy of strong customer service and continual innovation to meet the needs of an ever-evolving marketplace.

A Partner in Making History
When Richard Murphy's great-grandfather, Edward, bought his two horses and wagon in 1904, St. Paul was

a growing industrial center situated along the Mississippi River. Operating out of the family home, the business began as a city delivery service, hauling goods between companies and off paddleboats on the river and delivering building materials to the new state capitol construction in St. Paul. As demand grew, Edward Murphy continued to reshape his business with the introduction of motorized truck service in 1910—one of the first such uses of these vehicles in St. Paul.

By the time Edward Murphy's company was incorporated as the Murphy Transfer Company in 1913, the firm had become a success, and the company's founder was a prominent figure in St. Paul. Both triumph and tragedy, however, lay ahead for the Murphy family—the Great Depression, a violent labor uprising in Minneapolis during the 1930s, the post–World War II economic boom, the trauma of transportation industry deregulation in the 1980s, and many generational handoffs.

"I believe the Murphy family has survived because of our core values—courage and imagination in taking chances; pride, persistence, and humility during good and bad times; and, above all, integrity in every matter," states Richard Murphy.

Innovative Logistics Solutions

Though much has changed since 1904, the Murphy Warehouse Company continues to operate under the same principle as its predecessor companies: create the most efficient and effective way to manage, store, and ship a customer's products.

Murphy Warehouse handles more than 3.4 billion pounds of products each year via 76,000 truck and 10,000 railcar shipments. The company works across a wide variety of industries, including food, retail, medical, health, paper, beverage, recreation, forest products, and plastics. Murphy Warehouse also handles products throughout their life cycle, from raw materials to in-process goods to finished products for food, consumer, or industrial markets. The company's wide-ranging services include packaging and labeling, warehousing, transportation, consolidation, cross-docking, and pool distribution.

Murphy Warehouse understands that a strong supply chain system is important to the health of a customer's business. That is why this company is ISO 9001 Certified, OSHA–MNSHARP Certified, ASI inspected, and U.S. Customs bonded. Inventory control is a core competency, and high sanitation requirements are followed in all facilities. Quality control is critical to Murphy Warehouse's food- and medical-industry customers, and the company ensures it through strict lot and rotation controls.

Depending on customer needs, Murphy Warehouse can provide dedicated warehouse space in one of its facilities, custom-build a distribution center in a key location, or manage a company's logistics needs—a solution that makes sense for an increasing number of businesses. All this is supported with Murphy Warehouse's multimodal transportation services,

including its own truck fleet. Richard Murphy explains, "When a company allows us to operate their logistics functions, they can focus on their core business, not on managing freight."

Regardless of the scope of the assignment, Murphy Warehouse offers customers real-time access to

Above: Pictured are two of several Murphy Warehouse Company supply chain facilities in the Twin Cities. In total, Murphy Warehouse handles more than 3.4 billion pounds of products each year via 76,000 truck and 10,000 railcar shipments.

Above: In 2004, Murphy Rigging and Erecting, Inc., the sister company of Murphy Warehouse, gave a two-ton bronze eagle sculpture an assist in flight to its new home at Lookout Park in St. Paul by providing transportation and a crane lift. Murphy Rigging and Erecting's wide range of services includes the specialized transportation of delicate objects such as large art pieces and medical equipment.

inventory, order, and receipt information via the Internet, full EDI (Electronic Data Interchange) support, and GPS (Global Positioning System) technology to track their products.

Murphy Warehouse provides its international customers with more flexibility to ship and receive goods through its Midwest International Logistics Center (MILC), activated in 1989 as the area's first General Purpose Foreign Trade Zone. Goods moving through the MILC are considered to be on foreign soil and can be worked on for value-added activities

and/or customs corrective measures. Murphy also offers a U.S. Customs Examination Station, a U.S. Customs Container Freight Station, and a U.S. General Order Facility within the MILC.

Murphy Warehouse has several warehouses equipped with indoor rail sidings, which offer shippers a more cost-effective and secure way to bring products from remote locations into key markets. This is a big plus for the many paper companies that ship heavy paper, pulp, and other forest products. Murphy Warehouse is the

second-largest rail user in the Upper Midwest today, and close to half of its rail loads carry paper-related products, while the other half carry goods such as beverages, food, building materials, furniture components, and water treatment supplies.

Given all of that paper, it is no surprise that Minnesota is the fourth largest printing market in the United States, and area printers and paper suppliers look to Murphy Warehouse's storage and "just-in-time" (JIT) capabilities. The company's rail, warehousing, and transportation services allow many remote plants to store finished paper rolls for delivery to printers throughout the nation and region. Murphy Warehouse's locations in the Twin Cities offer access to multiple transportation resources needed to meet the paper industry's tight schedules.

In terms of mass-merchant retail support, Murphy Warehouse—via a 160,000-square-foot distribution center—helps customers such as xpedx (a division of International Paper) supply all 1,300-plus Target stores across the country with the materials needed to run the stores, including uniforms, bags, sales and promotional materials, and training manuals.

Murphy Warehouse also offers retail supply chain services to food retailers. One example includes creating end-of-aisle sale-promotion displays and multi-vendor pallets for area grocery stores. Murphy Warehouse combines complementary products and brands, such as pastas and sauces, onto display-ready pallets, which are in turn cross-docked and distributed to stores. Food manufacturers such as Amport; Anheuser-Busch, Inc.; Malt-O-Meal Company; and United Sugars Corporation look to Murphy Warehouse for support, storage, and shipment from its secure, climate-controlled facilities, which maintain the freshness of raw and finished products.

In the medical arena, Murphy Warehouse distributes customized surgical kits for various hospital teams, ensuring JIT delivery to surgical suites. The company also distributes medical and health care supplies to hospitals, primary care facilities, and nursing homes.

While many logistics companies may have limited capabilities in moving unusually large or heavy goods, Murphy Warehouse is fully equipped to transport goods of any weight, with no limit. In these cases, Murphy Warehouse's sister company, Murphy Rigging and Erecting, Inc.—also headquartered in Minneapolis—becomes a partner in service.

Moving the Future

Murphy Rigging and Erecting is a rigging and millwright contractor with 100 years of experience, specializing in machinery moving and erecting, millwright services, plant setups and relocations, maintenance, heavy lifts, and specialized transportation for such delicate objects as art pieces and medical equipment.

"Rigging requires a mixture of science, art, and experience, and most of the people working for Murphy Rigging and Erecting have learned the business from the generations preceding them," states Richard Murphy.

Today, typical customers for Murphy Rigging and Erecting include high-tech medical companies and hospitals installing MRI (magnetic resonance imaging) units or sterilizers, top-secret government suppliers, energy plants installing new equipment, and manufacturers with many assembly lines and tight schedules.

Even many of the Twin Cities' notable features—from the large concrete lions at the front door of The Minneapolis Institute of Arts to the KSTP-TV radar dome to the tunnel air-exchange units for the

light rail line—were supported by Murphy Rigging and Erecting's services.

As community partners, both Murphy companies pride themselves on giving back to their neighbors. In 2004, Murphy Rigging and Erecting gave a two-ton bronze eagle sculpture an assist in flight to its new home at Lookout Park in St. Paul by providing transportation and a crane lift.

"A core value that the Murphy family lives by is giving back to our community, which has blessed us in business and allowed us to support the lives of so many other community members as employees, suppliers, customers, and friends," states Richard Murphy.

Though the legacy of the Murphy family of companies began more than a century ago, the Murphys continue to meet and exceed the demands of

customers in an ever-changing business world. Murphy Warehouse Company and Murphy Rigging and Erecting, Inc. are two of the most trusted names in their respective fields, and both are focused on using their expertise to help their customers grow and prosper over the next 100 years.

This page, all: Murphy Warehouse Company— an industry leader in retail supply chain operations— provides pick and pack service, quality control of in-process foods, and logistics management of rail and JIT ("just-in-time") paper roll shipments.

Sun Country Airlines

Excellent service, upgraded amenities, a dedicated staff, and a future-forward commitment to continued growth distinguish this Minnesota-based airline, which offers scheduled flights to New York, Florida, the southwestern states, and the West Coast and, in season, to Mexico, the Caribbean, and Alaska.

Incorporated in 1982 following the bankruptcy of Braniff International Airways, Sun Country Airlines was formed by a small group of former Braniff employees and the principals of Main Line Travel to serve Main Line's charter needs. The group leased a Boeing 727 jetliner, and Sun Country began operations in July 1982. Sun Country's first revenue-producing flight was a Sioux Falls, South Dakota, to Las Vegas, Nevada, charter on January 20, 1983, and within six weeks of operation the company turned a profit.

From the beginning, this was an airline that inspired loyalty and pride. Each of the airline's 33 employees became a jack-of-all-trades. Flight attendants stocked liquor kits and prepared meals in the commissary, while pilots updated manuals and assisted with catering. Everyone pitched in to clean the planes and help unload baggage. The camaraderie formed in those early days was a key component of the company's success and continues to be a defining factor within Sun Country today.

The carrier thrived and prospered as a charter airline. However, financial troubles, as well as the post–September 11, 2001 economy, plagued the airline, and Sun Country suspended operations in December 2001 and went into bankruptcy.

One of Sun Country's founders, Robert Daly, a Twin Cities businessman, developed a plan to keep the airline viable and attract investors. In early 2002, the carrier slowly restarted operations with flights to Laughlin, Nevada, and a month later to Las Vegas and destinations in Florida. A small workforce was formed, and many of the original employees returning to their jobs experienced déjà vu as they wielded mops and vacuums to clean the planes, as they had 20 years prior. By the first quarter of 2003, Sun Country had become profitable.

Today, the airline offers scheduled service to more than 30 core destinations, including popular business locations such as New York, Los Angeles, and Dallas and, in season, to Mexico, the Caribbean, and Alaska. Amenities such as low-cost upgrades to first

class, full meal service, and new Boeing aircraft with roomy leather seats, as well as easy access to the Humphrey Terminal at Minneapolis–St. Paul International Airport, have attracted new customers to Sun Country. The Sun Country Web site (www.suncountry.com)

will continue to be a focus of growth as more and more people book flights online via the Internet. The company's future is bright and includes a conservative growth plan calling for additional Boeing 737–800 aircraft and additional scheduled flights and destinations, based on demand.

The employees of Sun Country Airlines continue to be the company's strongest asset. The airline's team— one of the most enthusiastic and dedicated in the industry—provides exceptional service that makes each experience on a Sun Country Airlines flight a memorable experience.

This page: Chairman Robert Daly (seated) and CEO Shaun Nugent, with the invaluable contributions of their dedicated employees, have guided Sun Country Airlines into its position of prominence in the competitive aviation industry. Opposite page: Sun Country is proud to be the hometown airline of the Twin Cities. With a fleet featuring new Boeing 737s, Sun Country is the anchor tenant of the spacious new Humphrey Terminal at the Minneapolis–St. Paul International Airport.

Metropolitan Airports Commission

Operating Minneapolis–St. Paul International Airport and six reliever airports throughout the Twin Cities, this commission serves the community by providing air travelers with facilities and services designed to ensure efficiency, safety, and security and by contributing to the region's economy.

Above: Minneapolis–St. Paul International Airport—operated by the Metropolitan Airports Commission—is consistently ranked among the nation's best airports, according to customer-satisfaction surveys.

The Metropolitan Airports Commission operates one of the largest airport systems in America. This system includes the world's seventh-busiest airport in takeoffs and landings—Minneapolis–St. Paul International Airport—and six reliever airports, serving the area's general and business aviation needs. The commission's airports accommodate nearly 1.2 million takeoffs and landings per year.

Linking Minnesota to the World

Created by the Minnesota legislature in 1943, the commission provides safe, efficient aviation services in the seven-county metropolitan area. In 1996, the state legislature voted to expand Minneapolis–St. Paul International Airport at its present site rather than develop a new airport elsewhere. In response, the commission launched the

$3.1 billion 2010 airport expansion program. As of 2005, this program has achieved numerous improvements, including construction of a fourth runway, a new Humphrey Terminal, a major expansion of the Lindbergh Terminal, and new air cargo facilities.

The commission has now begun to address future growth needs. The next generation of improvements for Minneapolis–St. Paul International Airport will be met through 20/20 Vision, a program designed to provide additional terminal capacity for the 55 million travelers expected to use the airport annually by 2020. The program is an $850 million effort that will advance in three stages over 15 years, ultimately expanding both terminals and providing 46 new aircraft gates, additional parking, improved passenger amenities, and the infrastructure for more efficient security screening.

Minneapolis–St. Paul International Airport is served by nearly every major airline and is a major hub for Minnesota-based Northwest Airlines.

The airport ranks second nationally in nonstop destinations per 100,000 area residents, with service to cities around the globe. The airport supports more than 150,000 jobs and annually generates $10.7 billion in business revenue, $6 billion in personal income, and $626 million in state and local taxes.

Easy Access to the Metropolitan Area

Centrally located, Minneapolis–St. Paul International Airport is bound by four major highways and also is served by a light rail system that extends to downtown Minneapolis and to the Mall of America in Bloomington. Minneapolis–St. Paul International Airport is ranked among the world's top airports for customer service, food and retail facilities, and snow removal.

The reliever airports are located in Blaine, Crystal, Eden Prairie, Lake Elmo, Lakeville, and St. Paul.

The Metropolitan Airports Commission provides a Web site (www.mspairport.com) with information about its activities and its airports.

Jefferson Lines

A hometown success for more than eight decades, the Minneapolis-based Jefferson Lines provides first-class passenger, express, charter, tour, and convention transportation services, plus counter-to-counter small-package delivery service, to 11 states in the American heartland and the province of Manitoba, Canada.

Above, left to right: Whether the year is 1924, 1978, or 2005, Jefferson Lines' sleek, distinctive motor coaches have always been state-of-the-art. Jefferson Lines and its sister company, Jefferson Tours, are operated by Jefferson Partners LP, a Minneapolis, Minnesota–based family company. Top right: Charles A. Zelle, who serves as president and CEO, is the third generation of the Zelle family to lead Jefferson Lines.

Founded in 1919 in Minneapolis, Minnesota, Jefferson Lines is a pioneer and a modern-day standard-setter in the transportation industry. This company owns and operates a fleet of modern motor coaches that transport people on scheduled runs throughout 11 states and to Manitoba, Canada. Jefferson Lines also provides group tours and charters. The company's package express service makes deliveries to every city on its bus route—with connections to more than 4,000 destinations.

Managing this impressive transportation network is President and CEO Charles A. Zelle, an MBA graduate from the Yale School of Management and the third generation of the Zelle family to lead Jefferson Lines. Zelle states, "Jefferson Lines understands what people want and need when traveling, and we provide the services that exceed their expectations. In addition, Jefferson Lines has a rich history of civic and philanthropic involvement in the communities we serve."

Customer service and community support are integral to this company's corporate culture and operating philosophy, but they are only the beginning. Additional values that guide Jefferson Lines' principals and staff members include reliability and trustworthiness in all business and personal matters; respect for every individual; receptivity to great ideas from every level of the company; exemplary community citizenship; environmental responsibility; and responsibility for one's success and the success of the company.

As an industry leader, Jefferson Lines demonstrates an unwavering commitment to safety—the American Bus Association ranked this company in the top 1 percent among all registered U.S. carriers. This ranking and Jefferson Lines' overall excellent reputation are achieved by adhering to all U.S. Department of Transportation regulations for operator shifts, by administering random drug and alcohol tests, by providing emergency training, and by maintaining a 24-hour emergency hotline for its drivers, who are put through one of the most extensive training programs in the industry.

Jefferson Lines' admirable corporate values, its commitment to safety, and its success in delivering an excellent travel experience have earned this company an industry-leading position in motor coach transportation.

Energy
Profiles of Corporations and Organizations

Great River Energy

This standard-setting energy generation and transmission cooperative—with expert employees and an entrepreneurial culture—provides its members and customers with an ever-growing array of energy solutions for the present and well into the future.

Great River Energy partners with the communities it serves through 4,400 miles of transmission line and more than 100 transmission substations. Distinguished as Minnesota's second-largest electric utility, Great River Energy meets the energy needs of 60 percent of Minnesota, geographically, as well as parts of Wisconsin.

Based in Elk River, Minnesota, Great River Energy employs more than 700 workers in two states—Minnesota and North Dakota—and encompasses 28 member distribution cooperatives. Collectively, these cooperatives provide electricity and related services to 580,000 members and customers, from the outer-ring suburbs of the Twin Cities to the far reaches of Arrowhead County.

What makes Great River Energy and its member cooperatives unique is that they are owned by the consumers they serve. As not-for-profit organizations, Great River Energy and its cooperatives have a joint mission to provide reliable, affordable energy services. With proactive load-management efforts, they make conserving energy, protecting the environment, and developing new sources of energy their top priorities.

As a power provider, Great River Energy generates electricity at power plants and transmits that electricity across high-voltage transmission lines. Its electric transmission system—which is consistently ranked among the most reliable in the United States—includes a 430-mile HVDC (high-voltage direct current) line that runs from Coal Creek Station in central North Dakota to the Dickinson Converter Station near Buffalo, Minnesota.

Overall, Great River Energy provides 2,500 megawatts of generation capability using a broad mix of fuels, including coal, refuse-derived fuel, natural gas, and wind generation. With an eye toward the future, Great River Energy also participates in advanced research. For example, the U.S. Department of Energy selected Coal Creek Station to participate in a clean coal technology project using waste plant heat to reduce moisture in the lignite fuel supply, thereby reducing the amount of coal required to generate electricity.

In addition, Great River Energy has entered an agreement to purchase power from Minnesota's first commercial-scale, landowner-developed wind farm. The Trimont Area Wind Farm in southwestern Minnesota will produce 100 megawatts of energy.

By providing good jobs in the communities it serves, by participating in advanced energy research and development, and by working to keep its cooperative organization strong, Great River Energy continues to successfully meet the increased demands for energy and energy services in the region.

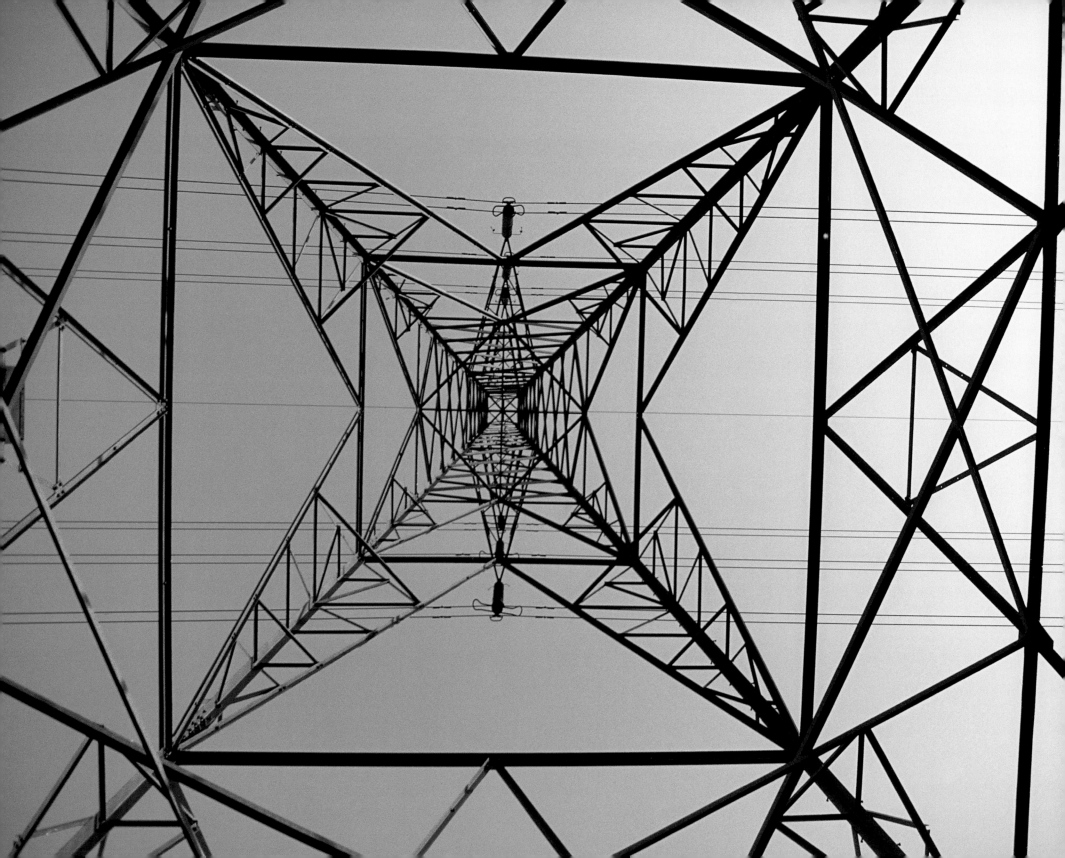

PATRONS

AAA Minneapolis*
Allen Interactions Inc.*
Alliance Steel Service Co.*
Allianz Life Insurance Company of
  North America*
American Medical Systems*
Augsburg College*
AXA Advisors, LLC*
Basilica of Saint Mary*
Best & Flanagan LLP*
Best Buy*
BKV Group*
Blake School, The*
Bloomington Convention & Visitors
  Bureau*
Boston Scientific*
Briggs and Morgan, P.A.*
Carlson Companies*
Durrant*
Ellerbe Becket, Inc.*
Elness Swenson Graham Architects
  Inc.*
Entegris, Inc.*
Eschelon Telecom, Inc.*
Foley Companies, The*
Gage*
G&K Services*
General Mills*
Gilbert Mechanical Contractors, Inc.*
Goodin Company*
Gray Plant Mooty*
Great River Energy*
Health Dimensions Group*
Hennepin Avenue United Methodist
  Church*
Hubert H. Humphrey Metrodome,
  The*
ING*
Jefferson Lines*
Kaltec of Minnesota, Inc.*
Lindquist & Vennum PLLP*
Lupient Automotive Group*
Manley Companies*
Marsh Inc.*

McCaa, Webster & Associates, Inc.*
McLaughlin Gormley King Company
Messerli & Kramer P.A.*
Metropolitan Airports Commission*
Minneapolis Foundation, The*
Minneapolis Grain Exchange*
Minneapolis Historic Houses of
  Worship*
Minneapolis Regional Chamber of
  Commerce*
Minnesota Vikings*
Mount Olivet Lutheran Church–
  Minneapolis*
Murphy Warehouse Company*
Nash Finch Company, The*
Normandale Community College*
Norman G. Jensen, Inc.*
North American Properties*
Opus Group, The*
Our Lady of Lourdes*
Padilla Speer Beardsley*
Parker Durrant International*
Patterson, Thuente, Skaar &
  Christensen, P.A.*
Pearson Education*
Personnel Decisions International*
Plymouth Congregational Church*
RSP Architects*
Saint Mark's Episcopal Cathedral*
Select Comfort Corporation*
Sofitel Minneapolis*
Star Tribune*
Sun Country Airlines*
Target*
Temple Israel*
Thomson West*
University of Phoenix–Minneapolis*
Upsher-Smith Laboratories, Inc.*
U.S. Bancorp*
Wagnild & Associates, Inc.*
Washburn-McReavy Funeral Chapels*
Westminster Presbyterian Church*
Wilkerson, Guthmann + Johnson, Ltd.*
Winslow Capital Management, Inc.*

*For additional information about these companies/organizations, please refer to the index on pages x–xi.

Cherbo Publishing Group

Cherbo Publishing Group's business-focused, art book–quality publications, which celebrate the vital spirit of enterprise, are custom books that are used as high-impact economic development tools to enhance reputations, increase profits, and provide global exposure for businesses and organizations.

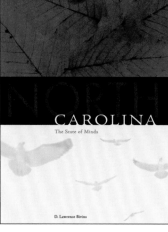

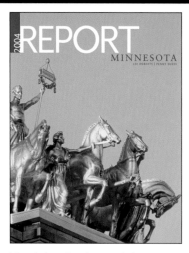

The Story Behind Cherbo Publishing Group (CPG)

Jack Cherbo, Cherbo Publishing Group president and CEO, has been breaking new ground in the sponsored publishing business for more than 40 years.

"Previously, the cost of creating a handsome book for business developments or commemorative occasions fell directly on the sponsoring organization," Cherbo says. "My company pioneered an entirely new concept—funding these books through the sale of corporate profiles."

Cherbo honed his leading edge in Chicago, where he owned a top advertising agency before moving into publishing. Armed with a degree in business administration from Northwestern University, a mind that never stopped, and a keen sense of humor, Cherbo set out to succeed—and continues to do just that.

CPG, formerly a wholly owned subsidiary of Jostens, Inc., a Fortune 500 company, has been a privately held corporation since 1993. CPG is North America's leading publisher of quality custom books for commercial, civic,

historical, and trade associations. Publications range from hardcover state, regional, and commemorative books to softcover state and regional business reports. The company is headquartered in Encino, California, and operates regional offices in Philadelphia, Minneapolis, and Houston.

Who Uses CPG's Services?

CPG has created books for some of America's leading organizations, including the U.S. Chamber of Commerce, Empire State Development, California Sesquicentennial Foundation, Chicago

O'Hare International Airport, and the Indiana Manufacturers Association. Participants have included ConAgra, Dow Chemical Company, Lucent Technologies, Merck & Company, and BlueCross/BlueShield.

About CPG Publications

CPG series range from history books to economic development/relocation books and from business reports to publications of special interest.

The economic development series spotlights fast-growing areas, showcasing the outstanding economic and quality-of-life advantages of a city, region, or state. The annual business reports provide an economic snapshot of individual cities, regions, or states. The commemorative series marks milestones for corporations, organizations, and professional and trade associations.

To find out how CPG can help you celebrate a special occasion, or for information on how to showcase your company or organization, contact Jack Cherbo at 818-783-0040, extension 26, or visit www.cherbopub.com.

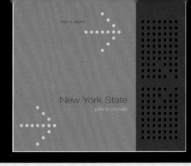

Select CPG Publications

VISIONS OF OPPORTUNITY
City, Regional, and State Series

AMERICA & THE SPIRIT
OF ENTERPRISE
Century of Progress, Future of Promise

CALIFORNIA *Golden Past, Shining Future*

CONNECTICUT *Chartered for Progress*

DUPAGE COUNTY, ILLINOIS
Economic Powerhouse

EVANSVILLE *At the Heart of Success*

GREATER PHOENIX *Expanding Horizons*

INDIANA *Crossroads of Industry and Innovation*

LUBBOCK, TEXAS *Gem of the South Plains*

MARYLAND *Anthem to Innovation*

MICHIGAN *America's Pacesetter*

MILWAUKEE *Midwestern Metropolis*

MISSOURI *Gateway to Enterprise*

NEW YORK STATE *Prime Mover*

NORTH CAROLINA *The State of Minds*

OKLAHOMA *The Center of It All*

UPSTATE NEW YORK
Corridor to Progress

WESTCHESTER COUNTY,
NEW YORK
Headquarters to the World

LEGACY
Commemorative Series

BUILD IT & THE CROWDS
WILL COME
Seventy-Five Years of Public Assembly

CELEBRATE SAINT PAUL
150 Years of History

THE EXHIBITION INDUSTRY
The Power of Commerce

THE NATIONAL RURAL LETTER
CARRIERS ASSOCIATION
A Centennial Portrait

NEW YORK STATE ASSOCIATION
OF FIRE CHIEFS
Sizing Up a Century of Service

VISIONS TAKING SHAPE
Celebrating 50 Years of the Precast/ Prestressed Concrete Industry

Annual Business Reports
MINNESOTA REPORT
2004

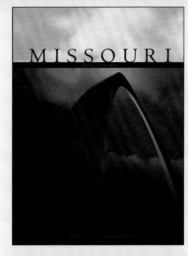

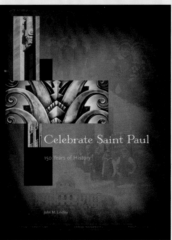
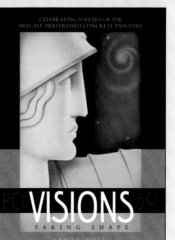

BIBLIOGRAPHY

"ADC Reports Fourth Quarter 2004 Results." ADC Telecommunications (press release), December 14, 2004. <http://www.adc.com/investorrelations. newsandcommunications/newsreleases/show.jsp?RELEASEID=150510> (2005).

"American Express Financial Advisors Hires Leaders of Strategic Planning and Investor Relations." American Express Financial Advisors (press release), March 16, 2005. <http://home3.americanexpress.com/corp/pc/2005/aefa_hire.asp> (2005).

"American Express Plans to Pursue Spin-Off of American Express Financial Advisors." American Express (conference call remarks transcript), February 1, 2005. <http://home3.americanexpress.com/corp/corpinfo/pdfs/aefa_spinoff_tp.pdf> (2005).

"American Medical Systems Reports Record $209 Million Sales for 2004." American Medical Systems (press release), February 17, 2005. <http://www. corporate-ir.net/ireye/ir_site.zhtml?ticker=Ammd&script=410&layout= 6&item_id=676501> (2005).

American Public Transportation Association. "Minneapolis—Greenway Trolleys." From Rail Transit Online, May 2004. <http://www.heritagetrolley.org/planMinneapolisRTOL1.htm> (2004).

"Analysts International Reports Profitable Results for 2004 with Fourth Consecutive Quarter of Profitability Improvement and EPS at High End of Recently Updated Guidance." Analysts International (press release), February 24, 2005. <http://phx.corporate-ir.net/phoenix.zhtml?c=111374&p=irol-newsArticle_print&ID=678553&highlight=> (2005).

Anfinson, John O. "12,000 Years at St. Anthony Falls: Spiritual Power to Industrial Might." Minnesota History, 58, nos. 5 and 6 (Spring/Summer 2003): 252–69.

———, and Theodore Blegen. The River We Have Wrought. Minneapolis: University of Minnesota Press, 2003.

Anfinson, Scott F. "Archaeology of the Central Minneapolis Riverfront." The Minnesota Archaeologist, Vol. 48, No. 1–2, 1989. <http://www. fromsitetostory.org/sources/papers/mnarch48/48inv-h-c.asp> (2004).

Atwater, Isaac. History of Minneapolis. New York: Munsell Publishing Co., 1895.

Beatty, Susan (vice president, Piper Jaffray). Interview by author (Sauerwein). April 14, 2005.

"Bemis Buys South American Packaging Company." Business Journal (Minneapolis/St. Paul), January 5, 2005. <http://twincities.bizjournals.com/twincities/stories/2005/01/03/daily25.html> (2005).

"Bemis Company Acquires Majority Ownership of Dixie Toga, Expanding Presence in South American Packaging Market." Bemis (press release), January 5, 2005. <http://www.corporate-ir.net/ireye/ir_site.zhtml?ticker= bms&script=410&layout=0&item_id=659104> (2005).

"Bemis Company Reports Record 2004 Sales and Earnings Per Share." Bemis (press release), January 26, 2005. <http://www.corporate-ir. net/ireye/ir_site.zhtml?ticker=bms&script=410&layout=0&item_id= 666735> (2005).

Bergsmark, Daniel. "Minneapolis, The Mill City." Economic Geography, 3, no. 3 (July 1927): 391–96.

Berman, Hyman, and Linda Mack Schloff. The People of Minnesota: Jews in Minnesota. St. Paul: Minnesota Historical Society Press, 2002.

Black, Sam. "Honeywell Expands Local Division." Business Journal (Minneapolis/St. Paul), July 27, 2001. <http://twincities.bizjournals.com/twincities/stories/2001/07/30/story5.html> (2005).

Blegen, Theodore. Minnesota: A History of the State. Minneapolis: University of Minnesota Press, 1975.

Boman, Alissa (marketing administrator, AmeriPride Services). Interview by author (Sauerwein). March 14, 2005.

Brady, Bill (spokesman, Cargill). Interview by author (Sauerwein). March 3, 2005.

Brandt, Steve. "Empty Nesters Leave Suburbs for Convenient Roost." Star Tribune, December 23, 1996, sec. B.

Broehl, Wayne G., Jr. Cargill: Trading the World's Grain. <http://cargill.com/about/history/history.htm> (2005).

"Business at the Next Level." Eschelon Telecom. <http://www.eschelon.com/products/Eschelon%20Overview%20-%203-26-03.pdf> (2005).

Buzenberg, Bill. "Mr. Foshay's Legend." Minnesota Public Radio, February 1, 2000. <http://news.minnesota.publicradio.org/features/200001/31_buzenbergb_foshay/> (2004).

Cagle, Erik. "Service with a Smile." Printing Impressions, June 2002. <http://www.mboamerica.com/media4.html> (2005).

Cannon, Elizabeth (director of risk management and real estate, Valspar Corporation). Interview by author (Sauerwein). March 2, 2005.

"Capella University Named One of America's 500 Fastest-Growing Privately Held Companies by Inc. Magazine for the 5th Consecutive Year." Capella University (press release), October 2, 2003. <http://WWW.CAPELLA.EDU/cec/news/news/03-10-02_inc500.aspx> (2004).

"Capella University to Relocate Downtown Minneapolis Headquarters to 225 South Sixth Building." Capella University (press release), February 23, 2004. <http://WWW.CAPELLA.EDU/cec/news/news/02-23-04_relocation.aspx> (2004).

Cargill. "A Summary of Cargill's History." <http://cargill.com/about/history/history.htm> (2005).

———. Collaborate, Create, Succeed. <http://www.cargill.com/about/index.htm> (2005).

"Cargill Reports Fourth-Quarter and Fiscal 2004 Earnings." Cargill (press release), August 10, 2004. <http://www.cargill.com/news/news_releases/2004/1040810_earnings.htm#TopOfPage> (2005).

Carlson Companies. "A History of the Radisson Hotel." <http://www.hotel-online.com/Neo/News/SpecialReleases1998/HistoryRadissonHotel_Jan1998.html> (2004).

Carr, Dan. "Medical Teamwork: Minnesota's Close Ties in Med-Tech Create New Successes Like ev3." Twin Cities Business Monthly, July 2002. <www.ev3.net/docs/Medical_Teamwork_-_Dale.pdf> (2004).

"C. H. Robinson Reports Fourth Quarter and Annual Results." C. H. Robinson Worldwide (press release), February 8, 2005. <http://phx.corporate-ir.net/phoenix.zhtml?c=97366&p=irol-newsArticle&ID=671964&highlight=> (2005).

Ciresi, Michael (partner, Robins, Kaplan, Miller & Ciresi LLP). Interview by author (Sauerwein). March 17, 2005.

Conzen, Kathleen Neils. The People of Minnesota: Germans in Minnesota. St. Paul: Minnesota Historical Society Press, 2003.

Dakota Electric Association. "2004 Facts and Stats: Dakota Electric Association." <http://www.dakotaelectric.com/PDF/2004Facts&Stats.pdf> (2004).

Danbom, David B. "Flour Power: The Significance of Flour Milling at the Falls." Minnesota History, 58, nos. 5 and 6 (Spring/Summer 2003): 270–85.

"Dayton's Loses a Name, Minnesota a Tradition." Minnesota Daily, January 16, 2001. <http://www.mndaily.com/daily/2001/01/16/editorial_opinions/e0116/> (2004).

Demma, Jay (vice president, Maxfield Research, Inc.). Interview by author (Soderstrom). January 25, 2005.

"Digital River Announces 52 Percent Annual Growth and Raises 2005 Revenue and EPS Guidance." Digital River (press release), January 26, 2005. <http://www.digitalriver.com/corporate/press_releases/pr_452.shtml> (2005).

Doan, Jason (compensation and benefits administrator, Campbell Mithun). Interview by author (Sauerwein). March 17, 2005.

Ely Lawrence, Deborah (spokeswoman, McGladrey & Pullen). Interview by author (Sauerwein). April 13, 2005.

"Eschelon Launches Elite Partners Agent Program in Portland." Eschelon Telecom (press release), March 15, 2005. <http://www.eschelon.com/about_us/section_detail.aspx?itemID=4778&catID=220&SelectCatID=200&typeID=6> (2005).

"Eschelon Telecom, Inc. Announces Fourth Quarter 2004 Operating Results." Eschelon Telecom (press release), March 7, 2005. <http://www.eschelon.com/about_us/section_detail.aspx?itemID=4598&catID=220&SelectCatID=220&typeID=6> (2005).

Falch, Linda (corporate communications, Ceridian Corporation). Interview by author (Sauerwein). March 14, 2005.

Federal Writers' Project of Minnesota. "Education and Religion." From Minnesota: A State Guide. American Guide Series. <http://newdeal.feri.org/guides/mn/ch09.htm> (2004).

Federal Writers' Project of the Works Progress Administration. Minnesota: A State Guide. New York: Hastings House, 1947.

Ferguson Otis, Jane (vice president of communications and information services, Minnesota Council on Foundations). Interview by author (Sauerwein). April 28, 2005.

"Fire Safety Requires Common-Sense Plan." Minnesota Daily, November 15, 1994. <http://www.mndaily.com/daily/gopher-archives/1994/11/15/B%25-2F~LN.TXT> (2004).

Fisher, Gwendolyn (vice president, Tyco Plastics & Adhesives). Interview by author (Sauerwein). March 1, 2005.

Ford-Martin, Paula Ann. "Minnesota Multiphasic Personality Inventory (MMPI-2)." In *Gale Encyclopedia of Medicine*, 2002. Reprinted on HealthAtoZ.com. <http://www.healthatoz.com/healthatoz/Atoz/ency/minnesota_multiphasic_personality_inventory_mmpi-2.jsp> (2004).

"G&K Services Reports Fiscal 2004 Fourth Quarter and Total Year Results." G&K Services (press release), August 17, 2004. <http://www.corporate-ir.net/ireye/ir_site.zhtml?ticker=GKSRA&script=410&layout=6&item_id=604521> (2005).

Garrison-Sprenger, Nicole, Sarah Mckenzie, and Sam Black. "Local Firms Likely to Profit From American Express Spinoff." *Business Journal (Minneapolis/St. Paul)*, February 4, 2005. <http://www.bizjournals.com/twincities/stories/2005/02/07/story2.html> (2005).

General Mills. "Our Milling Roots and Beyond." *History of Innovation*. <http://www.generalmills.com/corporate/company/history.apx> (2004).

———. *75 Years of Innovation, Invention, Food, and Fun*. <http://www.generalmills.com/corporate/company/history.apx> (2004).

———. *2004 Report: Champions for a Stronger Community*. <http://www.generalmills.com/corporate/commitment/community.aspx> (2005).

Gillik, Kevin (head of corporate marketing, Datacard Group). Interview by author (Sauerwein). February 9, 2005.

Gjerde, Jon, and Carlton C. Qualey. *The People of Minnesota: Norwegians in Minnesota*. St. Paul: Minnesota Historical Society Press, 2002.

"Governor Tim Pawlenty Proclaims January 2005 as Bell Mortgage Month." Bell Mortgage (press release), no date. <http://www.bellmortgage.com/about/news.html> (2005).

Gray, James. *The University of Minnesota: 1851–1951*. Minneapolis: University of Minnesota Press, 1951.

Green, Cindy. "Nutraceuticals and Pharmaceuticals: Market is Growing Rapidly for Medicinal Foods." *Ag Innovation News*, January–March 2003. <http://www.auri.org/news/ainjan03/08page.htm> (2004).

Hallowell, Bryce (spokesman, Alliant Techsystems). Interview by author (Sauerwein). March 3, 2005.

Hasselmo, Nils, Emeroy Johnson, et al. *The Swedes in Minnesota*. Minneapolis:

T. S. Denison and Co., 1976.

Henehan, Brendan. *Minneapolis Past*. © 1993 by KTCA. Video recording.

Iles, Chris (communications specialist, HealthPartners). Interview by author (Sauerwein). April 15, 2005.

Infoplease. "National Political Conventions Since 1856." <http://www.infoplease.com/ipa/A0781449.html> (2004).

Info.Resource, Inc. "Minnesota BioHistory." MinnesotaLifeScience.com. <http://www.minnesotalifescience.com/biohistory.htm> (2004).

"Is There a Monorail in Minneapolis' Future?" *Southwest Journal: Southwest Minneapolis' Community Newspaper*, February 3, 2004. <http://www.swjournal.com/articles/2004/02/03/news/news02.txt> (2004).

Jacobson, Don. "Making Gold out of Ethanol Waste." *Profits Journal Online*, December 6, 2002. <http://www.profitsjournal.com/story.asp?storyid=492> (2004).

Jensen, Teresa (director of marketing services, Personnel Decisions International). Interview by author (Sauerwein). April 12, 2005.

Johnson, Tara (spokeswoman, General Mills). Interview by author (Sauerwein). March 8, 2005.

Jordan, Lani (spokeswoman, CHS). Interview by author (Sauerwein). March 3, 2005.

Kaeding, Mary (company historian, Kraus-Anderson Companies). Interview by author (Sauerwein). April 15, 2005.

Kane, Lucille. *The Falls of St. Anthony: The Waterfall That Built Minneapolis*. St. Paul: Minnesota Historical Society Press, 1987.

Kirbyson, Geoff. "DQ—Blended." Brandchannel.com, September 27, 2004. <http://www.brandchannel.com/features_profile.asp?pr_id=199> (2004).

Klehr, Dawn (corporate public relations, The Toro Company). Interview by author (Sauerwein). March 1, 2005.

Korstange, Jason (director of corporate communications, TCF Financial). Interview by author (Sauerwein). April 13, 2005.

Kroll, Karen M. "Man About Town." *Minnesota Technology*, Tech 2002 Special

Issue. <http://www.minnesotatechnology.org/publications/Magazine/2002/SpecialIssue/man_about_town.asp> (2004).

Kuhlmann, Charles Byron. *The Development of the Flour-Milling Industry in the United States, with Special Reference to the Industry in Minneapolis.* Clifton: A. M. Kelly, 1973.

Lamb, Debby (administrative services manager, Malt-O-Meal Company). Interview by author (Sauerwein). March 3, 2005.

Lanegran, David A., and Ernest R. Sandeen. *The Lake District of Minneapolis: A History of the Calhoun-Isles Community.* Minneapolis: Living Historical Museum, 1979. Reprint, Minneapolis: University of Minnesota Press, 2004.

Langer, Christelle (vice president of marketing and communications, The Minneapolis Foundation). Interview by author (Sauerwein). May 2, 2005.

Larson, Don W. *Land of the Giants: A History of Minnesota Business.* Minneapolis: Dorn Books, 1979.

Larson, Susan (president, Evans Larson Communications). Interview by author (Sauerwein). March 17, 2005.

Lerner, Maura. "'U' May Overhaul Health System." *Star Tribune,* September 3, 2004. <http://www.startribune.com/stories/1556/4998303.html> (2004).

Lindman, Sylvia. "Diversity Matters: How Minnesota Grantmakers Are Supporting Diversity." *Giving Forum,* Spring 2001. <http://www.mcf.org/mcf/forum/diversity.htm> (2005).

Mack, Linda. "Riverfront Revival: The Minneapolis Mill District is Finding New Life as a Cultural Center." *Star Tribune,* September 7, 2003, sec. A.

"Malt-O-Meal Adds Jobs at Manufacturing Facility in Tremonton, Utah." Malt-O-Meal (press release), September 2, 2004. <http://www.malt-o-meal.com/ARTICLE20.HTM> (2005).

Markoff, John. "Computer Whiz Seymour Cray." *New York Times.* October 6, 1996. <http://www.cgl.ucsf.edu/home/tef/cray/obit.html> (2005).

"MCAD Only Art and Design Institution Named Best Midwestern College." Minneapolis College of Art and Design (press release), August 24, 2004. <http://www.mcad.edu/publicrelations/pdfs/20040824_bestmidwestern_web.pdf> (2004).

McDonough, John. "Campbell Mithun at 70." *Advertising Age* (special advertising section), March 10, 2003. <http://www.campbellmithun.com/

featured/cm_70.pdf> (2005).

"McKnight Commits $20 Million to Statewide Affordable Housing and Community Development." The McKnight Foundation (press release), April 6, 2005. <http://www.mcknight.org/arts/news_detail.aspx?itemID=2412&catID=57&typeID=2> (2005).

McLaughlin, Peter. "Update on the Midtown Greenway." <http://www.co.hennepin.mn.us/vgn/portal/internet/hcnewsarticlemaster/0,2301,1273_1736_103883277,00.html> (2004).

Meier, Peg. "They Built This City: Mill City Museum Celebrates Minneapolis's Riverfront, Industry, People." *Star Tribune,* September 7, 2003.

"Mesaba Airlines Celebrates 60th Anniversary." Mesaba Airlines (press release), July 6, 2004. <http://www.mesaba.com/mescom/home.nsf/main?openframeset&Frame=main&Src=/mescom/home.nsf/splash/investment?opendocument> (2004).

Mesaba Holdings, Inc. *2003 Annual Report.* <http://www.mairholdings.com/index.asp?Type=B_BASIC&SEC={0E148FB8-1747-4C49-B5DF-C1FB2C59D19F}> (2004).

Metropolitan Council. "Transportation Policy Plan." <http://www.metrocouncil.org/planning/transportation/TPP/tppindex.htm> (2004).

Metz, Jennifer (marketing coordinator, Faegre & Benson). Interview by author (Sauerwein). April 13, 2005.

"Midtown Greenway Coalition Advocates for Rail Trolleys in the Greenway and a Western Alignment for the Southwest Corridor." Midtown Greenway Coalition (press release), December 6, 2002. <http://www.midtowngreenway.org/greenway/Press/press_release_transit_2002_12_06.html> (2004).

Miller, G. Wayne. "Celebrating a Creator of Medical Miracles." *Providence Journal,* October 23, 2004. <http://www.projo.com/news/content/projo_20041023_heart23.25a03a.html> (2004).

Miller, Melanie (vice president and assistant treasurer, Bemis Company). Interview by author (Sauerwein). February 11, 2005.

Minneapolis Public Library. "Air Transportation." *A History of Minneapolis: Transportation.* <http://www.mplib.org/history/tr5.asp> (2004).

———. "Banking and Finance." *A History of Minneapolis: Business and Industry.* <http://www.mplib.org/history/bi2.asp> (2004).

BIBLIOGRAPHY

———. "Central Business District (Part II)." *A History of Minneapolis: Business and Industry*. <http://www.mplib.org/history/bi5.asp> (2004).

———. "Conventions and Organizations." *A History of Minneapolis: Tourism*. <http://www.mplib.org/history/to2.asp> (2004).

———. "Hotels." *A History of Minneapolis: Tourism*. <http://www.mplib.org/history/to1.asp> (2004).

———. "Intercity Transit and Highways." *A History of Minneapolis: Transportation*. <http://www.mplib.org/history/tr3.asp> (2004).

———. "Intercity Transit and Highways (Part II)." *A History of Minneapolis: Transportation*. <http://www.mplib.org/history/tr4.asp> (2004).

———. "Libraries." *A History of Minneapolis: City Government*. <http://www.mplib.org/history/cg6.asp> (2004).

———. "Medicine." *A History of Minneapolis: Religion, Social Services, and Medicine*. <http://www.mplib.org/history/rs3.asp> (2004).

———. "Milling." *A History of Minneapolis: Business and Industry*. <http://www.mplib.org/history/bi1.asp> (2004).

———. "Museums, Galleries, and Institutions for the Arts." *A History of Minneapolis: Arts and Entertainment*. <http://www.mplib.org/history/ae3.asp> (2004).

———. "Other Industries." *A History of Minneapolis: Business and Industry*. <http://www.mplib.org/history/bi3.asp> (2004).

———. "Professional Sports." *A History of Minneapolis Sports*. <http://www.mplib.org/history/sp2.asp> (2005).

———. "Public and Private Schools." *A History of Minneapolis: Education*. <http://www.mplib.org/history/ed1.asp> (2004).

———. "River Transport." *A History of Minneapolis: Transportation*. <http://www.mplib.org/history/tr1.asp> (2004).

———. "University of Minnesota." *A History of Minneapolis: Education*. <http://www.mplib.org/history/ed2.asp> (2004).

Minnesota Council on Foundations. *Minnesota Council on Foundations: 25 Year Anniversary*. 1995.

———. *Social Memory: The Five Percent Club—The Minnesota Keystone Awards: An Historical Review (1975–1987)*. 1987.

Minnesota Department of Transportation. "Basic Facts: Hiawatha Light Rail Transit Line." <http://www.dot.state.mn.us/metro/lrt/facts4print.html> (2004).

———. "Ports & Waterways." <http://www.dot.state.mn.us/ofrw/waterways.html> (2004).

Minnesota Higher Education Services Office. "Minnesota Grades High in National Higher Education Report Card." <http://www.mheso.state.mn.us/pPg.cfm?pageID=1446> (2004).

Minnesota Historical Society. "Minnesota History Topics: Southdale Mall." <http://www.mnhs.org/library/tips/history_topics/72southdale.html> (2004).

———. "Twin City Rapid Transit Company: An Inventory of Its Corporate Records at the Minnesota Historical Society." <http://www.mnhs.org/library/findaids/00207.html> (2004).

Minnesota Hospital Association. "Key Facts about Minnesota Hospitals." MNHospitals.org. <http://www.mnhospitals.org/index/tools-app/tool.160> (2004).

Minnesota Partnership For Action Against Tobacco. *2005 Annual Report Card Review*. <http://www.mpaat.org/index.asp?Type=B_BASIC&SEC={06DA7AC3-4786-4AC5-96AC-13760439DF22}> (2005).

Moore, Janet. "Minnesota's Pioneers of Cardiac-Related Technology." *Star Tribune*, October 17, 2004. <http://www.startribune.com/stories/535/5035251.html> (2004).

"MTS Reports Fiscal 2004 EPS of $1.35 on Strong Fourth Quarter Results." MTS Systems Corporation (press release), November 17, 2004. <http://www.mts.com/Pr/2004/pr20041117.htm> (2005).

Murphy, Jarrett. "A Conventional History Lesson." CBSnews.com, July 23, 2004. <http://www.cbsnews.com/stories/2004/07/23/politics/main631468.shtml> (2004).

Murray, Jean. "A River Runs Through It." *Minnesota Medicine*, July 1998. <http://www.mnmed.org/publications/MnMed1998/July/Murray.cfm> (2004).

"Nash Finch Reports Fiscal 2004 Results." Nash Finch Company (press release), March 2, 2005. <http://corporate-ir.net/ireye/ir_site.zhtml?ticker=NAFC&script=410&layout=0&item_id=681065> (2005).

National Academy of Engineering. "Internet: Greatest Engineering Achievements of the 20th Century." <http://www.greatachievements.org/greatachievements/ga_13_2.html> (2004).

National Center for Public Policy and Higher Education. "State News Summary: Minnesota." *Measuring Up 2004: The National Report Card on Higher Education*. <http://measuringup.highereducation.org/statedir.cfm?myyear=2004&stateName=Minnesota> (2004).

———. "State Reports: (Minnesota, 2004)." *Measuring Up 2004: The National Report Card on Higher Education*. <http://measuringup.highereducation.org/stateprofilenet.cfm?myYear=2004&stateName=Minnesota> (2004).

National Retail Federation. "Top 100 Specialty Store Retailers." *STORES*, August 2004. <http://www.stores.org/m100specialty.asp> (2004).

Oliver, Myrna. "Ancel Keys Taught Public Importance of Eating Well." *Seattle Times*, November 28, 2004. <http://seattletimes.nwsource.com/html/obituaries/2002102816_keysobit28.html> (2004).

Olson, Dan. "Gentle Hands—Sister Kenny's Legacy." Minnesota Public Radio News, August 22, 2002. <http://news.minnesota.publicradio.org/features/200208/22_olsond_sisterkinney/part4.shtml> (2004).

"Onvoy History: Delivering Broadband." Onvoy. <http://www.onvoy.com/pdf/Onvoy_History.pdf> (2005).

"Partnership with State's Three Largest School Districts Revitalizes Science Programs." Medtronic (press release), January 11, 2005. <http://www.medtronic.com/foundation/news_0205.html> (2005).

Pennefeather, Shannon, ed. *Mill City: A Visual History of the Minneapolis Mill District*. St. Paul: Minnesota Historical Society Press, 2003.

Peterson, Deborah (librarian and donations coordinator, Shakopee Mdewakanton Sioux Community). Interview by author (Sauerwein). April 27, 2004.

Picone, Linda. "NRP in Middle Age: The City Has Changed during the First 10 Years of the Program." *Southwest Journal*, June 26, 2000. <http://www.nrp.org/R2/News/InTheNews/SWJ20010313.html> (2005).

"Pioneers of Heart Surgery." Nova Online. <http://www.pbs.org/wgbh/nova/heart/pioneers.html> (2004).

"Prince Timeline." *Pioneer Press*, March 14, 2004. <http://www.twincities.com/mld/twincities/entertainment/music/8163655.htm?1c> (2005).

Reilly, Mark. "Duluth Attempts to Hail Taxi 2000." *Business Journal (Minneapolis/St. Paul)*, January 9, 2004. <http://twincities.bizjournals.com/twincities/stories/2004/01/12/story3.html> (2004).

"Retek Announces a 100 Percent Sequential Increase in GAAP EPS." Retek (press release), January 27, 2005. <http://www.retek.com/press/press.asp?id=659> (2005).

Robinson, James W. *America & the Spirit of Enterprise*. Encino: Cherbo Publishing Group, 2001.

Rosheim, David L. *The Other Minneapolis: Or, the Rise and Fall of the Gateway, the Old Minneapolis Skid Row*. Maquoketa: Andromeda Press, 1978.

Roth, Debbie (vice president of sales and marketing, Japs-Olson Company). Interview by author (Sauerwein). April 12, 2005.

Rubenstein, Mitchell E., and Alan R. Woolworth. "The Dakota and Ojibway." In *They Chose Minnesota: A Survey of the State's Ethnic Groups*, edited by June D. Holmquist. St. Paul: Minnesota Historical Society Press, 1981.

Rustad, Dave (senior media relations, Thrivent Financial for Lutherans). Interview by author (Sauerwein). May 18, 2005.

Ryder, Franklin J. "Phantom of the River: Spirit Island's Life and Death." *Hennepin County History*, 31, no. 2 (Spring 1972): 17–21.

"San Francisco Bay Area Sails into Top Spot in Intel's 'Most Unwired Cities' Survey." Intel (press release), April 6, 2004. <http://www.intel.pressroom/archive/releases/20040406corp.htm> (2005).

Sanoski, Steve. "Taxi 2000." *Ripsaw News*, May 2004. <http://www.ripsawnews.com/index.php?sect_rank=1&story_id=180&volume_id=12> (2004).

Schauer, Kathy (marketing manager, Opus Corporation). Interview by author (Sauerwein). May 16, 2005.

Scholtes, Peter S. "First Avenue." *City Pages*, September 3, 2003. <http://www.citypages.com/databank/24/1187/article11480.asp> (2004).

Seas, Kari (director of corporate communications, Stellent). Interview by author (Sauerwein). February 8, 2005.

Shaffer, Lynda Norene. *Native Americans Before 1492: The Moundbuilding*

BIBLIOGRAPHY

Centers of the Eastern Woodlands. Armonk: M. E. Sharp, 1992.

Shakopee Mdewakanton Sioux Community. *Indian Gaming Working for Indian People and Minnesota: 2004 Donation Report*. <http://www.ccsmdc.org/pr_events/dr/dr04.pdf> (2005).

Smith, Joel J. "Mesaba Strives to Develop, Make Profit with Northwest." *Detroit News*, August 17, 2004. <http://www.detnews.com/2004/business/0408/17/c01-244338.htm> (2004).

Smith, Scott D. "Minnesota the Healthiest State in the Nation, Again." *Business Journal (Minneapolis/St. Paul)*, November 8, 2004. <http://www.bizjournals.com/twincities/stories/2004/11/08/daily4.html> (2004).

Smith, Stuart (media relations, Ellerbe Becket). Interview by author (Sauerwein). March 14, 2005.

Solem, Rebecca (executive assistant, UnitedHealth Group). Interview by author (Sauerwein). April 13, 2005.

Solomon, Patrick (corporate communications manager, Onvoy). Interview by author (Sauerwein). March 9, 2005.

Soucheray, Joe. "Metropolitan Stadium: The Park Built for Outdoor Baseball." From Hubert H. Humphrey Metrodome souvenir book, 1982. <http://www.msfc.com/ann_before_metropolitan_stadium.cfm> (2005).

Spencer, William H., III. "Profiles in Cardiology: Earl E. Bakken." *Clinical Cardiology*, May 2001. <http://www.clinicalcardiology.org/briefs/200105briefs/cc24-422.profile_bakken.html> (2004).

Splett, Larry (director for global marketing communications, Honeywell Automation and Control Solutions). Interview by author (Sauerwein). March 1, 2005.

"Sr. Elizabeth Kenny." Nurses.info. <http://www.nurses.info/personalities_srl_kenny.htm> (2004).

Steeples, Douglas. "Book Reviews: Investing for Middle America." Economic History Services, February 2003. <http://www.eh.net.bookreviews/library/0593.shtml> (2005).

Stipanovich, Joseph. *City of Lakes: An Illustrated History of Minneapolis*. Woodland Hills: Windsor Publications, Inc., 1982.

Swanson, Joel (senior communications consultant, Blue Cross and Blue Shield of Minnesota). Interview by author (Sauerwein). April 14, 2005.

"Systemwide Sales Grow 25 Percent to $26.1 Billion." Carlson Companies (press release), March 2, 2005. <http://www.carlson.com/press_releases/02_02_05.cfm> (2005).

"Target Corporation Fourth Quarter Earnings Per Share from Continuing Operations $0.90." Target Corporation (press release), February 17, 2005. <http://www.corporate-ir.net/ireye/ir_site.zhtml?ticker=TGT&script=410&layout=0&item_id=676235> (2005).

Tatge, Mark. "Fun & Games." *Forbes*, January 12, 2004. <http://www.forbes.com/free_forbes/2004/0112/138.html> (2004).

"Ted Williams." *USA Today*, July 8, 2002. <http://www.usatoday.com/sports/baseball/williams/2002-07-08-timeline.htm> (2005).

Tellijohn, Andrew. "Sun Country Targets Business Travelers." *Business Journal (Minneapolis/St. Paul)*, February 20, 2004. <http://twincities.bizjournals.com/twincities/stories/2004/02/23/story2.html> (2004).

TheCenter at the University of Florida. *Top American Research Universities 2004*. <http://thecenter.ufl.edu/research2004.html> (2005).

Thon, Jan (grants administrator, General Mills Foundation). Interview by author (Sauerwein). April 28, 2005.

Thornley, Stew. "Minneapolis Lakers." Stewthornley.net, 1989. <http://stewthornley.net/mplslakers.html> (2005).

———. "Minnesota Baseball History." MLB.com. <http://minnesota.twins.mlb.com/NASApp/mlb/min/history/minnesota_baseball_history.jsp> (2005).

——— and Mark Hugunin. "Minnesota Fillies." Stewthornley.net, 2005. <http://stewthornley.net/fillies.html> (2005).

Thorsgaard, Marybeth (media spokeswoman, General Mills). Interview by author (Sauerwein). March 2, 2005.

Tilton, Bill. "MWPDC News." Mississippi Whitewater Park Development Corporation, August 21, 2003. <http://www.whitewaterpark.canoe-kayak.org/082103News.html> (2004).

"Toro to Prepare Football Field for the 2005 Rose Bowl." The Toro Company (press release), December 22, 2004. <http://www.thetorocompany.com/companyinfo/pressrel/rose_bowl_12222004.html> (2005).

"Transport Corporation of America Reports Fourth Quarter Results." *Transport Corporation of America* (press release), February 8, 2005. <http://www.transportamerica.com/news> (2005).

University of Minnesota. *2003 Annual Report.* <http://process.umn.edu/groups/controller/documents/main/controller_home.html> (2004).

U.S. Army Corps of Engineers, St. Paul District. "Engineering the Falls: The Corps Role at St. Anthony Falls." <http://www.mvp.usace.army.mil/history/engineering> (2004).

"U.S. Bancorp Names Richard Hartnack as New Head of Consumer Banking Division and Joseph Otting to Lead Commercial Banking Division." U.S. Bancorp (press release), March 17, 2005. <http://phx.corporate-ir.net/phoenix.zhtml?c=117565&p=irol-newsArticle&ID=686858&highlight> (2005).

U.S. News & World Report. "Augsburg College at a Glance." America's Best Colleges 2005. <http://www.usnews.com/usnews/edu/college/directory/brief/drglance_2334_brief.php> (2004).

———. "Directory of America's Hospitals: Abbott Northwestern Hospital by the Numbers." USNews.com, 2004. <http://www.usnews.com/usnews/health/hospitals/directory/numbers_6610815.htm> (2004).

Voigt, Sarah (spokeswoman, Ryan Companies US). Interview by author (Sauerwein). April 14, 2005.

Wangensteen, Owen H., and Warren H. Green, eds. *Elias Potter Lyon: Minnesota's Leader in Medical Education.* St. Louis: W. H. Green, 1981.

Weintraub, Adam. "Merger Follows World Trend of Consolidation." *Business Journal (Minneapolis/St. Paul),* June 11, 1999. <http://twincities.bizjournals.com/twincities/stories/1999/06/14/story2.html> (2005).

Wentzell, David O. "Cargill: Trading the World's Grain." *The Region,* September 1992. <http://minneapolisfed.org/pubs/region/92-09/reg929d.cfm> (2004).

Wikipedia, the Free Encyclopedia. "U.S. Presidential Election, 1892." <http://en.wikipedia.org/wiki/U.S._presidential_election,_1892> (2004).

Wilson, Leonard G. "Minnesota's Top 10 Contributions to Medicine." *Minnesota Medicine,* December 1999. <http://www.mnmed.org/publications/MnMed1999/December/Wilson.cfm?PF=1> (2004).

Witmer, Mark (treasurer, Michael Foods). Interview by author (Sauerwein). March 3, 2005.

The Web sites of the following companies or organizations were also consulted:

About.com, Achieve!Minneapolis, ADC Telecommunications, Alliant Techsystems, Allianz Life Insurance Company of North America, Allina Hospitals and Clinics, American Express Company, American Medical Systems, America's Second Harvest, AmericInn, AmeriPride Services, Analysts International, Answers.com, The Association for Professional Basketball Research, Augsburg College, Baseball Almanac, Bell Mortgage, Bemis, Best Buy, Biographical Directory of the United States Congress, Biorefining, Bloomington Convention & Visitors Bureau, Blue Cross and Blue Shield of Minnesota, Boston Scientific, Buca, Buffets, Campbell Mithun, Capella University, Cargill, Cargill Dow, Carlson Companies, Carlson Wagonlit Travel, Cenex, CenterPoint Energy, CenterPoint Energy Minnegasco, Ceridian Corporation, Charles Babbage Institute, C. H. Robinson Worldwide, CHS, City of Minneapolis, Cray Inc., Dakota Electric Association, Dakota Woodlands, Datacard Group, Detroit Metropolitan Wayne County Airport, Digital River, Discovery Genomics, Disney Online, Dorsey & Whitney, Ellerbe Becket, Emergency Food Shelf Network, Emporis, Evangelical Lutheran Church in America, Faegre & Benson, Fairview–University Medical Center, Football.com, G&K Services, General Mills, Glass Steel and Stone, Greater Minneapolis Convention & Visitors Association, Hammel, Green and Abrahamson, HealthPartners, Hennepin County, Hennepin County Medical Center, Hickoksports.com, Honeywell, Honeywell Automation & Control Solutions, Hoover's, IMDb.com, INC.com, Industry Search, International Dairy Queen, Inver Hills Community College, Japs-Olson Company, The Jay and Rose Phillips Family Foundation, Kraus-Anderson Companies, Lileks.com, Lillehei Heart Institute, Loft, Major League Baseball, Mall of America, Malt-O-Meal Company, Marshall Field's, M. A. Mortenson Company, Mayo Clinic College of Medicine, MBBNet, McGladrey & Pullen, The McKnight Foundation, Medtronic, Mesaba Airlines, Metropolitan Council, Metropolitan Sports Facilities Commission, Michael Foods, Midcontinent Media, Midtown Greenway Coalition, Minneapolis College of Art and Design, Minneapolis Community and Technical College, Minneapolis Convention Center, Minneapolis Downtown Council, The Minneapolis Foundation, Minneapolis Grain Exchange, The Minneapolis Institute of Arts, Minneapolis Public Library, Minneapolis Public Schools, Minneapolis Regional Chamber of Commerce, Minneapolis–St. Paul International Airport, Minnesota Department of Employment and Economic Development, Minnesota Historical Society, Minnesota Lynx, Minnesota Orchestra, Minnesota Partnership for Action Against Tobacco, Minnesota Partnership for Biotechnology and Medical Genomics, Minnesota State Colleges and Universities, Minnesota State Fair, Minnesota State University–Mankato, Minnesota Telecom Alliance, Minnesota Timberwolves, Minnesota Twins, Minnesota Vikings, Mount Olivet Rolling Acres, MTS Systems Corporation, The Musicland Group, Nash Finch, National Baseball Hall of Fame, National Basketball Association, National Center for Public Policy and Higher Education, National Football League, National Park Service, Normandale Community College, Norstan, Northwest Airlines, Onvoy, Opus Corporation, Personnel Decisions International, Piper Jaffray Companies, The Princeton Review, Protein Design Labs, Ragamala Music and Dance Theatre, Retek, Robins, Kaplan, Miller & Ciresi, Ryan Companies US, Shakopee Mdewakanton Sioux (Dakota) Community, SkyWeb Express, Soo Line Historical and Technical Society, Southdale Center, The Sporting News, Sports Encyclopedia, Starkey Laboratories, Stellent, Sun Country Airlines, Supervalu, Syska Hennessy Group, Target Center, Target Corporation, TCF Financial Corporation, TheFreeDictionary.com, 3M, Thrivent Financial for Lutherans, The Toro Company, Touchstone Energy Cooperatives, Transport Corporation of America, Tyco International, Tyco Plastics, Ultimate Pros Network, UnitedHealth Group, University of Minnesota, University of Minnesota Medical School, University of Minnesota Services, University of Minnesota, Twin Cities, U.S. Bancorp, U.S. Bank, U.S. Census, Valspar, Vinny T's of Boston, Walker Art Center, Women's National Basketball Association, Wright-Hennepin Cooperative Electric Association, Xcel Energy, Yahoo Finance

INDEX

INDEX

PHOTO CREDITS

Unless otherwise noted, all images that appear on the same page are listed in a clockwise fashion, beginning from the top left-hand corner of the page.

Pages ii–iii: © Richard Sisk/Panoramic Images

Pages iv–v: © Keith Levit/Index Stock

Page vi–vii: © Layne Kennedy/Corbis

Page vii: © Chris Gregerson

Page viii: © Chris Gregerson

Page x: © René Mansi/iStockphoto

Page xiii: © Lise Gagne/iStockphoto

Pages xiv–xv: © Richard Cummins

Pages xvi–xvii: © Chris Gregerson

Page xviii: Courtesy, Minnesota Historical Society

Pages xx–xxi: © Bob Firth

Pages 2–3: Courtesy, Minnesota Historical Society

Pages 4–5: Courtesy, Minnesota Historical Society

Page 6: Courtesy, Minnesota Historical Society

Page 7: © Bettmann/Corbis

Page 8: Courtesy, Minnesota Historical Society

Pages 8–9: © Library of Congress Geography and Map Division

Page 10: Both images, courtesy, Minnesota Historical Society

Page 11: Both images, courtesy, Minnesota Historical Society

Page 12: Courtesy, Minnesota Historical Society

Pages 12–13: Courtesy, Minneapolis Public Library, Special Collections

Page 13: Right, courtesy, Minneapolis Public Library, Special Collections

Page 14: Courtesy, Minnesota Historical Society

Page 15: Courtesy, Minnesota Historical Society

Page 16–17: Courtesy, Minnesota Historical Society

Page 18: Courtesy, Minnesota Historical Society; courtesy, Minneapolis Public Library, Special Collections; courtesy, The Institute for Minnesota Archaeology

Page 19: Courtesy, Minnesota Historical Society; courtesy, Minnesota Historical Society; courtesy, Minneapolis Public Library, Special Collections

Page 20: Both images, courtesy, Minnesota Historical Society

Page 21: Left to right, courtesy, Minnesota Historical Society; courtesy, Minneapolis Public Library, Special Collections

Pages 22–23: All images, courtesy, Minnesota Historical Society

Pages 24–25: Courtesy, Minnesota Historical Society

Page 25: Map, courtesy, The Institute for Minnesota Archaeology; three remaining images, courtesy, Minnesota Historical Society

Pages 26–27: Courtesy, Minneapolis Public Library, Special Collections

Page 27: Top to bottom, © Library of Congress; courtesy, Minneapolis Public Library, Special Collections

Pages 28–29: All images, courtesy, Minnesota Historical Society

Pages 30–31: Courtesy, Minnesota Historical Society

Page 32: Courtesy, Minneapolis Public Library, Special Collections; courtesy, Minneapolis Public Library, Special Collections; courtesy, Minnesota Historical Society

Page 33: All images, courtesy, Minnesota Historical Society

Pages 34–35: Courtesy, Minnesota Historical Society

Page 35: Inset, courtesy, Minnesota Historical Society; right, courtesy, © Minnesota Historical Society/Corbis

Page 36: Courtesy, Minnesota Historical Society

Page 37: © Gordon Coster/Time Life Pictures/Getty Images; courtesy, The Bakken Library and Museum; photo by Bill Shrout/Reprinted from *The Saturday Evening Post* magazine, 1961 Saturday Evening Post Society, reprinted with permission

Page 38: Courtesy, Minnesota Historical Society; courtesy, the Charles Babbage Institute, University of Minnesota, Minneapolis; courtesy, Minnesota Historical Society

Page 39: © Chris Gregerson

Page 40: © Richard Cummins

Page 41: Top to bottom, © Joseph Sohm, ChromoSohm Inc./Corbis; © Bettmann/Corbis

Page 42: Left to right, courtesy, Mall of America; © Bill Ross/Corbis

Pages 42–43: © Bill Ross/Corbis

Pages 44–45: © Janet Bailey/Masterfile

Pages 46–47: © FK PHOTO/Corbis

Page 48: Both images, courtesy, Carlson Companies, Inc.

Page 49: Courtesy, Parker Durrant

Page 50: Left to right, © Bill Alkofer/Getty Images; courtesy, Mall of America

Pages 50–51: Courtesy, Underwater Adventures Aquarium

Page 52: Left to right, © Alan Schein Photography/Corbis; © Joel Koyama, courtesy Ellerbe Becket

Page 53: Left to right, © Tim Shaffer/Reuters/Corbis; © Masterfile

Page 54: © Getty Images

Page 55: Courtesy, Buca Inc.; © Russell Underwood/Corbis; © Peter Sickles/SuperStock

Pages 56–57: © Pete Leonard/zefa/Corbis

Page 58: Courtesy, University of Minnesota

Pages 58–59: © Brian Droeg/courtesy, Ellerbe Becket

Page 59: Insets, top to bottom, © Richard Hamilton Smith/Corbis; courtesy, University of Minnesota

Page 60: © Stephen Geffre/Augsburg College

Page 61: © Stephen Geffre/Augsburg College; © Don Wong; © Tim Mantoan/Masterfile

Page 62: Both images, © Chris Gregerson

Page 63: Top to bottom, © Don Wong; © Index Stock

Pages 64–65: © Boden/Ledingham/Masterfile

Page 66: © Chris Gregerson

Pages 66–67: © Photodisc

Page 67: Insets, top to bottom, © Ron Stroud/Masterfile; © Gary Buss/Corbis

Page 68: © Richard Cummins/Corbis

CPG

cherbo publishing group, inc.

Typography

Principal faces used: Univers, designed by Adrian Frutiger in 1957;
Helvetica, designed by Matthew Carter, Edouard Hoffmann,
and Max Miedinger in 1959; and Industria, designed by Neville Brody in 1989.

Hardware

Macintosh G5 desktops, digital color laser printing with Xerox Docucolor 12, digital
imaging with Creo EverSmart Supreme

Software

QuarkXPress, Adobe Illustrator, Adobe Photoshop, Adobe Acrobat, Microsoft Word,
Eye-One Pro by Gretagmacbeth, Creo Oxygen, FlightCheck

CTP, Printing, and Binding

Performed by Friesens of Altona, Manitoba, Canada
Neche, North Dakota, USA

Paper

Text Paper: #80 Luna Matte

Bound in Rainbow® recycled content papers from
Ecological Fibers, Inc.

Dust Jacket: #100 Sterling-Litho Gloss